# Dancing the Labyrinth

## Initiation in the Modern World

## Patricia Ariadne, Ph.D.

Author of
*Drinking the Dragon*
*Stories of the Dark Night of the Soul*

*Things outside you are projections of what's inside you,
and what's inside you is a projection of what's outside.
So, when you step into the labyrinth outside you,
at the same time, you're stepping into the labyrinth inside.*
                                         ~ **Haruki Murakami**

# OTHER BOOKS BY PATRICIA ARIADNE

*Drinking the Dragon: Stories of the Dark Night of the Soul*
*Women Dreaming-Into-Art: Seven Artists Who Create From Dreams*
*Marjorie Klemp: Her Spiritual Journey through Service* (ebook)

*The Transition Series*, interactive workbooks that include:
- *Bridging Night and Day: Decoding the Hidden Messages of Your Dreams*
- *Navigating Change: How to Go from Trauma to Transformation*

DANCING THE LABYRINTH
Initiation in the Modern World
by Patricia Ariadne, Ph.D.

© 2022 by Patricia Ariadne, Ph.D.

ISBN: 0-978-0-9974680-4-5

All rights reserved. No part of this publication may be reproduced, stored in a retrieval system, or transmitted in any form or by any means (electronic, mechanical, photocopy, recording, or any other) except for brief quotations in printed reviews, without the prior permission of the publisher.

Sothis Press
Encinitas, CA

# DEDICATION

*Dancing the Labyrinth* is dedicated to the Vairagi Adepts,
the ancient line of Masters who have imparted the wisdom teachings
and facilitated the initiation process
throughout the ages of time.

*An "Initiate" is someone who has crossed the boundary (or threshold). The greatest Initiates have crossed the boundary of death and have returned — they have been called the twice born, the born again, or those born from above. These Initiates are often referred to as the Enlightened. However, the spiritual voyage consists of many steps, and thus in reality there are many initiations that the seeker experiences on the path to knowing the Divine. Each initiation is the badge of having overcome some challenge or barrier.*

~ **Laurence Galian**

# ACKNOWLEDGMENTS

*Someday, after mastering the winds, the waves,
the tides and gravity,
we shall harness for God the energies of love, and then,
for a second time in the history of the world,
man will have discovered fire.*
~ **Pierre Teilhard de Chardin**

*At the heart of all things is love.*
~ **Sadaharu Oh**

I want to thank everyone in this lifetime who has taught me to love. This includes everyone I've ever met who has profoundly impacted my life (including those who brought headache or heartache). On the other side of this lifetime, I will be asked, "How well did you love?" and this is the question that each of us will be required to answer. Like many of you, I had in many ways a painful childhood, and in response to that hurt, I wrapped up my heart in gauze and grew a hedge around it. Finding a spiritual path that suited me and committing to it for over four decades, years of psychotherapy in early adulthood, a few devoted friends, and work that I love—all have served to mend and enlarge my heart; all my experiences and every person I've met can now fit inside of it.

A few of the heart-healers in my life are mentioned here, in connection with the writing of this book. The deep bond—forged by a shared family legacy—with my sister, Diana, has given me great comfort throughout this lifetime. I am grateful to my dear friend, Sandra Rogers, for her loyal support, friendship, and encouragement. She has been an unwavering friend through weal or woe, thick or thin. I want to thank my book collaborator, Judith Balian, whose expertise and attention to detail has helped me to bring several books to fruition and whose friendship continues to sustain me. My gratitude also goes to Susan Oddo for her editing expertise as well as her friendship, creative ideas, and advocacy. Finally, thank you to the many clients and persons whose stories I have used in this book to illustrate the profound changes wrought by following the ever-spiraling path of initiation.

**When all is said and done, initiation is meant to enlarge our capacity to give and to receive love.** This is the key to humanity's very survival. Everything else on the Path is to help us expand our current stage of consciousness, to equip us to be of greater service to other human beings, and finally, to facilitate our return to the Ocean of Love and Mercy and the Divine Source. I am so fortunate to have had the opportunity to explore the process of initiation and some of its many challenges and experiences in this book. And I am profoundly grateful for the guidance and instruction of the Masters of the Vairagi, who are the true attendants on the Labyrinthine Way.

# PREFACE

*The spirituality of the earth is an invitation to initiation,
to the death of what we have been
and the birth of something new.*

~ David Spangler

*The privilege of a lifetime
is to become who you truly are.*

~ Carl Jung

I began writing *Dancing the Labyrinth* with misgivings—dare I try to shed light on the initiation process, such a sacred and all-encompassing subject? My previous book, *Drinking the Dragon: Stories of the Dark Night of the Soul,*[1] touches on only part of this process: the necessity for many "to face their darkest corners," or to engage in shadow work (to *drink the dragon*), as part of their initiatory journey. Through stories and interviews in *Drinking the Dragon*, I hoped to show that the Dark Night—often triggered by shattering life crises—can ultimately (if honored and understood) lead to profound psychological and spiritual transformation. In *Dancing the Labyrinth*, I want to outline the stages and content of an ancient process of human spiritual development, from the First through the Fifth Initiation (the initiation of Self-Realization). My primary premise remains the same in both books: ***A true initiation process is always dependent upon achieving a connection with "living Spirit,"*** which facilitates the individual's attainment of greater wisdom and loving compassion and an ever-deepening desire to be of service to others.

It is only now, in my seventies, and after several years as a sixth initiate, that I feel I can make an effort to approximate how this innate design for human spiritual unfoldment, or *Magnum Opus* (Great Work), expresses itself in the lives of modern-day individuals. My greatest interest has always been: *How do humans change and grow, both psychologically and spiritually?* After a two-year experience of profound spiritual upheaval in my early thirties,[2] this question broadened to include the transformative effects of spiritual initiation. Consequently, *Dancing the Labyrinth* is the product of my own experiences over a 40-plus-year commitment to a spiritual path; biographical events shared by the clients I have worked with as a psychotherapist over many years; the reporting of the dozens of people I have interviewed for several book projects; the many published narratives by people describing their spiritual experiences during the early 20s decade; and various books on the subject of initiation (though many were obscure and nearly impenetrable). I am not simply reframing the scholarly thoughts and research of other authors on the theme of initiation, but I am drawing on the empirical accounts of people who are experiencing extraordinary spiritual changes while living their lives in the ordinary world.

There are many levels and types of initiation being offered today. Some are less comprehensive initiations, mere ritualistic inductions into fraternities and orders; others are adolescent rites into adulthood and society; and still others are deeply transmutational and profoundly spiritual in nature. It is the latter type of initiation that will be the focal point of *Dancing the Labyrinth*. I will attempt to meander through the maze of this many-sided esoteric process by featuring material that includes story, myth, dream, and art. Once experienced primarily in temples and sanctuaries, the rites and rituals of initiation are now the themes of our dreams and the tropes of our outer-life activities. I will explore how these universal patterns and challenges of the initiation process permeate our daily lives and activities. The book will also investigate experiences and understandings gleaned at certain stages along the initiatory path. I am interested in focusing on the empirical psychological effects and challenges of initiation rather than detailing the technical aspects of the spiritual unfoldment process. The last chapter will look at how deep-seated transformation on the individual level relates to far-reaching social and global change.

Individuals who persist in the transmutation process of initiation work diminish their karmic load, open their hearts to greater love, integrate Spirit[3] into the fabric of their daily routines (*earthing* Spirit[4]), and connect with spiritual energies for upliftment (*spiritualizing* Earth[5]). I have observed over many years as a psychotherapist that when a person sincerely wants to learn about themselves, everything in their inner and outer world rapidly responds to fulfill and further this desire: This is because the individual is doing what I call true *human work*. Everything outside of striving toward self-awareness is, in actuality, a distraction from or substitution for our *real* task, which is recognizing ourselves as spiritual beings. It is only with this recognition that we can see life events and tasks as lessons to advance us on a life journey that has now become an initiatory path.

The initiation process is not for the individual only; each person who gains spiritually by walking the long and winding road of initiation assists the *world initiate* to advance as well. The individuals who succeed in raising their own vibrational level do so by doing the hard work of clearing their own negative energies, enabling them to act as effective channels for the Light and Sound of Spirit[6] to enter into the world (which, in turn, assists in the clearing of negative Earth energies). The world is an initiate too, and often advances spiritually, just as individuals do, through hardships, calamities, and tumultuous times, shared on a global scale during the 20s decade. The relationship between individual and world is *reciprocal*: Persons act on society, and society acts on persons; countries act on one another; we are ever interconnected and interrelated. I have heard that only 1%, of the world's current population, currently at 7.8 billion—computing to around 78 million people—will need to be awakened spiritually (preparing for or already walking the Path of Initiation) to bring about a beneficial energetic upliftment to the planet. Those who follow the Labyrinthine Path are part of this force for positive change.

As a licensed psychotherapist, I have a vision that someday there will be a broad recognition of the tests and trials characteristic of the initiatory path, and that the singular symptoms and sufferings pertaining to spiritual advancement will be regarded as belonging to a special order of phenomena. I hope that in the coming decades, "spiritual emergencies" and related difficulties will not simply be consigned to a category of psychological pathology, dismissed as mere "mental breakdowns," or dulled and canceled with medications. I believe that there will be certain mental health professionals, once called *therapeutes*[7], who have already traveled the spiral path of initiation and will be guides for this process, wayshowers also known in ancient times as *hierophants*[8] or *psychopomps*.[9] These attendants will be able to create a *sacred space* for initiates who need specialized care. Just as nurses help with physical transitions, these guides can assist in the death of the initiate's old way of being and help to deliver for that person the birth of something new.

As increasing numbers of people undergo religious phenomena and mystical experiences upon the arrival of the Aquarian Age,[10] it's imperative that the transformative processes of initiation be better understood by the persons experiencing these events as well as by the professionals caring for those undergoing them. Initiation is a *divine blueprint* for humanity's psychospiritual evolution. **As humans rise in consciousness, many will dance the Labyrinthine Path of Initiation, which takes us beyond mere ego maturity to the energies of the Self and ultimately, to the very heart of God.**

*Preface*

# PREFACE ENDNOTES

[1] *Drinking the Dragon: Stories of the Dark Night of the Soul*. Encinitas, CA: Sothis Press, 2021, is available as text and as an ebook on Amazon. The *Drinking the Dragon Companion Workbook* is also available through Amazon.

[2] This two-year period, which occurred in the early 1980s, is described in detail in *Drinking the Dragon*.

[3] *Spirit* is meant as that energy that flows from the Godhead or Creator, which sustains and connects all manifestation.

[4] Examples of *earthing spirit*: taking a dream message and applying it to one's physical life or manifesting insights and ideas by writing a book.

[5] Examples of *spiritualizing earth*: prayer, meditation, dream work, journaling—anything that raises your vibration and helps you to see everyday events from a broader, more multifaceted perspective.

[6] Spirit is not Light only; it is also Sound. The Sound is the wave of pure energy that we "catch" on our way back to God, the Ocean of Love and Mercy; the Light illuminates the pitfalls and guideposts along the way.

[7] *Therapeutes* or *Therapeutai* ("Healers," or "Attendants" in Greek), was a Jewish sect of ascetics closely resembling the Essenes, who are believed to have settled near Alexandria, Egypt, during the 1st century AD.

[8] A priest/priestess who interprets sacred mysteries or esoteric principles. A *hierophant* brings religious congregants into the presence of that which is deemed holy.

[9] In Greek mythology, the *psychopomp* serves as a spiritual guide of a living person's soul and also as a guide of souls to the place of the dead.

[10] Some writers have speculated that the Great Conjunction of Jupiter and Saturn on December 21, 2020 was the true beginning of the Aquarian Age.

# DANCING THE LABYRINTH: TERMINOLOGY

*...whenever you think you have lost the path,
or whenever you feel confused by esoteric terminology or technique,
remember that all these techniques or teachings
are various ways to help you pay attention.*
~ Rick Fields

Depending on the spiritual book you are reading or the spiritual path you are taking, you will run across various terms and diverse meanings for those terms. I am mindful here of the quote by Achyut Mishra that, "Too much spiritual jargon all over the place, without any living experience, makes an individual demented." I am defining terms by using the understandings of my own spiritual path as well as the usages of many masterful works on initiation that have been written in the past. In some cases, however, I differ from a number of these writers in my efforts to simplify esoteric terminology. I did not want the jargon of spiritual advancement to supersede the emphasis on spiritual experience. For above all, initiation is the *experience of a living religion* rather than merely an exercise in parsing words. After innumerable existences living on the surface of life, our profoundest attention on the Path of Initiation has now turned from the world of outer things to the inner landscape of spiritual transformation.

**Note:** Some of these terms and their definitions also appear in the endnotes for each chapter.

**Archetypes:** Archetypes are inherited psychological blueprints and innate patterns of behavior, shared by all humankind. In Jung's theory, the experiences of a common past have made deep, permanent impressions, creating pathways or patterns for typical human expression. In other words, archetypes are primal energies that function to organize how we experience and respond to certain things in recognizably human ways. They appear as universal figures and symbols in the dreams of individuals, and collectively, in our fairy tales and myths. Common archetypes include: The Great Mother, the Witch, the Wise Old Man or Woman, the Child, the Hero, and the Devil. In this book, the Path of Initiation is considered to be an archetypal, or inborn pattern, of spiritual growth.

**Dark Night of the Soul:** Often triggered by an outside crisis, such as a divorce, death of a loved one, or a serious illness, the Dark Night of the Soul is the experience of a protracted period of depression, desolation, and despair. If the Dark Night is honored and explored (such as in psychotherapy), it can lead to deeply transformative inner changes and a complete revaluation of the individual's life. It is essentially a spiritual process, usually occurring in midlife or later. The Dark Night of the Soul is a feature of the Path of Initiation, sometimes occurring more than once. (This process is a different level and kind of psychological tumult, not to be confused with the chaos of mental dysfunction and inadequate socialization, although symptoms may seem to overlap and are sometimes hard to distinguish).

**Densities:** The various rates of vibration related to consciousness. Human waking consciousness is considered Third Density because most humans share this consciousness: self-awareness and sentience at the cost of feeling separate from one another and all other forms of life. Many humans today are moving into Fourth Density, which means they will retain the self-awareness of the Third Density, while gaining a new sense of harmony and unity, and a greater realization of how we create our own realities. The Fourth density brings a greater feeling of connection to each other, the culture, and to the environment.

*Terminology*

**Dimensions:** Often interchangeable with the term planes, according to theorist Dr. Alan Lew (quoted below). However, Dr. Joshua Stone claims that they are not the same but are dimensions of realty vs. planes of consciousness. We evolve through the planes via initiation, and dimensions are associated with human experiences. For example, the first dimension, Stone asserts, is a feeling of completion, the second can be associated with new beginnings, the third with magnification of experiences (for examination), and the fourth with flow. Joshua David Stone, *Beyond Ascension*. Light Technology Publishing, LLC, 1995, Ch.10.

According to the theorist Dr. Alan Lew, Dimensions 1-5 can be considered Collective Dimensions. Dr. Lew shared the following with me in a private email exchange on the subject:

> "…as best as I can tell, spiritual planes are the same as spiritual dimensions…. My belief is that guides/teachers who specify specific numbers of planes/dimensions are doing so to make the concept easier to understand for the human mind. Like the colors of the rainbow, there are infinite numbers of planes/dimensions, depending on how we define them…I personally like the idea that there are 7.8 billion different dimensions of our 3D human reality alone on Earth today…Drunvalo Melchizedek said he taught that there are 12 dimensions of reality, and each of those is divided into 12 levels…but I heard someone…say that a new teaching he received says there are 10 dimensions and each of those has 10 levels. In spirituality, any system will work if it makes sense to the human mind."

See Alan Lew, "The One Most Complete Guide to the Spiritual Dimensions of Reality" for further insights on this subject. December. 20, 2021. https://medium.com/new-earth-consciousness/explainer-what-are-the-different-spiritual-dimensions-of-reality-and-is-earth-moving-to-the-5th-2cd99d3dc319.

**God:** In *Dancing the Labyrinth,* God is regarded as Source and resides in the Ocean of Love and Mercy, to which all beings strive to return (with initiation as a means to achieve this). God is the One Essence that exists in everything, as an impersonal life force, consciousness, or energy (similar to "The Force" in the *Star Wars* movie series). *Its supreme energy and power flows out in intelligent waves of Light and Sound, that we know as Spirit or the Voice of God.* As the term is used here, God is beyond male and female designations and is the source of all creation throughout every plane, world, and dimension. God, or *IT,* is also known *"as 'the Great Formless One'…an active, creative BEINGNESS that answers to no marks or qualities, since all that can be said about IT is that IT exists."* (Quoted description by Sri Harold Klemp).

God is defined as an omnipresent, omnipotent, omniscient Force and Source of consciousness in which we live and move and have our being—IT is what we are made of. God is beyond all form manifestation; we cannot really be separate from God because all things are in the matrix of the Source! We only feel separate when we have forgotten our Divine Identity. Initiation is a process of gradually embodying the God presence within us.

**The Greater Guardian of the Threshold:** a luminous being—sometimes appearing similar to an angelic presence—that reveals itself to us when we are no longer under control of the world of the senses.

**Higher Self:** Sometimes called *The Greater Guardian of the Threshold,* the Higher Self has long been the mediator between the ego-personality and the Self or Soul, until, at the Third Initiation, this mediator is no longer needed. The Causal Body, which housed the Higher Self, is relinquished at the Fourth Initiation (which is experienced as a great loss) and is replaced by an immediate connection with Self/Soul. This is a merging and integration of mind-body-spirit and a direct communication with Spirit. The Higher Self or Soul "is neither spirit nor matter, but is the relation between the two, " states Joshua David Stone in his book, *The Complete Ascension Manual,* Light Technology Publishing, LLC: 1994, p. 105.

***Initiation:*** Initiation is spiritual graduate work, an agreement to unfold spiritually via gradual changes in consciousness. A true initiation process is always dependent upon achieving a connection with "living Spirit." Initiation facilitates the individual's attainment of greater wisdom and loving compassion and an ever-deepening desire to be of service to others. The Initiatory Path delineated in *Dancing the Labyrinth* is not affiliated with a traditional religion, but is both ancient and contemporary, a universal, nondenominational teaching that is a gateway to an expansion of awareness.

Initiation is generally recognized as an advanced program of human spiritual unfoldment, a profoundly experiential and transformational process, during which the initiate passes from one level or stage of consciousness to another, each "higher stage" transcending but including earlier stages. Marked by a series of occurrences, awakenings, crises, and energy impacts, the Path leads to Self-Realization and ultimately, to God-Realization. This book focuses on the basic nature of the first five major initiations of the ancient spiritual ascension program, called by some the *Secret Doctrine, Path of Wisdom,* or *Perennial Philosophy.* This program is essentially a system of gnosis (or inner knowledge) brought here by Masters of Old as a design for human evolution. It includes the Wisdom Teachings of the Ages, which are taught to us in the dream state as well the through the mundane lessons of daily living.

**Note:** The descriptions of the first five initiations in *Dancing the Labyrinth* are partially derived from my personal experiences of over 40 years on an initiatory path. In addition, extensive research was used, including various books in theosophy, anthroposophy, modern psychology (particularly C. G. Jung), parallel paths of initiation in other systems and cultures, and spiritual autobiographies. The book's description of the initiation process is not meant to be all encompassing, as experiences and interpretations can vary from person to person and from path to path. The emphasis is on the empirical—or *lived*—experience of the individual on the Path, or in other words, on the psychospiritual realities of the initiation process. I believe these experiences are relevant for the modern individual who is seeking deeper spiritual meaning and purpose.

**Planes:** A region, level, or according to some authors, a dimension of reality. A plane, as used in *Dancing the Labyrinth*, is a level of thought, existence, or development. The two most popular number of initiatory planes are 7 and 12, but there are, in actuality, infinite numbers of planes/dimensions. The planes separated into distinct levels of consciousness, as I have done in this book, is simply a way to wrap our minds around spiritual growth. (Some claim that there are thousands of dimensions.) As humans evolve in consciousness, they individually realize coarser to finer densities that affiliate them with certain planes.

**Self, Soul, Atman.** In *Dancing the Labyrinth*, the terms *Self* and *Soul* are used interchangeably to refer to the true, innermost spiritual essence of all beings. The Spiritual Self is universal, unchangeable, ever present, permanent, ageless, and awake. The psychiatrist Carl Jung uses the term Self to "represent the centre of psychic awareness that transcends ego consciousness and includes in its scope all the vast reaches of the psyche that are ordinarily unconscious," the personal consciousness as well as the objective or non-personal unconscious. Achievement of the goal of the Self, or finding God within, "has been regarded by all of the great religions of the world as the final goal."

**Shadow:** The Shadow is an archetype, an energic form that is hidden in the unconscious aspects of oneself, which the ego has either repressed or never recognized. We usually see these reprehensible traits only outside of ourselves as the faults of others. (The Shadow has a personally relevant component and is also a part of the larger collective unconscious.) In esoteric literature, the Shadow has been called *The (Lower) Dweller* or *The Guardian of the Threshold*. The Dweller is encountered when Initiates are ready to see themselves as they truly are (such as the revelation of untamed instincts, selfish desires, and egotistical wishes). This process enables Initiates to see themselves without delusion, and to realize the efforts required to free themselves from the hidden influence of these undesirable qualities.

**Spiritual Experiences:** Phenomenal experiences are important at the beginning of this journey, but they can become distractions as we spiritually mature. Dramatic spiritual experiences (such as spontaneous out-of-body journeys, near-death experiences, visions of light, rapturous experiences of union) serve to "wake us" up to realities beyond the surface life of everyday routine. However, as we progress on the Path of Initiation, ecstatic experiences that "carry us away" recede in the face of the inner work we must do in the here and now. Spiritual experiences can fill us with love and light and awe. They often come to us as blessings. But if we attempt to remain in the realms of light, we can become inflated (the misappropriation of spiritual energies to our egos, which feeds our need to be admired or special) and certainly ungrounded. This can lead us to do a "spiritual bypass," or "end run" around the work of confronting and healing our own lower human natures. Spiritual maturity requires recognition of the opposites in ourselves and in life; we do not advance without shadow work and struggle.

# TABLE OF CONTENTS

*Acknowledgments* ... vii
*Preface* ... ix
*Dancing the Labyrinth: Terminology* ... xv

**INTRODUCTION** ... 1
    The Spiritual Journey of Initiation ... 1
    Advanced Program of Spiritual Development ... 1
    Characteristics of the Initiatory Journey ... 3
    Parallel Paths ... 8
    How Dancing the Labyrinth Is Organized ... 9
    Introduction Endnotes ... 11

**CHAPTER ONE**
**ENTERING THE LABYRINTH: WHAT IS INITIATION?** ... 13
    Who Is the Initiate? Seekers and Boundary-Crossers ... 13
    What Is Initiation? Blueprint For Human Evolution ... 17
    What Are the Goals of Initiation? We Are Stars… ... 20
    Archetypes: Patterns of Human Behavior ... 22
    The Labyrinth: Symbol of the Spiritual Journey ... 24
    How Does Initiation Work? Mystery and Metamorphosis ... 28
    Initiation: A Transformation in Consciousness ... 30
    Initiation: Pathway To Freedom ... 33
    Chapter One Exercises: Is Your Life Guided? ... 37
    Chapter One Endnotes ... 39

**CHAPTER TWO**
**LIVING THE MYSTERY: INITIATION IN MODERN LIFE** ... 45
    The Challenges of Everyday Life ... 45
    Rick's Story: Into the Desert ... 47
    Sharon's Story: Baptism by Water ... 49
    Veronica's Story: Through the Fires ... 53
    Purification Through Trials and Tribulations ... 55
    The Role of Anxiety and Depression ... 57
    Something Funny Happened on the Way to the Supermarket ... 59

*Table of Contents*

To Do a Job and Do It Well ..................................................................64
Lily and Kelsey's Stories: Experiences of the Spiritual Kind ................68
Spiritual Experiences and the Road of Initiation ..................................73
Chapter Two Exercises: Learning in the School of Life ........................76
Chapter Two Endnotes ..........................................................................78

**CHAPTER THREE**
**MAPPING THE SPIRAL WAY: FIVE STAGES OF INITIATION**
**THE MASTER AND STAGE 1** ..........................................................83
    The First Five Stages ............................................................................83
    The Journey Begins ..............................................................................86
    The Master ............................................................................................91
    Who Is the Master? ..............................................................................91
    Why Do We Need a Master? ................................................................93
    How Do We Meet Up With the Master? ..............................................94
    How Can We Tell a True Master? ........................................................96
    What Are the Effects of the Master? ....................................................99
    Which Roles Does the Master Fulfill? ................................................102
    The First Initiation: Purification ........................................................104
    The Birth ............................................................................................104
    The Muladhara Chakra ......................................................................105
    The Physical Plane ..............................................................................106
    Listening to the Voice of Guidance ....................................................107
    Tasks ..................................................................................................110
        Identifying Your Hidden Selves ..................................................110
        Encountering the Shadow ..........................................................113
        Confronting Your Fears ..............................................................117
        Moderation and Discrimination ................................................118
    Summary: Cleaning Up ......................................................................120
    Chapter Three Exercises: Who or What Runs Your Life? ..................123
    Chapter Three Endnotes ....................................................................125

**CHAPTER FOUR**
**MAPPING THE SPIRAL WAY: FIVE STAGES OF INITIATION**
**STAGES 2 AND 3** ............................................................................129
    The Second Initiation: Commitment ................................................129
    The Svadhisthana Chakra ..................................................................130
    The Astral Plane ................................................................................131

Into the Abyss ... 133
Tasks ... 139
    Transmutation of Energies ... 140
    Seeing Through Glamour ... 139
    Falling into the Void ... 144
    Loneliness ... 146
Summary: Coming into Being ... 149
The Third Initiation: Integration ... 151
To Know Your Narrative ... 151
The Manipura Chakra ... 153
The Causal Plane ... 154
Climbing the Mountain ... 156
The Divine Child ... 157
The Cycle of Threes ... 158
Lower Mental Thought Processes ... 160
Tasks ... 163
    Seeing Through Illusions ... 163
    Integration ... 165
    Detachment ... 166
    Flexibility ... 170
Summary: The Light and Sound ... 171
Chapter Four Exercises: Falling into Spiritual Darkness ... 174
Chapter Four Endnotes ... 176

## CHAPTER FIVE
## MAPPING THE SPIRAL WAY: FIVE STAGES OF INITIATION
## STAGES 4-5 ... 181

The Fourth Initiation: Alignment With Self ... 182
Renunciation ... 182
The Anahata Chakra ... 184
The Fourth or Mental Plane ... 186
Tasks ... 189
    A Second Dark Night ... 189
    Pride ... 191
    Disillusionment ... 192
    Alienation ... 194
Summary: The Great Transition ... 198
The Fifth Initiation: Self-Realization ... 200

*Table of Contents*

    The Revelation.................................................................................................200
    The Throat Chakra..........................................................................................202
    The Fifth Plane.................................................................................................203
    Soul Recognition.............................................................................................204
    Tasks....................................................................................................................206
        Homesickness........................................................................................206
        Union........................................................................................................208
        Service......................................................................................................213
        Ordinariness...........................................................................................216
    Summary: The Ocean of Love and Mercy.............................................217
    Chapter Five Exercises: "You Are Here"..................................................219
    Chapter Five Endnotes..................................................................................221

# CHAPTER SIX
# FOLLOWING THE THREAD: INITIATION PATTERNS IN THE ARTS....227
    Art Is Transformational.................................................................................227
    Books of Struggle and Change...................................................................230
    *Wild: Lost and Found on the Pacific Coast Trail:* Disillusionment..........230
    *The Deliverance from Error:* Pride...........................................................232
    *The Golden Notebook:* Integration...........................................................235
    *The Yoga of Max's Discontent:* Alienation..............................................238
    Dream-Inspired Art: Images That Transform.......................................241
    Anna Halprin: Shadow Work.....................................................................243
    Ann McCoy: Alchemical Transmutation................................................245
    Deena Metzger: The Dark Night of the Soul........................................248
    Carolee Schneemann: Union.....................................................................251
    Initiation Themes in Film............................................................................253
    *Chasing Mavericks:* Finding a Mentor......................................................253
    *Seven Years in Tibet:* Learning Humility..................................................255
    *The Whale Rider:* Going Your Own Way.................................................257
    *Dune:* Facing Your Fears..............................................................................259
    Chapter Six Exercises: Your Life is a Story, Too...................................262
    Chapter Six Endnotes....................................................................................265

# CHAPTER SEVEN
# THE WORLD LABYRINTH: THE NEW HUMAN..................................271
    Ch-Ch-Ch-Ch-Changes (David Bowie)..................................................271
    The Fourth Turning........................................................................................274

The Current Crisis Era ........................................................................... 275
The Shift Age ......................................................................................... 277
Issues of the Shift Age ......................................................................... 278
Cycles of Evolution .............................................................................. 279
Consciousness Rising .......................................................................... 281
The New Human .................................................................................. 284
Connectivity ......................................................................................... 285
The New Religion ................................................................................ 288
Practical Spirituality ............................................................................ 291
Chapter Seven Exercises: Reflecting on Your Spiritual Journey ... 297
Chapter Seven Endnotes .................................................................... 298

*Epilogue* ..................................................................................................... 303
*About the Author* ..................................................................................... 309

# INTRODUCTION

## THE SPIRITUAL JOURNEY OF INITIATION

*We take spiritual initiation
when we become conscious of the Divine within us,
and thereby contact the Divine without us.*
~ Dion Fortune

*If we pursue a spiritual path in depth,
then it changes who and what we are.
There is no turning back. We can only move forward.*
~ Vivianne Crowley

## ADVANCED PROGRAM OF SPIRITUAL DEVELOPMENT

*Each of us is here to discover our true selves;
that essentially we are spiritual beings
who have taken manifestation in physical form;
that we're not human beings that have occasional spiritual experiences,
that we're spiritual beings that have occasional human experiences.*
~ Deepak Chopra

In *Dancing the Labyrinth* **many references will be made to *God*.** I have indicated on the Terminology Page, as well as in the endnotes, that I use the familiar term God to mean the Source or the One Essence. This Supreme Energy exists in everything as an impersonal life force, consciousness, or energy. I employ the word God to indicate the Force of Creation, Whose power and energy flows out in intelligent waves of Light and Sound (Spirit).

The Source resides in the Ocean of Love and Mercy, to which all beings strive to return, with initiation as a means to achieve this.

When many people think of initiation, they usually think of the rites, rituals, tests, and trials that usher young people into adulthood. Many areas of the world, including the United States, retain these initiation processes where we continue to observe the Jewish tradition of *Bar* and *Bat Mitzvah*, the Hispanic *Quinceanera*, the Amish *Rumspringa*, and the coming of age *Sweet 16* celebration. Conversely, in *Dancing the Labyrinth*, we are looking at an *adult* initiation process, an advanced program of spiritual development which increasing numbers of persons today are (consciously or unconsciously) joining.

In the chapters ahead, we will be exploring initiation as a sacred process created so that humans can receive divine wisdom over time and by degrees—for the purpose of remembering—and becoming who we truly are as spiritual beings! I dreamed one night that as I was entering the physical world to be born into this lifetime, the last words I heard from the spiritual realm were, "Remember God; remember God!" The danger is becoming so encumbered by life's minutia and so lost in our daily narratives, that we forget our wings!

At one time we naturally knew our Source, but over millennia, our lower, physical senses (physical needs, basic emotions, thought processes) developed at the cost of the direct perception of the higher, spiritual worlds. We were no longer able to enjoy direct contact with spiritual realities without effort and training. Today, we not only feel separated from the spiritual planes but from *ourselves*. Think of how many people you know who believe that once we die, that's truly the end of us!

How does initiation heal this split? Initiation is an ongoing *reciprocal* relationship[1] between the physical and the spiritual worlds that *strives to heal*

*Introduction*

*this rift.* We are at that crucial juncture in human history when we have progressed, in general, to a level of consciousness that allows material culture and the world of the spirit to be united *within ourselves.* This merging, at least in regard to the lower initiations, can now occur in masses of people, and is no longer only reserved for the special few. *What are the guideposts and special markers of the Initiation process? How do we know if we are on the Path?*

## CHARACTERISTICS OF THE INITIATORY JOURNEY

*The journey home to God is what life is about.*
*In a sense, it's not even a journey.*
*It's an ongoing experience.*
~ **Harold Klemp**

*The only journey is the journey within.*
~ **Rainer Maria Rilke**

While the Labyrinthine Path of Initiation cannot be reduced to checklists, you can survey your life to assess what spiritual experiences you are encountering, and whether they are part of the deeper process of initiation. Ram Dass wrote about how the spiritual journey begins: "Once you get that first glimpse of living Spirit, once your heart opens even for a moment to unconditional love, everything in your life becomes grist for the mill of your awakening…if you're a lawyer, you go on being a lawyer, but you begin to use being a lawyer as a way of coming to God."[2] A surefire way to know if you are on the graduate school path of initiation is that your whole life begins to bend, like a plant toward light, in the direction of service to others. You increasingly find that you are drawn to offering up your every thought, every action, and every word as a gift to God.

Whether you think that you are preparing for or are already treading the Labyrinthine Path of Initiation, the following discussion points will be relevant to you:

**1. The goal of life is Self-Realization.** "The spiritual journey is what the soul is up to when we attend to daily living." (Christina Baldwin). The ages roll by, and finally, we awaken in a lifetime to find that we can no longer ignore the spark that is hidden inside us, and in fact, in all humans. Our perception of reality shifts: what we once thought was "real" is only illusion; who we once thought we were is simply *persona* (our "social" facades). We now realize that we want to become a *conscious collaborator* with a journey that turns the spark into a burning fire for God. Daily life in the physical world must be lived, but we know in our hearts that, essentially, we belong to the Religion of the Lovers of God, and we are on the footpath to Home. The spiritual journey as initiation becomes the meaning and purpose in life.

**2. Awakening to the spiritual journey may come as a crisis.** Following the trauma and stress of the last few years, you may find yourself identifying with a Dark Night of the Soul experience. This is a protracted period during which we feel lost, forsaken, and separated from God. This stage either cumulatively emerges over time or strikes more swiftly due to a life crisis, such as an unexpected breakup or divorce, the sudden death of a loved one, immediate trauma, or an abrupt major life transition. During this time, we feel that we are "walking through the valley of the shadow of death," finding no point, no direction, and little purpose in life. You may feel isolated, alienated, despairing, exhausted, and abandoned. No longer interested in what supported you in the past, you ask, "What can sustain me now?"

This dark and chaotic time is often an invitation to step into a more meaningful existence; you are beckoned to become part of a process that does not allow you to remain on the surface of life. Fundamentally, the Dark Night is a *death and rebirth* experience; all that you once identified with

*Introduction*

must be stripped away so that you can emerge immaculate and raw. More detail on the Dark Night can be found in *Drinking the Dragon*,[3] my book which focuses on the exploration of this process.

**3. Everyday life serves as a field of tests and trials in preparation for the Path of Initiation.** If we see our lives as earning an education in the schoolroom of Earth, our daily experiences are then lessons in courage (e.g., giving a talk when we have stage fright); classes in endurance (e.g., braving a grave illness with grit and grace); and training in patience (e.g., almost any situation when raising children). We learn some lessons more quickly or slowly than others, but before we can move up to the next grade level, there are many tests:

- making correct decisions about what's good for us and what isn't
- putting what we learn into practice
- working hard instead of expecting to be taken care of
- expressing gratitude for what is given to us
- learning that difficult situations can teach us the most
- knowing that all spoken words and actions have consequences
- loving others makes life worthwhile
- giving back to life in service is a mark of inner maturity

**4. During the early stages of the Path (some have called these the Disciple phases), you will be required to do a lot of "clean up."** To better understand this concept, it's helpful to think of your personality as a house. Initially, you will need to get rid of the rubbish in the backyard (bad habits, negative patterns, childish behaviors) and refurbish the house's foundation to make sure the house is secure and stable (which in some cases, means the house needs to first be dismantled or torn down). This process creates havoc, just as it would if you renovated your bathroom or kitchen while living at home. This process is so the personality can be eventually used as an instrument for the Higher Self and eventually, Soul, which can only occur if the personality is well-made: sturdy, solid, and sure.

**5. The spiritual journey reveals itself in steps and stages.** There are recurrent cycles of expansion and enlightenment, and moments of intimacy with the Divine that transition into periods of constriction, isolation, and a state of feeling forsaken by God. The Path is one of struggle and effort, encompassing the challenges of identifying, cleansing, and transmuting aspects of yourself at intervals, followed by periods of managing the intensive work of reintegration. The initiate is a collaborative partner in what is fundamentally a spiritual process; at many points along the way, we cannot control, but only respond to, the profound changes being experienced. This intensely transformative work cannot be done by the initiate alone.

**6. *You will need a Guide*.** This work can be facilitated via some practitioners of transpersonal methods of psychotherapy, certain leaders of various spiritual belief systems and paths and, especially, through contact with a Spiritual Master or Guide (your own experience will help you test the authenticity of this Master). Frequently, such a Master of the Path will make him- or herself known to you once you begin transmitting certain frequencies (and thereby emitting greater intensities of light).

The process of Initiation is best guided by someone who has personally seen the Journey to its end and knows of its pitfalls and challenges. In addition, the spiritual student will require energy impacts which stimulate the Initiate's progress and are transmitted at the Master's discretion. The authentic Master extends, out of a deep and abiding love for all humans everywhere, a helping hand to those who long for God. (More on the Master/Guide in Chapter 1).

**7. *The length, tasks, and individual responses to the stages of Initiation may vary*.** Some initiates may complete earlier stages of initiation more quickly than later levels (due to having successfully achieved earlier initiations in previous lifetimes). A few initiates will only complete part of the Path, picking up the journey in future lifetimes. In *Dancing the Labyrinth*, we will look only at the first five of the initiatory stages, which brings us to

*Introduction*

Self-Realization. It is possible today for some to become Self-Realized (and beyond) in a single lifetime.

Tasks assigned in this book to each of the first five stages of initiation are not hard and fast. A number of initiates, needing more time to learn tasks associated with certain stages of initiation, may continue to work on these undertakings into the next stages. Because these stages are fluid, tasks from different stages can be presented together or simultaneously. Finally, these tasks are not all inclusive, but represent some of the main challenges faced by the initiate over time. Yet, even with these variations on the theme, there are enough significant similarities between individual journeys on the Path that particular patterns and comparable chronologies can be recognized and explicated.

**8. *There are observable behaviors, qualities, and traits that can be associated with progress on the Path.*** The purpose of the Labyrinthine Way is to find our way back to our true center of being. This requires that we temporarily disengage with the outer world to explore and develop an *inner life*. This turnaround from external to internal life begins a process (not entirely in our control) that encourages awareness of our own behaviors and reactions so that we can take responsibility for them. There are hallmarks of progress on the Path, as a transformed consciousness eventually manifests in changes that affect every aspect of our lives. We become committed to expressing deeper compassion and love, greater generosity and unselfishness, more tolerance and forgiveness, and enhanced patience and flexibility.

As Ram Dass has conveyed,[4] our entire nature becomes bent on submitting all that we do in life as an *offering to God*. When we wake up, we offer the coming day with its myriad problems as an offering to God; if we are dealing with a difficult customer service situation, we offer it up to God; when we are annoyed by our partner's messiness at home, we offer it up to be blessed; when we walk happily outdoors in the sunshine, we offer this up, too. We learn to develop an observing or witness consciousness that enables us to take a detached (objective) perspective in the midst of life's ups and downs. The deep burning love of God comes like a thief in the night; and before we know it, we are caught up in its flames.

## PARALLEL PATHS

> *Do not exalt any path above God.*
> *There are many paths that lead to God.*
> *So, people are capable of finding and following*
> *the ways that suit them, provided they do not stand still.*
> ~ Zalman Schachter-Shalomi

> *Regardless of time, place, or culture,*
> *the motifs and stages of initiation are the same.*
> ~ Miles Neale

There are many paths to God! The Initiatory Path delineated in *Dancing the Labyrinth* is not affiliated with a traditional religion, but is both ancient and contemporary, a universal, nondenominational teaching that is a gateway to an expansion of consciousness. This Pathway is generally recognized as an advanced program of human spiritual unfoldment, a profoundly experiential and transformational process, during which the initiate passes from one level of consciousness to another, each "higher stage" transcending but including earlier stages.[5] Marked by a series of occurrences, awakenings, crises, and energy impacts, the ancient Path of Initiation repolarizes the individual's consciousness from the lower self (ego-personality) to the Self. The Path leads to Self-Realization and ultimately to God-Realization.

Initiatory paths can vary on the basis of system and type, potency, number of initiations, and the potential for spiritual progress. Yet, many overlap in purpose, chronology and core curriculum. Similar, parallel paths include the ancient Mystery Schools such as the Egyptian, Eleusinian, Bacchic, and Orphic Schools; the Hawaiian Huna teachings; West African traditions; Native American and other types of shamanism; Spiritual or Transpersonal Psychology; the Islamic esoteric branch of Sufism; esoteric Christianity; some Hindi paths; the Judaic esoteric teachings of the Kabbalah; Buddhist wisdom traditions; and the ancient study and practice of alchemy.

*Dancing the Labyrinth* does not include a review of the many alternative pathways of spiritual development, but focuses on the basic nature of the first five major initiations of the ancient spiritual ascension program, called by some the *Secret Doctrine*, *Path of Wisdom*, or *Perennial Philosophy*. This program is essentially a system of gnosis (inner knowledge) brought here by Masters of Old as a design for human evolution. It includes the Wisdom Teachings of the Ages, which are taught to us in the dream state as well the through the mundane lessons of daily living. In general, *Dancing the Labyrinth* discusses what is meant by initiation, how modern humans are encountering the motifs and challenges of initiation in their everyday lives, including the arts, and what initiation means for Western culture and the world at large.

## HOW DANCING THE LABYRINTH IS ORGANIZED

*When we speak of the Path,*
*we mean much more than a course of study.*
*The Path is a way of life*
*and on it the whole being must cooperate*
*if the heights are to be won.*
~ **Dion Fortune**

The following is a brief overview of this book's contents by chapter:

**Chapter 1** describes the characteristics of an initiate and provides a framework for initiation as a blueprint for human development. An overview of the processes of initiation is presented, and the meaning of the labyrinth as an apt symbol for human development via initiation is discussed.

**Chapter 2** covers the images and themes of initiation in the everyday experience of modern Western humans. These patterns of initiation will be explored through the lived stories and anecdotes submitted by clients, acquaintances, friends, and the protagonists of published narrations.

**Chapter 3** will take the information in Chapter 1 and reorganize it with additional material to outline the First Stage of Initiation. An overview of the role of a Master or Guide of the initiation process will be included.

**Chapter 4** discusses the Second and Third Stages of initiation. This information includes tasks and other features that are characteristic of each Stage.

**Chapter 5** summarizes the Fourth and Fifth Stages of initiation, including the tasks and challenges distinguishing these levels of the Path.

**Chapter 6** looks at the theme of initiation as portrayed in the arts: novels, film, and the works of artists working in various media.

**Chapter 7** considers the importance of the initiation process on a global scale, for the present and future of humankind.

*Introduction*

# INTRODUCTION ENDNOTES

[1] Initiation functions as both an ascent for the physical world of the senses and, at the same time, a descent for the spiritual realms. The hard work aquired along the Path of Initiation (e.g., healing our splintered selves, transmuting shadow qualities, resolving karma) allows us to gradually ascend in consciousness so that hidden spiritual truths, blessings, and transformative energies can be imparted to us. As more and more people do the work of initiation, the secret teachings of the sacred dimensions can be made more readily available to all of us.

[2] Ram Dass. *Polishing the Mirror: How to Live from Your Spiritual Heart*. Boulder, CO: Sounds True, 2013, p.31.

[3] Patricia Ariadne. *Drinking the Dragon: Stories of the Dark Night of the Soul*. Encinitas, CA: Sothis Press, 2021.

[4] Ram Dass. "Making Every Act an Offering of Service," *Love, Serve, Remember Foundation*. https://www.ramdass.org/making-every-act-an-offering-of-service/

[5] More detail on the concept of "transcending but including" is covered in Ken Wilbur's book, *The Religion of Tomorrow: A Vision for the Future of the Great Traditions—More Inclusive, More Comprehensive, More Complete*. Boulder, CO: Shambhala Publications, 2017.

# CHAPTER ONE

# Entering the Labyrinth: What is Initiation?

*The word Initiation comes from two Latin words,*
*in, into; and ire, to go; therefore,*
*the making of a beginning, or the entrance into something.*
~ Alice Bailey

## WHO IS THE INITIATE?
## SEEKERS AND BOUNDARY- CROSSERS

*True initiation is a response to an inner calling;*
*it requires that you face personal challenges heroically*
*and experience a genuine rebirth into a new way of being.*
~ Albert Villoldo

***Many people today do not know that they are already on the initiatory path.*** Lecturer and author, Marianne Williamson, remarks that everyone is on a spiritual path just by simply living their lives, even though they may not be aware of this. Unknowingly on the path of initiation, everyday people may not be affiliated with a particular religion but nevertheless harbor deep spiritual longings. They are not content with merely living on the surface of life; they are seeking to live a "guided" life. They are sure that they will continue to exist in some form beyond physical death. They wonder if they have a "mission;" above all, they seek meaning and purpose. These individuals often make efforts to release themselves from grudges, to understand and resolve childhood setbacks, to develop compassion, to surmount their fears, to act on their desire to help others, to view obstructions as challenges, and to see life itself as a program of learning. They know that a Divine Source or Supreme Creator (beyond male and female designations) exists outside of time and space, and they long to return there, "to go home" again. They are seekers of higher truths. They may use prayer, meditation, or contemplation, spiritual literature, dream work, and other spiritually oriented practices to try to fill in what is, for them, a God-shaped hole in their hearts. Theirs is a natural unfoldment into initiation. Often, they do not even know why or how they came to know, wonder or to act on these things. Perhaps you recognize *yourself* in this description.

For some people, the invitation to embark on the labyrinthine path may begin with vague feelings of discontent, incompleteness, and disappointment. Such persons may also struggle with a chronic, low-level depression for which they cannot find a cause. They feel at odds with themselves and unhappy with the decisions they've made. The refrain "Is that all there is?" may secretly echo in the back of their minds. They may feel painfully alone, endure moods of emptiness and boredom, and find they are out of step with current activities and friends. To dull or diminish such feelings, many people today try to lose themselves in group activity; excessively use distractions such as social media and entertainment; or employ alcohol, prescription or recreational drugs, food, or sex to muffle their discomfort. Another typical response to psychological disquiet is to make major, sweeping changes by leaving jobs, swapping out spouses, moving to another state or country, or by rushing to rffect other drastic outer-life adjustments. Alternatively, a special few may have begun a process of self-exploration. They suspect that their uneasiness has an inner, spiritual cause and that these disturbing moods and feelings may be signaling that life is calling them to find and become their innermost spiritual selves.

Without knowing it, everyday persons facing the adversities of life are sometimes candidates for the initiation process. A number of people unconsciously embark on a process of initiation by experiencing an unexpected crisis in the outer, physical life, such as a divorce, death of a loved one, a passionate love for another that isn't returned, a life-threatening illness or catastrophic injury, or a devastating experience of social injustice. These difficulties often lead to inner tumult and chaos, which can impel a person into his or her own psychological depths. The events of the 2020s decade have brought every type of physical, emotional, and social illness and dysfunction to our attention and sometimes into our homes. While struggling with the sorrows, disappointments, and failures of life—sometimes called "walking through the fires"—certain people have not been defeated by such tests but rather purified and refined by them. Accordingly, in the preparatory or beginning stages of initiation, this process can be understood as *purification by fire*. When honored with attention and insight, these devastating incidents can trigger profound changes in our lives. What were thought to be merely injurious events can actually represent the *outer* complements to an *inner* need for a larger life, a "life that more closely resembles"[1] you.

The calamities of the last few years have compelled many people to reassess their lives and to reevaluate their priorities; they were stopped in their tracks by Covid-19 and its variants. However, the upside to the stay-at-home restrictions of the last few years is that many of us have been "forced back onto ourselves." Perhaps for the first time, there has been an opening of a space and time to go within—although parents of school-age children may disagree! Some people, especially those who have resigned from prior jobs or occupations, may have begun an inner journey of self-inquiry, possibly through psychotherapy, that initially seemed to be forced on them by circumstances. Yet many who found themselves doing this inner work have essentially been preparing for the journey of initiation. *In fact, some have been training to walk this Path their entire lives!* These same individuals likely spent many years cultivating an aspirational nature, demonstrating a bent for spiritually-oriented studies and practices, making efforts to help others, and striving to improve their character by fostering the qualities of diligence, courage, honesty, generosity, perseverance, patience, compassion, tolerance, and kindness. These are qualities necessary to begin the journey on the Labyrinthine Path of Initiation.

Those who take the initiative and step forward—two root meanings of the word, *initiation*—become "boundary-crossers" with one foot in the material world and another in the spiritual realms ("head in the clouds and feet on the ground"). This type of straddling, or living in two worlds, is especially difficult for results-oriented Westerners. During the initiation process, nothing is certain and the itinerary is unknown. The physical senses one has depended on throughout life are useless here. Many people who pass over the threshold into the labyrinth of initiation (and into their own unconscious depths) initially do so with an *outer-directed* consciousness (extroversion, ego-centeredness, focus on the materialistic world), but they soon find themselves walking along a deeply disorienting corridor that forces them ever more into an *inner-directed* consciousness (introversion, intuition, focus on the intangible world). Their everyday life experiences—along with perennial themes of initiation in their dreams and visualizations—induct them into the tests and trials of initiation that were once ritually enacted in the ancient mystery schools. At some crucial point in their journey, they are sustained in unexpected ways: They find supportive people, illuminating books, and guiding symbols from the unconscious. They may also find that a spiritual guide or master is close at hand to help them negotiate the meandering path that leads them into parts of themselves where they have not gone before.

Many tests of courage and trials of resolve are encountered along the Serpentine Path. Trembling and lost in the dank and mossy passages of the labyrinth, the wanderer at some point confronts the formerly hidden and objectionable parts of the lower self. This task, one among many, is for the individual to confront, acknowledge, mediate (make less harmful), and integrate these aspects of the psyche that are the most difficult to accept as one's own: envy and jealousy, rage, dishonesty, misuse of personal power, vanity, and more. Remorseful and in deep emotional turmoil, the wanderer eventually experiences psychological death and rebirth. Initiation leads to the death of a former way of being, which is always followed by a rebirth, a renewal as a consequence of having undergone a transmutation in every atom, nerve, and cell. That is why initiates were once called "twice born" or "born from above."

Helena Blavatsky, the founder of Theosophy,[2] stated that the true name of humans is "The Initiates." To become an initiate is the future of all humankind. It is the way of evolution for all humans, instituted during the mid-Atlantean era and accelerating at the onset of the Aquarian Age.[3] Initiation is an advanced course of human development, which is better understood as *unfoldment*, since qualities or virtues are not so much added as the negative accumulations of the ages are thrown off. When we finally reach the labyrinth's outer door, we are released into the cold, clear air, and we stand shiny and luminous. We now know that we are part of a larger whole, and that life is no longer about *us*, but that we are about *life*.[4]

## WHAT IS INITIATION?
## BLUEPRINT FOR HUMAN EVOLUTION

*Life, it seems, is nothing if not a series*
*of initiations, transitions, and incorporations.*
~ **Alan Dundes**

*The new blueprint is designed to accelerate that remembering,*
*like we are awakening from a dream. That's its purpose.*
*The initiations will anchor the new blueprint,*
*and the integration of that—with full alignment to that frequency.*
~ **Christine McCormick Day**

Initiation is linked to the basic structure of human life. It underpins everything we are and do. Initiation is an inherited destiny belonging to the human race as a whole. We start to awaken to the reality of initiation when we begin to ask the essential questions: *Is there more to my existence than day-to-day life? Is there an overarching design to my life? Do I have an unknown purpose? Is there a hidden meaning in my suffering?* The questions themselves open the door to spiritual awakenings that ultimately help us transcend our daily routines and to invite something sacred into our lives.

Many people think that they know themselves well—their likes and dislikes, their fears and doubts, their particular traits and their characteristic behaviors. However, this awareness is only centered in the personal consciousness or ego; there is another part of us that is hidden to most. That part is the most sacred facet of ourselves, identified by the psychiatrist Carl Jung as the Self,[5] our highest spiritual aspect. Most of us see the Self only *outside* of ourselves, in those religious figures we most revere: Jesus, Mohammed, Buddha, Osiris, Krishna, to name a few. These outer figures represent and reflect back to us the beauty and holiness of the Self that is our true essence. The primary events of their life stories often represent the *inner* path that all of humanity must take when walking the mysterious and uncertain Labyrinth of Initiation. **We must find the Divine Avatar within us.**[6]

In the Middle Ages, going within to find God was primarily done in nunneries and monasteries, which grew to be known as taking the path of *devotio moderna* (modern devotion), the idea that the inner life of the spirit was more important than obedience to ritual or religious law. This movement was particularly exemplified in the lives of the medieval mystics, including Mechtilde of Magdeburg, a Christian medieval mystic who had her first vision of the Holy Spirit at age twelve; Julian of Norwich, an English anchoress who wrote the first book in English by a known woman author; and Meister Johann Eckhart, a German theologian, philosopher, mystic, and the source of the quote, "If the only prayer you ever say in your entire life is 'Thank you,' it will be enough." Today, we do not have to be cloistered in seclusion or join a religious order to cultivate a personal relationship with the Divine. In the midst of everyday life, we can nurture a profound relationship to Spirit; while potting plants or washing dishes, we can begin the long, return pilgrimage to Source.

As mentioned earlier in this chapter, the Path of Initiation very often begins with crisis. That is why the events during the early years of the 20s decade have been so important, as these tumultuous times have created opportunities for many to reassess their lives and their relationship to the Divine. Gary Zukav points out in his inspirational book, *The Seat of the Soul*, that humans did not have to develop into spiritual realization via pain and trauma, but that this pattern evolved out of the choices that we made throughout time as a species. He reminds us that, as a consequence, the awakening of the personality for most humans now requires learning through fear and doubt instead of through wisdom. The current onset of the Aquarian Age, Zukav posits, will give humanity another opportunity to choose how it will learn.[7]

I am optimistic that in the coming years, many persons will choose The Path of Initiation—the *Way of Wisdom*—in order to develop and grow into wholeness. I foresee a day when a spiritual psychology develops that will make The Path of Initiation central to its psychological theories and psychotherapeutic methods. Such a school of psychology will employ the ancient system of initiation as practiced in the mystery schools of old, to recognize, understand, and realize the various stages of consciousness inherent to the initiation process. This approach to human psychology will be facilitated by *therapeutae*[8] (healers or attendants), who themselves have walked The Path. **The spiritual unfoldment once achieved by humans via crisis and the "Road of Ashes" will then be attained by those treading the healing "Path with Heart."**

# WHAT ARE THE GOALS OF INITIATION? WE ARE STARS...

> *I am a child of Earth and starry heaven,*
> *but my race is of heaven alone.*
> ~ The Orphic Mysteries

There are many goals of the initiation process including the following objectives:

**1. *One of the main goals of initiation is to realize our connection with Spirit through immediate and direct experience.*** When humans wonder where God is in their lives, they forget that they *themselves* are a spark of God; our very existence is predicated on God's essence within us. We have *never* been separated from God; it is only the distraction of the "10,000 things"[9] and a trick of the mind to think that we are. Through a true initiation process, we are linked to Spirit and find ourselves, as a channel for this energy, more capable of giving and receiving a higher (not merely romantic or filial) love, with every initiation.

**2. *Another major goal is to lose the fear of death.*** The Initiatory Way incorporates many psychospiritual deaths and rebirths. On the Path of Initiation, we are learning to "die in life." We intermittently shed people, possessions, positions, approval, and praise, and, accordingly, our last shred of pride! We also undergo several *into-the-void* dream experiences on The Path, where we find ourselves, as an example, in a car plummeting off of a roadside cliff. As we are hurling through dark, empty space, we feel powerless, disoriented, terrified, and alone as we anticipate certain death on the rocks below. Ultimately, after a few of these dreams, we realize while still in the dream or afterwards, that death does not really exist—and even if we *do* hit bottom, we can simply walk out of the physical body into another "body" of finer substance.

The fear of death is also resolved because some initiates are able to naturally and consciously leave and return to their bodies (sometimes called *soul travel*). This was a common ability among humans at one time, and later, when most humans became so tied to the physical world that they could no longer practice this art, *exteriorization* (as it is also known) was taught to initiates in temples and mystery schools. We already *unconsciously* leave our physical bodies while dreaming (which is why our skeletal muscles are paralyzed by neurotransmitters during REM sleep). In fact, most of us have had the experience of driving somewhere while thinking about something else, only to realize that we remember nothing or little about the trip after reaching our destination. This phenomenon is akin to being out-of-body (OOB) while still performing a task or functioning in the physical world. Many contemporary persons have also reported spontaneous OOBs while relaxing or meditating. These types of occurrences, along with near-death experiences (NDEs), are persuading persons to be less fearful of death, in general.

**3. *A third purpose for initiation is to know that God is love.*** Masses of people are turning away from oppressive religious beliefs such as: We live to please a jealous and angry God; we arrive into this world as unworthy sinners; and we have to "scrub the floors" to earn our way back to God. We exist because God loves us. It's as profoundly simple as that! I once heard that all of the nearly 300 mental disorders that are currently classified and categorized in the *Diagnostic and Statistical Manual* (DSM-5, 2013) can fundamentally be understood as *problems of love*! This means that humans desperately need to find a way to get to the "heart of the matter," which impels us to find a way toward greater openness, authenticity, and a deeper capacity to love.

We have many names for the life force that animates us and brings us to life, depending on the culture: *Prana* (Hindi); "*The Force*," (Star Wars series); *Chi* (Taoist); *Ki* (Japanese); vitality, Baraka (Islam); the *ECK* (Hindi); *Ruach Adonai* (Hebrew); *Mana* (Polynesian), and *Spirit* (Christian). All are ancient terms for the energy that flows around us and through us. In String Theory, the vibrational patterns or waves of energy that move "strings," the smallest physical units in the composition of atoms, are called *Qi* in Chinese Medicine.[10] I believe that this energy links us to each other and connects us to all beings on all planets, planes, and dimensions of the multiverse. Fundamentally, this energy is love.

**4. *A fourth goal of the initiation process is to achieve psychological wholeness*.** When whole, persons are less divided within themselves (suffer from fewer conflicts), and are more truly individuals (yet, paradoxically, can better relate to humanity as one among many). The ego is not destroyed, as we need an ego structure to maneuver the physical world; instead, it becomes submissive to the Self. The objective is for the Self to become both the sacred center of our personality and a stable container for the integration of all of the elements that make up the totality of the individual.[11] Jung referred to the route by which we achieve the realization of psychological wholeness as *individuation*, a process analogous to initiation. It is, above all, a *spiritual* process.

## ARCHETYPES: PATTERNS OF HUMAN BEHAVIOR

The real work toward wholeness is with the unconscious, which, on the various levels, houses the instincts, such as the uncontrolled drives of hunger, greed, sex, power urges, and aggression that can be seen in dreams (and in our psychological projections onto others) as the Shadow.[12] On other, deeper levels, there are ever more chaotic and powerful energies that act independently of the ego—and sometimes against it! Jung identified these subterranean layers of the unconscious as the *collective unconscious*, which can be negotiated by successfully recognizing and relating to the archetypes, as they successively appear in our dreams, for example. The collective unconscious is what Jung named the impersonal, deepest layer of the unconscious mind, which is *shared* by all human beings because of our common ancestral history. The archetypes, such as the Anima (which Jung designated as the feminine aspect in males) and the Animus (the masculine aspect in women), can create a bridge between the personal and collective unconscious. Common archetypes include the Great Mother, the Witch, the Wise Old Man or Woman, the Child, the Hero, the Devil, and many others. Because archetypes carry the energy of all human experience throughout the ages, they often evoke unconscious responses in people and consequently, have great power to influence human behavior.

Just what *are* archetypes? Archetypes are inherited psychological blueprints and innate patterns of behavior shared by all humankind. In Jung's theory, the experiences of a common past have made deep permanent impressions, creating pathways or patterns for typical human expression. In other words, *archetypes are primal energies that function to organize how we experience and respond to certain things in recognizably human ways.* They appear as universal figures and symbols in the dreams of individuals, and collectively, in our fairytales and myths. An interesting experiment to try is to write your own biographical story in the language of fairytales or myths; for example, "Once upon a time, there was a daughter whose father left her alone and whose mother did not love her…" Chances are you will find that your completed story bears a striking similarity to the archetypal theme found in a particular myth or fairytale!

Our most stirring and revelatory experiences in literature, art, theater, religion, music, and dreams occur when the characters, images, and themes symbolically embody universal meanings and archetypal human experiences. We are surrounded by archetypal themes (such as *The Quest, Rags to Riches, Rebirth and Renewal,* and *Voyage and Return* tropes) in the books we read, the movies we see, and in the lives we lead. If you compare various religious figures with the hero's (or savior's) story in myths, you will clearly see a recurring archetypal pattern: They were born of a miraculous or virgin birth; they were sons of a supreme god; stars appeared at their birthplaces; they were forced to flee from threats of death as infants or children; they spent time alone in the desert; they traveled to teach others; they had disciples; they performed miracles; they were persecuted and then crucified; they descended into hell after death; they appeared to others in visions after death; and finally, they ascended into heaven.[13] In every facet of our lives, archetypal images and themes are found, patterns that serve to guide us in living and understanding our lives as human beings.

In *Dancing the Labyrinth,* we are most interested in the particular *archetypal pattern of initiation.* Embedded in the fundamental design of human psychology, initiation is the stadial (yet paradoxically fluid) program by which humans grow and evolve. When strongly activated, the pattern of initiation provides a meaningful transition or rite of passage from one level of human awareness to the next (transcending but including the previous stages). When the spiritual seeker no longer knows where they are at or where they are going, the exploration of the archetypal symbols and themes in their visualizations, dreams, and daily lives will guide their uncertain steps on the narrow and precarious initiatory path.

## THE LABYRINTH: SYMBOL OF THE SPIRITUAL JOURNEY

*There's no need to build a labyrinth when the entire universe is one.*
**~ Jorge Luis Borges**

*A labyrinth is an ancient device
that compresses a journey into a small space.*
**~ Rebecca Solnit**

Why is the symbol of the labyrinth[14] used to portray the initiation process? The labyrinth's shape has been linked to the convoluted folds and grooves of the brain, which connects this symbol with a natural structure in humans. The labyrinth also symbolizes the journey we must take within ourselves to unlock the deeply encoded DNA data that reveals us to ourselves. These organic references mirror the mystery of human existence itself. We are unique expressions of humanity, like the lines on our hands or the swirls on our fingertips, yet we all share a common developmental pattern.

The labyrinth, which combines the imagery of the circle and the spiral, is associated with the long, meandering path to one's own center and to a reunification with the Source from which we originated. Long considered an image of wholeness containing the entirety of human experience, the labyrinth across cultures has variously denoted *the passage of time, spiritual unfoldment, enlightenment, involution* (leaving Source) *and evolution* (returning to Source), *connection to one's center, descent and ascent, death and rebirth, resurrection, emergence, progress, spiritual path, the "eternal return"* of *births and rebirths in cycles of reincarnation,* and *the process of initiation.* In attempts to recreate this ancient mystery walk, many persons today have constructed labyrinths in their own back yards and garden spots as models and metaphors for their personal life journeys. Sometimes called a "spiritual gateway," or portal, labyrinths are often built to induce contemplative states and mindful meditations.

Labyrinths have been found painted onto stones or cave walls, formed with tiles on the floors of churches, carved into cliffsides, etched on tombs, and constructed with stones or hedges in every continent in the world, with the exception of Antarctica. In 2017, a prehistoric painting of a labyrinth was discovered near a cave in Southeastern India. The labyrinth, dating back to the Neolithic period (about 12,000 years ago), was painted on a rock with seven circles in red ochre on white pigment, a motif similar to those found on the slabs of Bronze Age Megalithic tombs and rock surfaces in England, Ireland, Norway, Sweden, and Italy. The oldest rock art in North America is located at Winnemucca Lake, Nevada. The incised carvings on rocks, or petroglyphs, include images of labyrinths that are more than 10,500 years old. Another ancient labyrinth locale is the Temple of Artemis at Ephesus in Turkey. This great temple was built by Croesus, King of Lydia, 2,570 years ago, and because of its enormous size, was considered one of the Seven Wonders of the ancient world.

Well-known labyrinths of the ancient world include the Egyptian Labyrinth complex, previously thought to be a mythical structure. It is estimated to be over 3,300 years old, but probably dates well before this time. Its buildings are no longer standing, but it is speculated that the complex's subterranean portion was used for initiation rites performed in the Egyptian Mystery Schools. Another of the better-known labyrinths is located at Knossos on the Greek island of Crete. The Palace of Knossos is designed in the form of a vast labyrinth, and was used to host processions and rituals by the Minoan civilization, a Bronze Age Aegean people who flourished between the time span of 5,000 to 3,120 years ago.

The universality of the labyrinth is evidence that it has held collective meaning for various cultural systems in every place and in every time. This fascination continues today precisely because the labyrinth is an archetypal image, and so we respond to it with a sense of a profound recognition and resonance. For that reason, the labyrinth features in many contemporary movies, among them: *Inception* (2010), *The Shining* (1980), *Don't Look Now*, (1973), *Raiders of the Lost Ark* (1981), *Shutter Island* (2010), and *Harry Potter and the Goblet of Fire* (2005). There are also movies that focus on the labyrinth as the main plot device, such as *The Labyrinth of the Faun* (also known as *Pan's Labyrinth*, 2006) and *Labyrinth* (1986). The labyrinth is enthralling to us because it symbolizes *both a pattern of wholeness and the means to attaining this wholeness.*

Once the labyrinth is *entered into* (another root meaning of *initiation*), the twists and turns soon make it a mysterious and sometimes dark and frightening thing. We find dead ends, make wrong turns, and lose our bearings.[15] Trembling with fear and foreboding, we pray we won't be swallowed up by the darkness. At this point in the journey, we feel unbearably alone and irrevocably lost. The most ubiquitous instrument for inducing this type of ritual disorientation has been the labyrinth. Recently, science has confirmed what the ancients always knew: When we are lost, we are in an altered state that enables greater spiritual connection and communion. In this confused and unmoored state, the part of the brain responsible for the cognitive navigation of the outer world begins to shut down. A region near the front of the brain, the posterior superior parietal lobe, has been shown to decrease in activity whenever we are in a confused state brought on by an external inhibition of spatial perception.[16] In this altered fugue state, we may experience a temporary loss of identity and alignment; we disconnect from external realities and geographies. Our minds crack open, our boundaries collapse, and we are ready for the transformation.

The candidate for initiation today experiences the labyrinth as an *inner, psychological* journey rather than as a visceral wandering through the bounded walls of subterranean corridors or stony cavern passages. But the effects are the same: The spiraling pathways of the labyrinth ultimately leads the aspirant to the depths of their innermost being. There are dangerous tasks to perform along the way, among them the slaying of the Minotaur, symbolizing the aspirant's lower nature (shadow). The center of the labyrinth may hold creative madness, the loss of space and time, and the death of the conditioned (automaton-like) ego-self. Finally, the wanderer wearily trudges the slow and circuitous way out of the labyrinth, and this womb-tomb delivers the "new born" once more to the world at large. After a period of recovery and integration, the initiate may dare to share with others the insights and wisdom that were purchased with so great a sacrifice on the Labyrinthine Path.

## HOW DOES INITIATION WORK?
## MYSTERY AND METAMORPHOSIS

*To enter into the initiation of sound, of vibration and mindfulness,*
*is to take a giant step toward consciously knowing the soul.*
*~ Don G. Campbell*

*The word crisis is from the Greek,*
*meaning a moment to decide.*
*The recurrent moments of crisis and decision, when understood,*
*are growth junctures, points of initiation*
*which mark a release from one state of being*
*and a growth into the next.*
*~ Jill Purce*

**Initiation is dedicating your life to God.**[17] The challenge for the modern seeker is to live a spiritual life while going about life's daily business. Most of us do not have the choice of leading a spiritually-committed life within the protective and silent walls of a monastery, convent, ashram, or lamasery. Today's spiritual initiate must be able to shop for groceries, pick up their kids from school, and work at their jobs while quietly living a deeply sanctified life. **Spirituality isn't something that an initiate adopts or espouses; it's something that the initiate becomes.**

*It seems important here to head off a few misconceptions by cataloging what initiation is not.* For today's modern initiate, initiation is not simply a baptism by water, a transmission of secrets, or a secret ceremony where the participants are dressed in unusual garb. It is not a granting of psychic powers to reinforce feelings of superiority. It is not a one-time rite or ritual during which one becomes suddenly all knowing, wise, and judicious. It is not deciding to give up all possessions in the name of impoverishment, privation, or martyrdom. It is not (ever) a surrendering of personal freedom and sovereignty to another individual or group, regardless of how devoted the initiate is to a particular spiritual collective or teacher. And it is not leaving behind responsibilities or obligations to become a drifter or mendicant. Importantly, the path of initiation is *not glamorous or romantic!* The Tibetan teacher Chogyam Trungpa once began a talk in a San Francisco lecture hall by cautioning those in the crowd who hadn't already begun the spiritual path to leave. He described the true spiritual path as difficult and demanding. Only those who had begun a true path should stay, he explained, for once begun, it was best to finish.

To be initiated indicates that the hard work has only begun. In my book, *Drinking the Dragon,* I described initiation this way:

> *In fact, the path of initiation is both a turning point and a process during which people hope to achieve self-mastery, or power over themselves. Initiates are taught to see themselves more objectively, to accurately evaluate themselves and the situations around them, to handle life events with less distress and more understanding of their meaning and value, to overcome long-standing fears, to deepen their connection to loved ones, to transform destructive relationships, and to lose the fear of death. Yet, because there is always one more step to take on the spiritual path, the initiate must suffer from the knowledge of his or her own imperfections.*[18]

Whether the initiation process is activated via a life crisis, by an unrelenting search for meaning, or is a naturally-occurring progression of unfoldment, initiation is the destiny that all humans will encounter in the fullness of time. Michael Washburn, a philosopher who integrates psychology with religion, emphatically maintains that sooner or later, we *cannot avoid* a spiritual life.[19] The purpose of initiation is to become more conscious of the Divine Plan that shapes the world as well an increased desire and capacity (acting as a *Co-Worker*) to further this Plan. The ultimate goal of initiation is to lead the initiate to a homecoming with God. The most profound initiation process is overseen by a Master who not only guides and protects the initiate throughout the pilgrim's journey, but facilitates the activation of the initiate's energy centers, thereby coupling the person with potent spiritual forces. In *Drinking the Dragon*, I further defined initiation:

> *Initiation is the process of being linked to Divine Spirit, which gradually brings about, in graded steps, an expansion of consciousness. In a true initiation process, the spiritual forces within an individual are activated, and these energies bring about a total transformation of a person over time. Initiation opens all of your inner "channels" so that you can more easily receive the messages of Spirit in dreams as well as in daily life. Importantly, initiation brings a person into immediate experiences of God.*[20]

## INITIATION: A TRANSFORMATION IN CONSCIOUSNESS

The transformed consciousness of the initiate allows for the person to become a *practitioner* and *experiencer* of Spirit (also known as the Light and Sound), rather than simply a title- or officeholder for spiritual achievement. Just what are such immediate, authentic and visceral experiences of Spirit? They include recognizing the meaningful signs and messages in your dreams, which, as an initiate, will become more organized and significant: You may dream of wearing a different body in another distant time and place and feel strongly that you have loved and been loved there. Another common dream theme is of visiting great temples of learning where universal laws and spiritual teachings are imparted. You may also experience being guided through situational mock-ups to help you better manage certain challenges occurring in your physical life experience.

Other spiritual messages or signs may occur in a "waking dream."[21] A waking dream is something that you experience in your physical life that is startling or unusual, that catches your attention and makes you wonder.

You might ask yourself, for example: *What is the message behind my losing my wallet, not just once but three times in a row? Or why is it, whenever I think of my deceased mother, a hummingbird arrives to hover in front of me?*

As people passing near to you are talking, you may suddenly hear a sentence or phrase that has deep meaning and relevance for you (known as *Golden-Tongued Wisdom*). You are becoming mindful of the truth that the Sufi poet Rumi conveyed when he declared, "Each moment contains a hundred messages from God."

As your consciousness continues to open, you will become more intuitive, more finely tuned to others. You may find yourself becoming more sensitive to what another might *not* be saying in their communications, such as somehow being aware that you've unintentionally hurt someone's feelings—and being more susceptible to feeling badly about it when you do! While driving, you may hear a disembodied voice (or get an inner nudge) urgently directing you to make a quick turn so that you just miss being in a car accident. You may naturally and easily "visit" other places, people, and even various planes and planets when you deeply contemplate or meditate. You may sense, without seeing, that a Spiritual Guide or a Master Teacher is around you and is in contact with you. You find that your heart is opening, and you have a greater capacity to feel compassion for others. You slowly begin to realize that there is nothing meaningful left to you in life but to be of service to humankind. A person who was newly committed to a spiritual path recently shared this story with me:

> *One evening after work, I was extremely hungry. I decided to stop at a fast-food drive-through. I ordered fried chicken, cold slaw, and a biscuit. I quickly ate one piece of the chicken and then hurried home with the rest. When I was getting out of my car, I noticed an old Black man pushing a grocery cart filled with all of his worldly belongings. I experienced a strong nudge to*

*offer him my dinner, but I did not want to give up my food. The nudges persisted, but I continued to resist. Finally, I called out, "'Are you hungry?'" The old man stopped and turned to look at me. With a surprised look on his face, he said, "Yes, I am." I began to list everything that was in the box for him before handing it over. He asked me, "Are you an angel?" Without thinking, I answered, "Well, tonight, I am."*

This person realized that in spite of herself, she was growing into her higher nature where love rules and fried chicken comes second!

At each further step of initiation, revealed teachings, life lessons, and new understandings are disclosed to the initiate. Learnings must not only be mentally understood or emotionally grasped before moving on to the next spiritual level; the initiate must manifest and *apply learnings* to everyday behaviors and actions to ground them in physical life. A complete self-inventory of the initiate must be undertaken. *How can the spiritual student reduce pride and vanity?* Perhaps the individual's sources of personal income begin to dry up, and it becomes humbling to ask for financial assistance from family and friends. *In what ways can people learn to regard others with greater respect?* Perhaps the spiritual seeker is instructed in a dream to address people, plants, and animals with a silent "thou," as a way of metaphorically bowing one's head to others in an act of reverence. These types of lessons occur in everyone's lives, but the initiate, who has committed to an individualized program of intensified spiritual instruction, learns to quickly bridge outer life occurrences to inner spiritual conditions. Many people have heard that everything that happens is a lesson to be learned and everyone who is met is a teacher in disguise, and the initiate is compelled to recognize this truism every day and in every moment.

Initiation is not simply about the individual stiving to become shipshape through a code of conduct or a list of rules. The initiate doesn't simply try to be good. Initiation is a powerful process of transmutation. This is a change so profound that it is analogous to an (al)chemical[22] process. Initiation is a *mystery;* we can collaborate with this process, but we cannot control it. After a few years, initiates may barely recognize the persons they once were. The people, habits, or habitats that previously attracted them but did not benefit them are no longer a part of their lives. They do not respond to the same things in the same way, including certain types of entertainment (raucous parties, recreational drug use, or slasher/horror movies); certain types of people (those who enjoy hurting others, are hateful and full of rage, or are excessively fearful); and certain types of activities (jobs that clearly exploit or harm others or the environment, involvement in abusive relationships, or attachment to addictions). These are often not "willed" changes but are naturally occurring adjustments, even though individual efforts toward self-purification and self-command are still required.

## INITIATION: PATHWAY TO FREEDOM

As the initiate moves through various stages of initiation, the process is comparable to condensing the life experiences of several lifetimes into one. For some, a new level of initiation will bring with it a completely new set of circumstances: a fresh job, a changed residence, and different people with whom to interact. In this way, the initiate lives abridged versions of several "lifetimes," with the lessons and experiences from each life compressed into a finite span of time. This is why the journey of initiation is sometimes called the "short path," because it can shorten the number of future incarnations required to graduate from Earth School. In one sense, initiation can be understood as a program of "forced progression," a process in which personal efforts are combined with a series of energy impacts that accelerate spiritual growth within a rigorous program of self-purification and esoteric learning.[23] This program of spiritual education and development ultimately makes possible the initiate's mastery of every plane of existence that progressively lies beyond the physical, which continues for the spiritual student even after physical death.

A plane, as used in *Dancing the Labyrinth,* is a level of thought, existence, or development; a region or level of reality. The two most popular number of initiatory planes is 7 and 12, but there are, in actuality, infinite numbers of planes/dimensions. The planes as separated into distinct levels of consciousness, as I have done in this book, is simply a way to wrap our minds around spiritual growth. As humans evolve in consciousness, they individually realize coarser to finer densities that affiliate them with certain planes. Human waking reality is considered Third Dimensional reality or 3D, because most humans share this consciousness; this is a level of reality in which humans experience being individuals with an ego and body that is separate from others. "Technology, scientific rationalism, individuality, personal pride, and political and military power"[24] are all associated with the solar Plexus Chakra and 3D consciousness. When most humans wake up to our non-physical, spiritual dimensions, then Earth consciousness, as a whole, will reflect this.

The Labyrinthine Path is a way of freedom, a means for release from the *Wheel of Awagawan*, the ages-long cycles of births and deaths known as reincarnation. A contemporary movie that depicts this Cycle of Eternal Return is *Cloud Atlas*. The visionary film was directed by Tom Tykwer and siblings Lana and Lily Wachowski. Inspired by the novel of the same name by David Mitchell, the movie intersects six stories taking place over nearly 500 years, between 1849 and 2346. The complex theme of the movie portrays how the actions of several individuals impact one another in ways that create ripple effects across the centuries. In their various incarnations, six persons appear in different bodies (including both sexes) and varying ethnicities, yet they are inextricably connected to one another through their interactions in distinct time frames and diverse circumstances. These relationships are demonstrated through time by a repetitive phrase of music, a dream, a diary, or an image (such as a birthmark) as well as by residual memories. The movie dramatizes how it is possible for human beings to evolve over lifetimes, as a former murderer becomes a hero, and another progresses into a revered figure of revolution. *Cloud Atlas* emphasizes the role of love, sacrifice, and forgiveness in transforming the habits of cruelty and oppression that keep persons treading the *Wheel of 84*, or reincarnating.[25] The film's most basic message? As we travel through time, our continuing existence is a thread that is tied to other Souls (some of whom we recognize on our journey and others that we do not). We are ultimately responsible for all that we say and do along the way—our impact on others—so we must make our story about love.

If you've seen the 1991 movie, *Defending Your Life,* with Meryl Streep and Albert Brooks, you have an idea of this review process (though it is played in the movie for comedic effects). In the movie, individuals who have recently died meet in Judgment City to participate in their life review. They review scenes from the lives they've just exited to evaluate whether or not they have successfully overcome their fears. How well they have mastered their deepest fears determines whether or not they will be required to reincarnate to live another life on Earth or be allowed to move on to the next phase of existence. Near the end of the movie, Albert Brook's character advances spiritually because he carries out a decisive act, driven by love.

The effects of a life review are illustrated by a woman who recounts a near death experience (NDE) while in surgery for a ruptured ectopic pregnancy. As she exited her body in the operating room, she found herself reviewing her life up to that time. This review included an incident that occurred during her younger years when she sweet-talked a guy into driving her to a party that didn't exist, because she wanted a ride home. After reviewing how she had run inside, ditching him, she commented, "I was grieved to see how totally selfish, thoughtless, and downright cruel I had been. I felt his complete panic and fear, and his change as he became less trusting. I was sickened. I had such total guilt that I tried to pull my view away." She shared further:

> *Most things were pleasant to see; some things made me very embarrassed. In fact, revulsion and guilt took away any good*

*feelings, making me so very sorry for certain things I had said or done. I hadn't just seen what I had done, but I felt and knew the repercussions of my actions. I felt the injury or pain of those who suffered because of my selfish or inappropriate behavior.*[26]

The Path of Initiation allows for individuals to review the consequences of their thoughts, words, and actions *before* physical death. As initiates, we do not have to wait until we die, or nearly so (as in an NDE), before we meet up with the consequences of our actions. As we unfold spiritually, we receive "instant feedback" regarding our thoughts and words. We not only quickly receive prompt spiritual feedback, but we have periodic reviews of our state of being (particularly before another initiation). Eventually what we do hurts *us* as much or more than the other person involved. We are our *own* judges. **It is helpful to keep in mind that at the end of life, we will be asked, "What was the quality of your love?"**

# CHAPTER ONE EXERCISES

## Is Your Life Guided?

You may want to use a journal as you explore the exercises at the end of each chapter.

1. What experiences in life lead you to think that you are already an initiate or preparing to be one? Be as specific as possible. (Hint: Reread the first part of this chapter.)

2. Make two columns on a page in your journal. In one column, write down the qualities you believe that you have already developed to a good degree (see paragraphs under the subtitle "Who is the Initiate? Seekers and Boundary Crossers") In the same column write under each quality an example of how you have applied this quality in your outer life. In the second column, list the qualities you want to further develop. In the same column, under each quality, write down how you can acquire or improve upon this quality in your life.

3. Discuss in your journal what you might do to support your spiritual development and upgrade your inner spiritual communication.

4. Do you fear death? How has becoming a conscious spiritual student (a disciple or initiate) helped you to diminish this fear? Have you ever had a spontaneous out-of-body experience or a near-death experience? Respond to and expand on these questions in your journal.

5. Do you feel that you are living a *guided* life? What makes you think so? Have you had any kind of communication with a Guide or Angel? Use your journal to describe these experiences.

6. Are you aware of having made a *sacred contract* or life design for this life? This could mean that you agreed to experience certain events to awaken you to your pre-incarnational pledge to help others in order to give back in some way. Write your thoughts about this topic in your journal.

# CHAPTER ONE ENDNOTES

[1.] A wonderful phrase written by Elizabeth Gilbert in her book, *Eat, Pray, Love*. New York, NY: Penguin Group, 2006, p.11.

[2.] Theosophy is a religion established in the United States by the Russian immigrant Helena Blavatsky in the late 19th century. It combines Western esoteric writings and Neoplatonism philosophy with teachings of Hinduism and Buddhism.

[3.] Some have made the claim that the onset of the Aquarian Age was at the Great Conjunction of Jupiter and Saturn on December 21, 2020. Others posit that the Aquarian Age will formally begin in 2050.

[4.] Paraphrase of a quote by Richard Rohr: "You know after any truly initiating experience that you are part of a much bigger whole. Life is not about you henceforward, but you are about life."

[5.] The terms *Self, Soul, Atman*. In *Dancing the Labyrinth*, *Self* and *Soul* are used interchangeably to refer to the true, innermost spiritual essence of all beings. The Spiritual Self is universal, unchangeable, ever present, permanent, ageless, and awake. The *Higher Self*, on the other hand, (sometimes called the Greater Guardian of the Threshold), has long been the mediator between the ego-personality and the Self or Soul, until this mediator is no longer needed. The Causal Body, which housed the Higher Self (called soul with a small "s" in some literature), is relinquished at the Fourth Initiation (which is experienced as a great loss). After that, there is a merging and integration of mind-body-spirit and a direct communication with Spirit.

[6.] "Within the Western Christian framework, the ideal that is relevant to the initiation process is to become *ourselves* the Christ, to lead the Christ-life, to go through the tests and trials of the Gospel story, which can be seen as a 'a mighty drama of the Initiation of the Spirit.' In the early days of the Christian Church, these mysteries were promulgated." Annie Besant in *Initiation: The Perfecting of Man*, London: Theosophical Publishing, 1912: p. 86.

[7.] Gary Zukav. *The Seat of the Soul*. New York: New York: Simon & Schuster, 1989: p. 191-194.

[8.] In the first century the Therapeutae was a religious sect, similar to the Essenes, with a main settlement at Lake Mareotis, near Alexandria, Egypt. A pre-Christian group of Jewish ascetics, the Therapeutae were dedicated to spiritual study and contemplation and were highly skilled healers. They were considered to be not only healers of the physical body but also "physicians of souls."

9. In Zen Buddhist and Taoist philosophies, "the 10,000 things" refers to the manifest forms of the material world. My particular use of this phrase makes a reference to the multiplicity of daily distractions while living in the physical world.

10. "What is Qi and Why Does It Matter?' Nov.8, 2017. *The Hayo'u Method* https://www.hayoumethod.com/blog/good-vibrations-quantum-physics-meets-qi/

11. The psychiatrist Carl Jung uses the term Self to "represent the centre of psychic awareness that transcends ego consciousness and includes in its scope all the vast reaches of the psyche that are ordinarily unconscious," the personal consciousness as well as the objective or non-personal unconscious. Achievement of the goal of the Self, or finding God within, "has been regarded by all of the great religions of the world as the final goal." Esther Harding, *Psychic Energy*, New York, NY: Princeton University Press, Bollingen Foundation Series, 1963.

12. The Shadow is the archetype, an energic form that is hidden in the unconscious aspects of oneself, which the ego has either repressed or never recognized. The reprehensible traits are usually only seen outside of ourselves, as the faults of others. In esoteric literature, the Shadow has been called *The (Lower) Dweller or The Guardian of the Threshold*. The Dweller is encountered when Initiates are ready to see themselves as they truly are (such as the revelation of untamed instincts, selfish desires, and egotistical wishes). This process enables Initiates to see themselves without delusion, and to realize the efforts required to free themselves from these shadow qualities. The Greater Guardian of the Threshold, on the other hand, is a luminous being, that reveals itself to us when we are no longer under control of the world of the senses.

13. The recurring mythological themes imbedded in the lives of the god-men who have inspired the world's major religions can be researched in books by Joseph Campbell, such as *The Hero with a Thousand Faces*, and in *The Golden Bough* by James George Frazer. The existence of a recurring archetypal theme does not prove whether these were fictional or actual men, however, even though some writers attempt to make a case for either one or the other. Information for the list of world saviors was gleaned from Edward Carpenter's book, *Pagan and Christian Creeds*. Daly City, CA: Book Tree, 1999: p. 50.

14. Labyrinth also comes from the word "labyrs," meaning double axe. The labyrinth is sometimes known as the "house of the double axe." In ancient Crete, the double axe was only carried by women as an important sacred symbol in the Minoan religion.

15. I mention dead ends and wrong turns here, which are characteristic of *mazes*, which have multiple paths that branch off and do not necessarily lead to the center. Labyrinths have a single, continuous path which leads to the center and then out again. However, I am talking about the *psychological* experience of a labyrinthine journey of initiation here, not a walk through an actual labyrinth, so I have taken some liberties.

16. The posterior superior parietal lobe has been closely tied with the occipital lobe to help us with aspects of attention and visuospatial perception. It has been scientifically shown that damage to this area can cause visuo-spatial deficits, so that we might have difficulty finding our way around new, or even familiar, places. The parietal lobe houses the somatosensory cortex, which receives information sent from our senses. If we become disoriented and lost, we are not able to send messages to this part of the brain to help us locate ourselves in space. An excellent article that discusses this phenomenon has been written by Will Hunt in the *Atlantic Magazine*, "Getting Lost Makes the Brain Go Haywire," Feb. 21, 2019, which is adapted from his book, *Underground: A Human History of the Worlds Beneath Our Feet*. NY: Random House, 2019.

17. *God* is understood in this book as the non-gendered Source of All That Is. The energy and power of the Supreme Essence flows out in intelligent waves of Light and Sound, that which we call Spirit or the Voice of God. "It is also known as 'the Great Formless One' that resides in the Ocean of Love and Mercy. It is an active, creative BEINGNESS that answers to no marks or qualities, since all that can be said about IT is that IT exists." Quoted description by Harold Klemp.

God is defined as an omnipresent, omnipotent, omniscient Force and Source of consciousness in which we live and have our being—it is what we are made of. God is beyond all form manifestation; we cannot really be separate from God, because all things are in the matrix of the Source! We only feel separate when we have forgotten our Divine Identity. Initiation is a process of gradually embodying the God presence within us.

18. Ariadne, Patricia. *Drinking the Dragon: Stories of the Dark Night of The Soul*. Encinitas, CA: Sothis Press, 2021, p. 205.

19. Washburn, Michael. *The Ego and The Dynamic Ground: A Transpersonal Theory of Human Development*. NY: State University of New York Press, 1995.

20. Ariadne, op. cit., pp.203-204.

21. Both dreams and waking dreams are further explained in my self-help workbook, *Bridging Night and Day: Decoding the Hidden Messages of Your Dreams*. Encinitas, CA: Sothis Press, 2021.

22. Alchemy was a philosophy and tradition practiced in Egypt, Europe, Africa, and throughout Asia. Alchemy, the medieval prototype of chemistry, was based on the transmutation of matter, such as turning nonprecious metals into gold. In essence, alchemy was the process of transforming something ordinary into something extraordinary; this process not only occurred in the laboratory using metals, but also occurred *inside* the alchemist. Many of the processes performed by the alchemist are replicated in the transformation of the unconscious when humans undergo deep-seated change. A classic book on this subject is

*Alchemy*, by Marie-Louise von Franz (Toronto, Ontario, Canada: Inner City Books, 1980) Von Franz, who died in 1998, was close a friend and colleague to C.G. Jung.

[23.] Some classic thinkers in this area write that the serpentine, spiral, or labyrinthine ways represent the *long* path that most humans tread via countless incarnations, while the path of initiation is a shortcut. They use the symbol of the caduceus to illustrate this by identifying the outer spirals of the two snakes to indicate the involution and evolution of the Self (Soul) (i.e., the entering of the Soul into physical incarnations and the eventual return of Soul to the Divine.) The Initiate, however, follows the staff by going right up the middle, "the straight and narrow way," eliminating the need for further incarnations. I have taken the prerogative of using all of these designations for the Path of Initiation, but I am acknowledging this differentiation.

[24.] Quote is from Alan Lew's writing, *The One Most Complete Guide to the Spiritual Dimensions of Reality*, Dec. 25, 2021. https://medium.com/new-earth-consciousness/explainer-what-are-the-different-spiritual-dimensions-of-reality-and-is-earth-moving-to-the-5th-2cd99d3dc319

[25.] Ram Dass tells a story which illustrates the extensive, wearying road of evolution for the masses of humanity:

> When the Buddha described how long humanity has been on the journey, as he spoke of reincarnation he talked of a mountain six miles wide, six miles high, six miles long. Every hundred years a bird would fly with a silk scarf in its beak and run it over the mountain once. The length of time it takes the scarf to wear away the mountain is the length of time you have been on the path. (Recounted in "Promises and Pitfalls of the Spiritual Path," by Ram Dass in *Spiritual Emergency: When Personal Transformation Becomes a Crisis*. Stanslov Grof and Christina Grof, Eds. Los Angeles, California: Jeremy Tarcher, p. 176).

[26.] "All is Everything, Everything is One," International Association for Near-Death Studies Inc., NDE Accounts, IANDS.org., April, 2015.

Another interesting example of an after-death life review is disclosed by Dannion Brinkley in his account of his own NDE experience in the book, *Saved by the Light*, NY: Random House, 1994, p.14. While reviewing his behavior up to the time of his NDE, he found himself not only reliving his experiences, but vividly reliving them from the perspectives of the persons he had hurt.

Dannion was led to comprehend both the future as well as the past effects of his actions. In his review, he saw himself unloading weapons in a Central American country and watching as the guns were used to kill both soldiers and civilians alike. He witnessed the results of his role in the war, including children crying because their fathers were dead, killed by the guns he had supplied.

> "Not only could I feel the way both I and the other person had felt when an incident took place, I could also feel the feelings of the next person they reacted to. I was in a chain reaction of emotion, one that showed how deeply we affect one another."

# CHAPTER TWO

## Living the Mystery: Initiation in Modern Life

*It could be shown...that the festivals and celebrations of society,*
*its public ceremonies, spectacles, sports competitions,*
*youth organizations, propaganda by pictures and slogans,*
*literature for mass popular consumption—*
*all still preserve the structure of myths, of symbols, of rites,*
*although they have been emptied of their religious content.*
~ Mircea Eliade

*You are one thing only,*
*You are a Divine Being. An all-powerful Creator.*
*You are a Deity in jeans and a t-shirt,*
*and within you dwells the infinite wisdom of the ages*
*and the sacred creative force of*
*All that is, will be, and ever was.*
~ Anton St. Maarten

## THE CHALLENGES OF EVERYDAY LIFE

*Every test successfully met is rewarded*
*by some growth in intuitive knowledge,*
*strengthening of character,*
*or initiation into a higher consciousness.*
~ Paul Brunton

The preparatory and beginning stages of the initiation process are no longer limited to the closed chambers and secret sanctums of the ancient mystery schools. Today, the tests and trials of initiation confront us in the challenges of our workplaces, the contests of our sporting events, and in the mythic themes and motifs of our arts. The ordeals of everyday life sometimes bring in their wake profound change and transformation, which is at the heart of initiation. At important times in history, when we are compelled to become more spiritually mature, *life itself accelerates the initiatory process!* At these crucial junctures in the culture, such as the one we are living through now, we are confronted with occurrences so shocking that we are thrown out of our routines, and realizing that we no longer have the answers, we must ask ourselves what can spiritually support us when we can no longer support ourselves.

The events of the early 2020s decade presented a series of adversities that brought many people to their knees. Bewildered and shaken, some individuals acted out, behaving in ways that hurt themselves or others; many, when thrown back on themselves during the period of quarantine, used this time to rethink their lives, including their jobs and relationships. This is essentially an invitation to know ourselves on a deeper level, to rediscover ourselves as spiritual beings. As the Buddhist teacher and author Pema Chodron has observed, "Most spiritual experiences begin with suffering… they begin when the rug has been pulled out from under us." We may find ourselves feeling like we are wandering in a desert, lost like the three individuals below who found that the pile up of alarming personal and national events impelled them to confront their deepest fears. Ultimately, all three endured the death and rebirth experience of initiation.

# RICK'S STORY: INTO THE DESERT

> *God takes everyone he loves through a desert.*
> *It is his cure for our wandering hearts,*
> *restlessly searching for a new Eden.*
> ~ **Paul E. Miller**

At some point in your life, may find yourself feeling like you are trapped in a desert wasteland, lost and alone in a vastness without direction. Like the *World Stranger*[1] or Wanderer, you feel like you no longer fit in, either because you have changed or the world around you has shifted (or both). During my first (and most severe) Dark Night of the Soul experience while in my early thirties, I profoundly felt the deep desolation and barrenness of what my life had become; all had been stripped away: money, housing, friends, position, and pride. I dreamed at this time that I was wandering in the wilderness, in the middle of nowhere, without hope of rescue or relief. The "dweller in the desert" experience is shared below by Rick,[2] who related that much of the bleakness he was undergoing had its roots in the events of the early 2020s, most particularly the Covid-19 pandemic.

> "My entire social/support network has collapsed in the last two years and I've been struggling a lot with that. It actually began five years ago when my back was broken and multiple people who I thought of as close friends left my life because, as one of them actually told me, 'This is all too much for me.'

> "Those who were left after that have drifted away, disappeared, or pulled back over the last two years as the pandemic drove many of us into isolation and much of the social fabric around us has been destroyed. I did pretty well for the first year, but being stuck alone inside my place for eight days during the Texas ice storm in 2021 threw me hard back into my C/PTSD[3] place,

and that's when I found that the remainder of my support network was absolutely unreliable if I was in need.

*"I am an exceptionally generous person, especially with people I've let into my close circle. Unfortunately, I've found that I tend to attract people who are happy to seek out and benefit from my generosity when they are in need, but who head for the hills or get angry and tell me to "snap out of it" when the shoe is on the other foot. Unfortunately, this includes a couple of siblings with whom I thought I had a good relationship. I've only begun to stop lying to myself and to feel the full impact of this reality recently, and it's hitting me quite hard."*

During this dismal period, Rick felt profoundly disappointed and *desert-ed*. Where it had once been fruitful, Rick now found his life futile. Those he thought would be there were gone, and when the whole world went into shutdown, it strongly intensified his sense of isolation and sterility. Rick was forced to examine his own dependency issues and to discern when his expectations of others, as well as his own gestures of generosity, were "too much." Most importantly, he needed to discover what he could count on to never forsake him. Where could he find solace when everyone around him seemed to have fled, and he was alone and parched in the dry and forbidding regions of life? It is during these meandering days in the badlands that it may come to us that **only more Spirit can quench our thirst for more life.**

Like others who suffered during this time, Rick had to traverse the desert of his inner landscape before finding his way back to the green land of the living. This was a death and rebirth experience; something had to be altered in his being to make way for something new and sustaining. The desert experience is a time when we lose (usually temporarily) what we hold most dear so that we can turn to things that are more spiritually oriented and life-sustaining. Drawing on the experiences of his abusive childhood, Rick has had success as an author, poet, men's coach, and podcast host. Now, he is examining his recent experiences in the wilderness for understandings that he can translate into lessons of value for those who come into contact with his work.

## SHARON'S STORY: BAPTISM BY WATER[4]

> *Deep, unspeakable suffering may well be called a baptism, a regeneration, the initiation into a new state. Suffering can be likened to a baptism—the passing over the threshold of pain and grief and anguish to claim a new state of being.*
> ~ **George Eliot**

Sometimes we find ourselves slowly sliding into a morass of melancholy and misery for no single, clearly discernable reason. Life's disappointments and disillusionments have accumulated into such a stranglehold on our life force that one morning we find that we can barely get out of bed. We feel physically exhausted, emotionally desolate, and mentally clouded. Sharon, a psychotherapist, related her story of falling into the abyss of anxiety and depression, a process of decline that began with the 2016 presidential election results and intensified with the surge of Covid-19 in the U.S.:

> "I have always been an anxious person, and on a daily basis my anxiety was being fed by conditions outside of my control. I began to obsess about what felt like multiple threats to my safety and survival. One night I had a panic attack. I said to myself: 'Just hang on. Just concentrate on your breath and take it moment to moment.'" Sharon rode it out, but the next morning she awakened with what she described as a "lead weight in my stomach." She added, "That weight dropped again and again; every time I heard something alarming on the news, the weight dropped."

*Sharon began experiencing multiple symptoms. Her natural empathy went into overdrive. "Hearing something sad or frightening or even just thinking about it would send this signal of terrible anxiety throughout my body." Her anxiety began to affect her sleep. After several sleepless nights, Sharon tried everything she could think of: "sleep" music on YouTube, wearing a sleep mask, trying to regulate her sleep time, and getting up and doing something instead of lying in bed. Finally, her doctor prescribed Ambien, but with a family history of serious addiction, she was afraid of taking the sedative and asked her husband to hide the bottle from her.*

*Sharon's anxiety was so overwhelming that she began to experience her life as unreal. Terrified, she prayed to God for clarity. She said, "I did not hear an answer. I felt that perhaps I was on a spiritual journey. But I also wondered if God had abandoned me." Sharon confided she had felt that she could no longer live like this. She wasn't planning suicide, but she felt increasingly despondent and hopeless.*

*Sharon sought help from a Jungian analyst, a psychotherapist she had previously seen. During her depression, Sharon let go of fear, anger, and grief, some of which was related to her childhood. Her brother had committed suicide when he was 33 years of age, an event around which she had done a lot of previous grief work. In her current therapeutic process, Sharon had the realization that she had always unconsciously felt, from the time she was a little girl, that she was responsible for her making her depressed mother happy. "My mother never really seemed to 'see' me nor did she ever truly support me. I was always being told by her to behave in a certain way, if only because I was a reflection or extension of her. I felt that sometimes she even competed with me," Sharon explained.*

At her analyst's urging, Sharon also contacted a psychiatrist to discuss her condition and to determine whether she could safely take medications for relief. The psychiatrist explained to Sharon that given her family history of depression, she was very likely genetically predisposed to experience bouts of depression. She began taking low-dosage medications for both her depression and anxiety with immediate positive effect: "I quickly responded to the medications, feeling better every day, until one day I actually felt joy!"

Assessing her experience, which she characterized as "six months in hell," Sharon declared, "This is where I am now: feeling happy, hopeful, and sometimes even joyful. But what is my takeaway message? Is there a deeper meaning here?" Sharon reflected, "I no longer feel so threatened by outer world events, although I do monitor how much news I take in." Appraising her own response to this life-changing passage, Sharon remarked, "I have a much greater belief in my own resiliency, as I stayed the course and sought my own healing."

After additional reflection, Sharon added that as a result of her own anguish and torment, she has a greater compassion for those who suffer from mental illness, stating, "I know the depths of misery that anxiety and depression can bring. I now have more compassion for my mother because I believe that she may also have suffered from anxiety and depression—but she had no one to talk to and was not able to get effective treatment." Sharon realized, "I have a much more profound appreciation for how connected we all are as human beings."

At certain points in the preparatory or beginning stages of the initiation process, deep-seated and disturbing emotions come up for review, sometimes preceded by a deep depression. Often, our most troubling emotions seem to be not only related to events that have occurred in our current life, but they are often bound up with emotions that still cling to unresolved childhood events and can even be related to unsettled issues from previous lifetimes. As a result, the emotions currently being experienced are both cumulative and intensified. These memories and emotions often come up to the surface of our awareness when we are strong enough to fully experience them. By reexperiencing the emotions and the events from which they originated, we can become more resilient and flexible, as Sharon noted about herself at the end of several months of therapeutic work. We more easily flow with life, and because we have integrated more of the unconscious, we simultaneously experience greater stability and strength. The tears of sorrow that we have shed have have washed away our impasse; they have now become the "waters of life."

Emotions as well as the unconscious part of ourselves (the part of ourselves we are not aware of in our day-to-day lives) are often symbolized—especially in dreams—by bodies of water, such as lakes, seas, and oceans. During a time of intense psychological distress, we may dream that a tidal wave or flood is threatening to overtake us, indicating that we feel overwhelmed by our emotional response to personal life problems or by disturbing events in the outer world. Water symbols herald the activation of an alchemical (psychospiritual) process that *dissolves, cleanses,* and brings *transformation.* Our own tears dissolve old, tired ego defenses and barriers, so that outworn emotions can then wash over us, through us, and are finally released. The mastery of our emotions indicates that we are no longer subject to being overwhelmed or "drowned" in our own watery depths.

# VERONICA'S STORY: THROUGH THE FIRES

> *Sometimes the elements of our life present us with a challenge*
> *that is an initiation in disguise, a fire walk*
> *that burns your lower nature right out of you*
> *so that you are able to adapt to a higher level of consciousness.*
> ~ **Caroline Myss**

In the past, when reading or hearing of someone else's crushing life experience—a death in the family, a serious accident, a financial crisis, a devastating natural disaster, or a violent incident—we may have thought to ourselves, "Yes, that person is definitely going *through the fires.*" Today, there are so many of us who have been hit with calamitous events that we are *all* becoming firewalkers. The process of initiation brings successive experiences of purification by fire: This phrase refers to life crises that burn away the dross or incinerate what is no longer serving us in our lives. These are traumatic experiences that bring deep-seated, fundamental, and life-shattering change. Just such a confluence of crises unexpectedly disrupted Veronica's seemingly well-ordered life:

> *After 25 years of marriage, Veronica was devastated to learn that her husband was having an affair. She had uncovered secret phone logs, credit card receipts, and other signs that he was cheating on her. Feeling blindsided, betrayed, and humiliated, she confronted her husband. He didn't deny the affair, admitting that he just hadn't known how to tell her. In an instant, Veronica realized her marriage was over.*
>
> *Veronica and her husband had been planning to move to another state to be near Veronica's family, and now she was facing these changes alone. She took on selling her house; sorting through 25 years of accumulated possessions for packing, storing, or unloading; beginning divorce proceedings; and arranging for a major*

move. Her beloved dogs went with her husband, and she said good-bye to longtime friends.

In just 39 days, Veronica's life was irrevocably changed. Once in her new location, she rented an apartment, stored her boxes of belongings, and allowed herself to fall apart. For four months, Veronica journaled and cried every day, taking the time to mourn all she had lost. "I had never been alone before—I had gone from one long marriage to the next," she acknowledged. "I decided to 'feel it to heal it.' I dug myself in to gain clarity." Formerly social and attracted to gatherings, Veronica now withdrew. "The pandemic was raging," Veronica offered, "so it was easier for me to stay inside where I slogged through my memories and my misery."

Veronica decided to go into psychotherapy to better understand the breakup of her marriage. She soon realized that she had been unhappy for years, and from an objective perspective, she sensed that her husband's betrayal might actually be a blessing. Importantly, after months of soul searching, Veronica came to another awareness: Her grief was much less about her broken marriage than about old childhood wounds.

Accomplished and successful on the outside, Veronica knew she needed to resolve deep-rooted insecurities. She explored old grief that remained from her relinquishment as a baby by her birth mother, her subsequent adoption, and her second abandonment at age ten by her adoptive father, who left her to be raised by an alcoholic, mentally unstable mother. Veronica cried a lifetime of tears, allowing herself to experience her own brokenness and vulnerability.

During the following months, Veronica continued to journal and sought support from psychotherapists. She created visualizations to reassure and care for the part of herself she perceived as the hurt and vulnerable child within. Her healing journey included reaching out to meet other women by joining groups in her new community. Veronica resumed her consulting work, presented workshops on journaling, and completed a course to earn a certificate as a grief counselor.

*Eight months after her divorce, Veronica bought a new house and began to tentatively explore a relationship with a new companion. "I am not out of the woods yet, but I am more comfortable in my own skin," she disclosed. "I have a greater sense of my own self-worth." Veronica added that she thinks of her ordeal now as a spiritual quest, a journey to feel more alive and to connect with the Divine. "It was the most painful experience of my life, but now I feel grateful, and I express this gratitude daily when I journal."*

Veronica recognized that the severe trials recently served up by her life were out of her personal control, but she elected to actively explore and *collaborate* with these experiences. Through her own process work, Veronica took responsibility for past decisions and squarely faced the reality of her marital relationship. She learned more about her own patterns and needs. By going deeply into her excruciating sorrow and disappointment, she attained greater self-confidence, perseverance, and strength. To accelerate her own healing, Veronica continued to journal. Ultimately, Veronica resumed her consulting work in marketing, presented workshops on journaling, completed a course in grief counseling, and made plans to continue her personal growth workshops.

## PURIFICATION THROUGH TRIALS AND TRIBULATIONS

Veronica's story is an example of how life's most devastating experiences can serve the purpose of inducing an important reorientation toward Spirit.

Such periods of personal darkness can bring a deeper understanding of ourselves as spiritual beings. Veronica's ordeal could be identified esoterically as *Purification by Fire*. This type of process is currently being faced by an increasing number of people who, through the ordinary challenges of everyday experience, more or less undergo an unconscious process of initiation via the difficulties they overcome. In recent years, thousands of people have experienced similar trials and tribulations, many brought on by the pandemic as well as by widespread social, political, financial, and environmental upheavals as well as global conflicts. While these conditions are devastating, they can also trigger profound transformations of a psychospiritual nature. We rarely change when things are status quo and all remains well with our world. In order for the golden nuggets of insight, empathy, understanding, and greater usefulness to the world to be extracted from the psyche, we must sometimes undergo what could be metaphorically understood as a smelting (melting) and refinement process.

Going *through the fires* can be seen as a *crucible* experience. A crucible is a ceramic or metal container used to melt down alloys into liquid form, which is then poured into new containers for alternative uses. The crucible of life melts down old, outmoded forms of thought, emotion, and behavior in order to remake them into more expansive and purer forms. The debris of outworn obstructive thoughts, emotions, and behaviors is melted down and transmuted into new potentials. The "heat" of the fire can be equated to the emotional turmoil and grief that you feel when life delivers a series of severe blows; fiery emotions are the fuel that forces you to *cook in your own juices*, eventually transforming your life into something more valuable and good.

**Our darkest experiences can bring us the greatest light.** For necessary psychological work to be inaugurated, a profound depression may first occur. Such depressions can cause us to temporarily withdraw from outer life. In American culture, which is largely extroverted, social withdrawal is sometimes seen as deviant or unhealthy. Even without experiencing a depression, scheduling into your life intermittent quiet times provides space to journal, contemplate, work with your dreams, visualize, and to hear inner thoughts, all of which provide important guidance in living our busy, daily lives. (This was one of the benefits of having had so much time indoors over 2020-22, even though this "forced retreat" brought distress and difficulty to many).[5] Creating a private place during a depression is even more important, as this allows old memories, feelings, and bits and pieces of our childhood that require healing to float to the surface. Sharon commented that the need to stay inside during the pandemic was a source of frustration for her, but that these conditions suited her depressed mood and ultimately, gave her time to reflect and ruminate. It helps immeasurably to find an ally or psychotherapist, as both Veronica and Sharon did, to help you navigate the "black dog" of despair, which is what Winston Churchill named his recurrent dark and disabling depressions.

## THE ROLE OF ANXIETY AND DEPRESSION

Our inner work, especially during an initiation journey, forces us to deal, at intervals and in increments, with everything in us that remains unresolved. We must first "go back," or revisit, those issues that are "stuck" in our childhoods before we can move forward and advance on the spiritual path. Interestingly, the very psychological issues that seem to hold us back can impel us forward; this is because the emotional energy once invested in these experiences, when sufficiently resolved, can be released as life force. As the poet Rilke so beautifully expressed, "Perhaps everything terrible is in its deepest being something helpless that wants help from us." Loving ourselves—and the problems that seem to belong to us—make it possible to transform the darkest moments of our life's journey to points of light that illuminate our pilgrimage along the Initiatory Path.

Sometimes the unresolved thing in the unconscious that wants to make itself known to us first announces itself through bouts of anxiety. Anxiety signifies that the memory or event is on the threshold between what is known (conscious) and what is unknown (unconscious). It's important to learn to let these contents come into view (this is more easily and safely done with a psychotherapist) because anything that remains in the depths of the watery unconscious still affects us in unknown ways, sometimes adversely influencing our decisions and reactions. This is one reason working with our night dreams is so important, as dreams come to us from the unconscious; when dreams are worked with and their messages understood, they augment consciousness. Dreams provide a "fast track" to self-awareness. The path to greater consciousness leads to an understanding of ourselves as unique and distinctive individuals, but ultimately, as Sharon experienced, it generates a real sense of interconnection to all humans, everywhere.

It is only through the experience of death and annihilation that, according to Carl Jung, something indestructible rises within us, a solid center of gravity. We are unassailable, come weal or woe: this means that no matter what happens to us, we have a stationary core. We can bend but we won't break. In alchemical texts, the achievement of our innermost Center (the Self) is called *The Philosopher's Stone,* for this very reason, that something infinite and indomitable has taken its place within us. Just as the winds weather the sea cliffs, the stormy winds of trouble and tumult have sculpted us into new shapes of strength and resilience.

In my book, *Drinking the Dragon: Stories of the Dark Night of the Soul,*[6] I include many interviews and vignettes of individuals who, similarly to Veronica and Sharon, experienced periods of intense and protracted suffering.[7] These persons sought to find the deeper meaning hidden in their anguish, collaborating with a process that was like tumbling into a dark and unknown abyss. Many found help from psychotherapists or other mental health professionals. All searched out ways to better understand their process: meditation and prayer, spiritually-oriented tapes, books or other media of this nature, journaling, gardening, and other methods. Significantly, they all relied on spiritual beliefs, practices, and exploration. In every case, the Dark Night of the Soul journey was a spiritually transformative process.[7] Ultimately, they emerged from this subterranean passage with increased self-awareness, a more profound connection to their spiritual centers, and a pressing need to give back to life. Triggered by recent life events in the lives of millions, the Dark Night process is being experienced today by ever greater numbers of people in Western culture. If understood and utilized as catalysts of inner transformation, such Dark Night experiences can propel global human consciousness to a level that is new and revelatory.

## SOMETHING FUNNY HAPPENED ON THE WAY TO THE SUPERMARKET[8]

> *Initiation "involves not only the religious life of an individual… it involves his entire life."*
> ~ **Mircea Eliade**

The previous vignettes in Chapter 2 bring an understanding that initiation, as author and lecturer Carolyn Myss puts it, has gone mainstream. The tests and trials of initiation can be seen in the challenges faced in everyday life, by everyday people. These trials are familiar to many, and include:

- Obstacles in the workplace or the loss of employment
- The end of a relationship or the death of a loved one
- Physical or mental illness
- Homelessness
- Natural catastrophes
- Economic hardships
- Substance abuse and addictions
- Political corruption
- Racially-motivated slurs and assaults

Even seemingly positive experiences can test our mettle: being idolized in public life; immigrating to a new life in an unfamiliar country; or taking on a blended family. We can also regard certain commonly-shared milestones as initiatory experiences: marriage, giving birth, the death of a parent, graduating from educational institutions, starting one's first job, receiving an award for a job well done, retirement, and achievements in athletics. **Life itself is a school of tests, tears, and trials, and we ourselves are the path.**

The rites, rituals, and symbols of initiation are evident in many public events and collective social experiences.

- Public festivals and celebrations such as Fourth of July festivities and the Olympics.
- Various youth organizations such as scouting.
- Media propaganda, ads, and commercials use slogans and iconic, recognizable scenes from daily life (such as a family on a picnic together) to promote their products and services.
- Our literature, musical, performing, and visual arts all utilize the structure and archetypes of the initiation process (although they are today experienced as secular rather than as spiritual experiences).
- The Olympics require long and demanding training programs, all of which include tests of stamina and fearlessness, guidance via coaches and mentors, and (hopefully) bringing home the coveted prize—all are are preparatory approximations to a spiritual initiation process.
- Business competitions, beauty contests, artistic creations (more on the initiation motif in the arts in Chapter 6), as well as meeting the challenges of a higher education or work training program.[9]

We are learning many important spiritual qualities needed for the initiation process through the requirements of our everyday lives. We can learn *patience* as we raise our children, stand in line, wait for a red light, or try to straighten out an issue using an online site or a call center (who hasn't yelled at an auto-attendant while using a call menu!)

We can learn *trust* when we have done all we can (including prayer) and our pet is still missing, or when we have scrambled to get the rent together and we're still a few dollars short. In cases such as these, trust is closely connected to *surrender*. As a spiritual practice toward greater trust, you can ask that if it is in the best interests of everyone involved (and in alignment with Spirit) that your need is met, and then—this is *key*—say *Baraka Bashad* ("May the blessings be") or the alternative "Let go and let God" to surrender the situation to Spirit. And if your need is *not* met, then you can accept this outcome, too.

We can all learn *gratitude* by thanking the grocery clerk, acknowledging the person who opened a door for us or allowed us into a parking space at a shopping center; or by unexpectedly calling up a parent to thank them for raising us (especially through our teen years!); or sending a card of thanks to a teacher who provided guidance at some point in our lives (writing or even calling is more personal so more meaningful). When was the last time you were truly thankful for a car, to be able to buy groceries (even at sky-high prices), or to have shelter over your head? When did you say thank you to the ocean, the trees, the birds, the clear skies, the sod under your feet?

We can learn *compassion* more easily if we have gratitude for what we have been *gifted* with in this life. Compassion is the "trembling of the heart," a living energetic flow of refined love for all beings, everywhere. Compassion allows you to forgive someone in your past who betrayed you, to quietly help a person who is down-and-out, to allow for someone to be an exception to the rule instead of rigidly adhering to the rules, to tolerate someone's point-of-view because you accept them for who they are.

The pattern of initiation can also be seen in modern dreams. The well-known historian of religion, Mircea Eliade, asserted that initiatory themes remain alive chiefly in modern man's unconscious. Though the living, experiential, and transformative aspects of initiation are no longer part of today's organized religions, initiation rites as they were once practiced in the mystery schools continue to appear in the modern unconscious.

The dreamer may enter a library to study ancient spiritual texts, participate in sacred rituals, learn a mysterious language, be anointed with one's spiritual name, meet with mentors, guides, and angelic beings, take part in mystery rites such as of baptism, drink from a sacred chalice, be an honored guest at a sacred ceremony or feast; fly through the air; or visit different realms or dimensions of existence. These scenarios were once aspects of ancient initiatory religions such as the Egyptian, Eleusinian, Dionysian, Orphic and the Mithraic Mysteries.

Modern dreamers are sometimes baffled or even frightened by bizarre dream imagery that seems to have little to do with their everyday lives. Persons may be unsettled and disturbed by dreams that show themselves being disemboweled and embalmed, dismembered, or flayed (dream scenarios often described by shamans as part of their training). Dreamers may experience themselves transforming into a wild animal; see themselves as a deformed creature or skeleton; or undergo roasting in a blazing fire. Such imagery has significance for the dreamer because these events usually refer to extraordinary processes of psychological transmutation and as such, are often seen in the dreams of persons undergoing preparation for or who are in the first stages of initiation. Many of these motifs represent the cleansing and passing off of old states of consciousness to make room for higher, more comprehensive levels of spiritual understanding.

Today's dreamers may undergo the types of tests described by holy persons, high priests, spiritual teachers, and shamans everywhere in the world, the very same trials with which initiates once confronted as contrived or engineered challenges to test their readiness and resolve for spiritual advancement. Individuals may dream of perilous journeys, life or death ordeals, descents into caves, canyons or catacombs. Dreamers might cross a fiery burning ground; jump into a fathomless abyss; swim across a wide and rapid channel of water; find their way through a dark and hazardous labyrinth, or stand, quaking in fear, in front of a towering tsunami, an overwhelming wall of water from which there is no escape.

Like Indiana Jones in *The Last Crusade*, the dreamer might make a leap of faith by stepping out onto an invisible bridge spanning a bottomless gorge. Or like Pi, in the movie, *Life of Pi,* everything and everyone previously known are suddenly torn away, and the dreamer floats in a lifeboat, lost and alone at sea, and in Pi's case, with a Bengal tiger on board! Such dream trials invite persons to confront and conquer fears—especially the fear of death—enabling them to live in the physical world with more creativity and freedom.

The archetype of initiation is deeply embedded in the fabric of our lives. That this pattern of unfoldment is inextricably ingrained in everything we experience makes it apparent that *over all of our lifetimes, and through everything we undergo, we are ultimately being prepared for the tests and trials of spiritual initiation.* If Earth life comprises a school, we are learning life lessons at every grade level, passing from one level to the next, life after life, until we are ready for the graduate school that is initiation. Eventually, we may matriculate out of Earth School; this feat of spiritual maturity is achieved through initiation.

# TO DO A JOB AND DO IT WELL

*Don't ask what the world needs. Ask what makes you come alive and go do it, because what the world needs is people who have come alive.*
~ **Howard Thurman**

*Everyone has been made for some particular work, and the desire for that work has been put in every heart.*
~ **Rumi**

The daily jobs and vocations by which we make a living are helping us to become more aware of how life itself works, and in doing so, are preparing us for the journey of initiation. The higher qualities we learn through working, especially at something we love, include initiative, perseverance, follow through, attention to detail, dependability, thoroughness, creativity, competency, skill, and a drive towards excellence, which are all qualities necessary for the trials, tests, and tasks of initiation. Many people today are candidates for initiation (or are disciples unconsciously engaged in the first two initiatory stages) who are going about their work, learning through their daily tasks and challenges to become of greater benefit to the broader human family.

By the time we are ready for induction into the Great Path, we are looking for ways to be of service and to execute what we do for the sake of the greatest good. We do not need to run off to volunteer at Mother Teresa's Foundation to serve in the streets of India; we can be of service anywhere, and in the humblest of jobs, if we have first transformed our inner selves. This is possible because, as Jungian analyst Rachel Wooten notes, "The spiritual development of a single individual has the power to transform everyone around them."

Once, I sat down and wrote out what I thought were the higher "octaves" (higher frequencies or vibrations) of the work we do in the physical world, which I include in chart form below. The job list is not all inclusive, and the higher octaves are subjective reflections, but you will get the general idea. I have always been fascinated by what originally attracted people to their line of work: *Why is a firefighter attracted by the fire element? Why is a pilot drawn to the skies? Why does someone have the inner drive to become a comedian? Of all the possible parts of the human body, why did a person focus their interest on teeth and become a dentist?* Some people, of course, naturally go into the family business, a field of endeavor that is common to their bloodline (and aligns with their life path); while others work at jobs that they are neither content with nor happy to be doing. In this section, I am primarily referring to people who feel that their work accurately (for now) reflects their skills, interests, and temperament.

In fact, it is not so much *what* we do as *how* we do it and the qualities we develop while we're doing it. Looking at the spiritual octave of a line of work is considering what might be the spiritual significance or higher purpose of such an occupation. Everything in life, including our vocations and avocations, has as its true objective the realization and development of ourselves as spiritual beings. *Ask yourself what qualities you might be learning in your job or profession. What do you think is the spiritual octave of the work you do?*

| Physical World Occupations | Higher Octave/Spiritual Significance |
|---|---|
| athlete | learning discipline, self-regulation, dedication, endurance and fitness for the Spiritual Path of Initiation |
| police officer | to help others learn and keep the Spiritual Laws (principles) of Life |
| salesperson | to become a "Salesperson for God," promoting the rewards of living a Higher Life |
| bureaucrat | learning how to be a "Co-Worker" for God, or a World Server |

| Physical World Occupations | Higher Octave/Spiritual Significance |
|---|---|
| chef | to help humans learn that "spiritual" food is the true nourishment for humankind |
| pilot | to free humans from the lower worlds; aspiration, Soul Travel |
| farmer | preparing and tilling the fields, or creating fertility in persons so that they grow from seeds of awareness into spiritual awakening; all in the fullness of time |
| dentist | to help people take in (chew on) and assimilate (understand) life experiences |
| politician | to help humans learn to self-govern; to protect human sovereignty and freedom |
| physicist | to help persons see God's Universal Laws, or the workings of Spirit in the material world |
| comedian | to lighten the human spirit; to help people observe and question the larger meaning of daily human experience |
| miner | digging deep to find what's hidden to the surface; mining for the gold of Self-Realization, the wholeness of the Self (The Philosopher's Stone); precious metals and gems as the currency of love |
| architect | to promote the understanding of God's Universal Design for humans to unfold as spiritual beings (God is sometimes called the Grand Architect). |
| warrior; armed forces | to become spiritual warriors for God; to protect and serve the greater destiny of all beings |
| prostitute | to more fully love and to give oneself, finally, to God |
| nun | to more fully love and to give oneself, finally, to God |
| journalist | to find the lessons in human events; to help people see their lives as "human interest" stories, or fodder for Soul |
| fisherperson | to find the treasures of Spirit by plumbing one's depths |
| teacher | helping others to see and realize themselves as Soul via the Wisdom Teachings |
| physician | healing, via Spirit, the ills of the lower bodies so as to aid humans on The Spiritual Path of Initiation |
| psychotherapist/ psychologist | guide and helper to those on The Spiritual Path of Initiation |

| Physical World Occupations | Higher Octave/Spiritual Significance |
|---|---|
| artist: painter, musician, dancer, writer | giving expression to the beauty and joy of Soul (our true selves); revealing through art the deeper meaning and significance of life |
| firefighter | tending to the fire of God in one's heart; the burning away of impurities to assist the flame of Spirit to more brightly shine in the world |
| actor | to mirror human experience for the schooling of Soul |
| businessperson | to finally understand that all business is God's business; there is no agenda that isn't part of a greater spiritual design |
| clergy, ministry | to minister unto others and their needs (listening); service to others as service to God; inspiring humans to aspire to the things of Spirit |

**Reminder**: *God is expressed here as the Great Source, where all creation throughout every plane, world, and dimension has been created (sometimes via hierarchies of beings). God is beyond male or female designations and dwells in what has been called the Ocean of Love and Mercy, from where we came and to where we return via the Path of Initiation. God is beyond form manifestation; we can never be separate from the Source because all manifestation takes place within the Source!*

When we ponder the higher octave, or purpose of the work we do, we are elevating this work, *lifting up* or *spiritualizing*, an aspect of the physical world. Conversely, when we work with our dreams and apply their messages to everyday life; or when we meditate or practice mindfulness during our daily routines; we are *bringing down* or *earthing* spiritual energies to integrate into our physical lives. Our occupation, whether we know it or not, is actually a way of integrating the spiritual and material worlds. True work is an expression of the deepest self when we do it with purpose, passion, and a desire to help others; then it has become a *calling*.

# LILY AND KELSEY'S STORIES: EXPERIENCES OF THE SPIRITUAL KIND

*You are Soul, a particle of God*
*sent into this world to gain spiritual experience.*
~ **Paul Twitchell**

*If I may take the risk of defining what a spiritual experience is,*
*it is one in which pure awareness reveals itself*
*to you as a maker of reality – where you suddenly discover through*
*insight or meditation or a freak accident*
*that your essential nature is spiritual, non-material.*
~ **Deepak Chopra**

When asked about their religious identity, more and more Americans describe themselves as "spiritual but not religious."[10] The Pew Research Center reports that while the overall public is becoming less traditionally religious, among Americans who are unaffiliated (without membership in a traditional religion), "half…have had a religious or mystical experience—that is, a moment of religious and spiritual awakening."[11] Spiritual experiences at the beginning of The Path are a means to awaken our attention and to draw us in, a way to break through the hypnotic hold of our electronic devices, our social media addictions, our online shopping habits, and our ongoing daily diversions.

Spiritual experiences are sometimes known as religious experiences, sacred encounters, supernatural, or mystical experiences. Spiritual experiences, as understood here, are subjective experiences which often occur unexpectedly and in the absence of drugs or physical illness. They may involve visions; "miraculous" healings; what Jung called Big or Archetypal Dreams; a near-death experience (NDE); a spontaneous out-of-body experience (OBE); a meeting with an angel, guide or other resplendent personage; a feeling of awe while contemplating the infinity of the cosmos; a sense of "union" (a defining characteristic of mystical experience) with the Divine or with nature, and even contacts with extraterrestrial beings which can result, according to some reports, in transformational experiences of a spiritual nature.[12]

Many of these experiences serve to introduce individuals to the truth of realities and states of being beyond the physical. They may elicit feelings of connection to a higher power. Some may inspire people to become seekers in life, moving them to "remember" their spiritual purpose or life design. Some spiritual experiences occur early in life, bringing guidance, encouragement or support. It is this last type of spiritual experience that Lily had when she was a young girl during one of the most difficult times of her life.

> *Lily shared that, when she was a child, her parents presented the façade of "idyllic family life" to their Florida beach community. "In reality," she revealed, "there was the darkness of molestation, of my mother's pill popping, and the fear of my father's out-of-control anger, which at times was so great that my younger brother and I would push a heavy desk in front of our bedroom door after we had locked it for the night."*

> *One night when Lily was nine years old, she sobbed alone in her bedroom, her heart broken by the secret suffering in her family. "As I fell asleep crying, I repeated to myself that I wanted to go home—because I knew that this was not where I belonged." Later, in the darkest hour of the night, she was awakened by a voice coming from the end of her bed: "The voice was musical, soothing, and loving. I felt no fear. As I looked toward the voice, I saw two light beings, a man and a woman." Lily sat up, wide awake now. The woman spoke to her kindly, "You said that you could do this. You can go if you want to, but you said you could do this." For a moment Lily thought about this. "I remembered that I had said that I could live this life, and as soon as I made*

> the decision to honor this commitment, the light beings disappeared." Lily was left with a profound calm and the understanding that these two beings "had been there for her and that they would always be there."

This childhood experience later influenced Lily to study world religions, where she searched "for a belief system that resonated with me, that could explain my life experiences and give me some answers to my 'why' questions." She began to explore the possibilities of life after death, reincarnation, and the evolution of the spiritual Self. Lily stated, "My lifelong mantra became 'I said I could do it and I will.'"

People today are recognizing spiritual experiences in the midst of everyday life, many of which are triggered by common occurrences seen from an unexpected perspective. In a recent article in a digital issue of *Refinery29*, Millennials were asked to define their spirituality.[13] The article's author pointed out that the most frequently submitted definition had to do with *being a part of something larger than oneself*. One person related a recent spiritual moment when "looking into her nephew's face" soon after he was born. The writer marveled, "I could actually feel myself looking at the world in a different way." Another contributor described "sitting in a lawn chair in the middle of a New Mexico desert, staring up at the stars…" The star-gazer began thinking, 'There must be a God, because somehow everything has worked out for this moment to exist, and without a God, nothing this perfect could ever happen." Someone else wrote in that during a visit to her veterinarian's office to have her pet euthanized, she felt "a happy, loving, and peaceful presence fill the room" as the cat passed away. "It felt like her soul was giving me a final and last goodbye. I walked out of the vet's office feeling oddly happy." Yet another person submitted that the television show, *Cosmos*, led to the mystical experience of feeling "how everything is connected and we are just stardust." This reader admitted that watching episodes brought tears, explaining, "It's just so amazing learning about how the universe started and evolved" and to realize that humans are "trying to make meaning out of something that's so wonderful that it cannot yet be fully explained."

A spiritual experience that Kelsey remembered from childhood has had a lasting effect on her life. She shared with me that she was adopted at an early age, but never felt comfortable with her troubled adoptive family which struggled with mental illness and substance abuse. She remembered a childhood experience that, similarly to Lili's meeting with the light beings at the foot of her bed, helped her navigate a life in which she often felt vulnerable and lost:

> "I'm blessed (and also cursed) that I remember events, feelings, and people from the time I could walk. Before I could speak, I could read minds. Some of the messages I picked up through telepathy were good, other messages were not. I was confused that I could read others' minds—but that they could not read mine. But this is how I became a fixer of animals and people, although I was a child and often didn't know what to do. I spent most of my time outside or with animals, knowing that immersing myself in nature centered me and gave me insight, direction and solace. Nature was a place of safety. Once, while wishing I could fly away from a situation, I actually willed it to happen. As birds gathered on a branch above me, I took a deep breath, exhaled, and felt myself no longer connected to the ground. I became weightless, floating up as light as air until I was eye level with the birds. I was thrilled and terrified at the same time; what if I lost focus and fell? The sudden realization of my achievement frightened me. I gently descended to the ground. I never spoke of this event to anyone, but I knew that what I understood as my guardian angel had facilitated this experience and was keeping me safe."

Kelsey felt that she had "secret" friends and that she was never completely alone, even though she often felt that she didn't belong. Kelsey knew with certainty that there was a world of unseen and magical things; she would return to the memory of "visiting the birds" whenever she needed solace. This experience also prompted her to look for validation from nature and animals instead of the people around her.

There are as many reasons for why modern individuals are becoming more aware of spiritual experiences as there are types of spiritual experiences. Two major reasons, however, can be identified. One is the importance of the period of history in which we are now living. We are living in a critical time, or juncture, which is known as *kairos*, an ancient Greek word meaning the right or most opportune moment. At their most dire, scientists warn that if we do not take action to ameliorate environmental and weather conditions, there is a possibility of a sixth mass extinction by 2100, or the Holocene Extinction.[14] Such an event, they claim, would largely be due to our tardiness in dealing with environmental conditions, such as the current amount of carbon-load in our oceans and the ongoing eradication of entire species of insect, bird, and animal life.

While I personally do not see catastrophe on that level ahead of us any time soon, we *are* living on the edge. Our attention to the healing of our planet in the 20s decade should be among our greatest concerns. Added to ecological issues is the urgent need for the renovation of almost every area that makes up human life—political, financial, educational, medical, psychological, and social and global relationships. We are at a pivotal moment, and it is ultimately up to us to make vital decisions about what direction we want to go. It is imperative that humans quickly become more self-aware; spiritual development embraces a greater realization of our connection to all things, and this understanding results in wiser decision-making and more rapid change. (This topic is further explored in Chapter 7.)

The second reason why humans are reporting an increasing number of spiritual experiences is that there is an escalation of the "thinning of the veils." This esoteric phrase, cautiously reframed in scientific terms, indicates that we may be living in intersecting realities. The theoretical framework of Superstring Theory, for example, posits that the universe exists in eleven different dimensions, according to physicist Dr. Brian Greene.[15] Others say that there are dimensions beyond counting.[16] Recent discoveries in physics and astronomy, he submits, point to the idea that our universe may be one of many universes, or a *multiverse.*

Harvard University physicist Lisa Randall includes in her scientific explorations the possibility of the existence of extra dimensions as well as parallel universes.[17] Randall is careful to separate spiritual beliefs and scientific facts (that is, until science has corroborating proof), but scientific inquiry in the last two decades is looking into questions of reality that were once only proposed by science fiction writers—and have been shared by spiritual explorers since the beginning of recorded history. From a spiritual point of view, the slow, steady upward progression in overall human consciousness is enabling the merging of different planes, levels of existence, or regions of reality, particularly apparent to people who are intuitively sensitive. Simply put, more humans are becoming aware of extraordinary psychospiritual states and extranormal phenomena outside of physical world norms.

## SPIRITUAL EXPERIENCES AND THE ROAD OF INITIATION

> *The whole point (of spiritual practice)*
> *is not to get visions but to get realizations.*
> *A realization is a white transparent light at the center of the prism;*
> *not the rainbow colors around it.*
> ~ **Tenzin Palmo**

Unusual and uplifting spiritual experiences can awaken us to the probability of other realities and bring to us a reassurance of ourselves as spiritual beings. Some spiritual experiences are moments of revelation, giving us a glimpse of our own possibilities. These experiences are meant to encourage us to double-down on our spiritual studies and practices. They give us the momentum and drive to begin the *hegira,* our personal journey toward human wholeness. Most spiritual experiences are intended to bolster our resiliency, our resolve, and our compassion. Most importantly, we are shown by our spiritual experiences that it is possible to pursue a relationship with the Divine that is personal and immediate. The author Paul Brunton (pen name of Raphael Hurst), stated that no one "who has lived through a temporary spiritual experience is ever likely to forget it." He concluded that such a person would need "to seek out ways and means of repeating it" to find peace.

Spiritual experiences are at their most valuable when we integrate them into our everyday lives, creating in this way a fusion of our inner and outer worlds. We must incorporate the extraordinary while living an ordinary existence—a tall order! The effort to integrate spiritual experiences creates stability, steadfastness, and a centralized solidity within ourselves. Without this effort, we are tempted to use these experiences to set ourselves apart from others as "special." In this regard, the psychologist and Buddhist teacher Jack Kornfield remarks:

> *"A bulging portfolio of spiritual experiences matters little if it does not have the power to sustain us through the inevitable moments of grief, loss, and change. Knowledge and achievements matter little if we do not yet know how to touch the heart of another and be touched. Wisdom is alive only as long as it is lived, understanding is liberating only as long as it is applied."*[18]

Spiritual experiences can fill us with love and light and awe. They often come to us as blessings. But if we attempt to remain in the realms of light, we become inflated (the misappropriation of spiritual energies to our egos, which feeds our need to be admired) and certainly ungrounded.

This can lead us to do a *spiritual bypass* or end run around the work of confronting and healing our own lower human natures. Spiritual maturity requires recognition of the opposites in ourselves and in life; we do not advance without shadow work and struggle.

*Where do spiritual experiences fit in for those who enter upon the Way of Initiation?* Phenomenal experiences are important at the beginning of this journey, but they become distractions as we spiritually mature. Dramatic spiritual experiences may sometimes still occur, but they become secondary as we progress on The Path. Ecstatic experiences that carry us away recede in the face of the inner work we must do in the here and now. At some point on the Path, spiritual travelers find they cannot go any higher than they can go low; they must "touch the bottom of their own wells" in a Dark Night of the Soul experience before they can climb up the "Mountain of God."

The Long Road of Spiritual Initiation is a difficult one; we have been walking toward this Road forever. The poet Anne Sexton wrote, "I cannot walk an inch without trying to walk to God." All humans are destined to progress through the stages of initiation during their evolution. If we commit to this Path, we will have intermittent feelings of great joy and will realize a larger capacity to give and receive love. But the work of maturing into greater consciousness will always test us at our "growing tip" where we are most vulnerable and weak. The phenomena we once thought were fascinating and exciting have lured us in—and now we find that we are at spiritual boot camp! Along the way, it is reassuring to remember that as we meet each challenge, we are becoming our truest, most authentic Self. We hold a secret happiness in our hearts, knowing that we are "making ourselves more beautiful" for God.

# CHAPTER TWO EXERCISES

## Learning in the Schoolroom of Life

1. In your journal, describe an experience you have had that could be characterized as going through the fires. This would be an ordeal in which you felt that everything in you that was old or no longer useful was "burned off" through emotional suffering. Discuss how you "rose from the ashes" afterward: What types of things helped you to get through this ordeal? Once it was over, how did you feel that you had changed?

2. When did you feel overwhelmed and emotionally vulnerable, perhaps to the extent that you were not able to reliably function on a day-to-day basis? Did this experience lead you to insights you might not otherwise have realized? In what ways did you look for help (e.g., journaling, psychotherapy, dream work)? What emotions were most difficult to deal with? Did anger, jealousy, revenge, resentment, shame, guilt, or rejection come up for review? What were your takeaways or insights from this period of emotional tribulation? Do you believe that you have resolved any deep-seated emotional issues?

3. Do you feel that your line of work was a *calling*? Does it fulfill you? If not, what would you be happiest doing? How can you make this a reality in your life, now or later?

4. Reread the paragraphs under the subtitle, "Experiences of the Spiritual Kind." Have you had an experience you would categorize as an *awakening*? This would include experiences of transcendence or oneness or uplifting moments of wonder and awe. You may have been unaccountably filled with great love and tenderness for Earth and all life on the planet. When astronauts see the Earth from space, for example, they often report having an experience known as the *Overview*

*Effect.* This experience is a feeling of awe and clarity with a sense of cosmic interconnectedness and unity. In your journal, describe in detail your own spiritual awakening experience.

## CHAPTER TWO ENDNOTES

[1.] In Tobias Churton's book, *The Invisible History of the Rosicrucians,* there is reference to the term of *cosmoxenus,* or "The World Stranger." Also known as *Wanderers* (as in *The RA Material* books), they are seekers after the Light. Though they may lose everything in life, they go on to serve the greater good. The cosmoxenus is an individual in the world but not of it. (Rochester, Vermont: Inner Traditions, 2009, p.383).

[2.] "Rick" is a given name, but all other names of persons whose stories I relate in this book are pseudonyms. (This was each interviewee's choice).

[3.] Complex Post-Traumatic Stress (c-PTSD or CPTSD) is a condition where the individual experiences the usual symptoms of PTSD along with additional symptoms, such as: difficulty controlling emotions, feeling very angry or distrustful towards the world, avoiding friendships and relationships, or finding them very difficult, etc. Some people with this syndrome have experienced severe trauma such as war conditions, mass shootings, or like Rick, childhood abuse.

[4.] The *Desert Trial, Fire Trial, Water Trial,* and *Air Trial* are tests along the Path of Initiation. The Water Trial, for example, is the esoteric name for accomplishing a task without any apparent external support. (Some esoteric writings put the Fire Trial before the Water Trial). The *Air Trial* comes next, which is a test in which the initiate must successfully accomplish a task straightaway, without hesitation or compunction. (Ordeals by Water and Fire were also torture-tests in medieval times to test for guilt or innocence). I use the water trial more as a reference to emotional processing and clearing.

[5.] Many Americans are so busy with responsibilities (including childcare, home teaching, household maintenance, and working from home) that finding such quiet times are next to impossible. (During a therapy session, one client laughingly commented that only by retreating to the bathroom could she ever find a few moments to herself!). Having time for yourself, however, allows you to reflect and process; otherwise, many are unwittingly pulled into a depression in order to do this necessary work. We are cyclic beings, with organic rhythms, not robots who work without rest or pause.

[6.] Patricia Ariadne. *Drinking the Dragon: Stories of the Dark Night of The Soul.* Encinitas, CA: Sothis Press, 2021, p. 203.

[7.] Some people do not return from the abyss. It largely depends on factors such as whether the individual has previously had a stable history of mental health (and has been able to hold jobs and maintain long-term relationships); currently has a network of support; and has an adequate ego structure to contain the extreme psycho-emotional turbulence that a Dark Night can bring. Importantly, the individual needs a *spiritual orientation,* in whichever form is natural for that person, to weather what is essentially, a spiritual process. This process is a different level and kind of psychological tumult, not to be confused with mental dysfunction and inadequate socialization (Although symptoms may seem to overlap and are sometimes hard to distinguish). The field of psychology needs to expand its awareness regarding these various states and stages, and a slight inroad has been made with the inclusion in the A.P.A.'s *Diagnostic and Statistical Manual* (*DSM5*) of the category of "Religious or Spiritual Problem." (See books by Stanislav and Christina Grof, such as the *Stormy Search for Self*, Westminster, London, England: Penquin Publishing Group, 1992, to get a better idea of this differentiation).

[8.] The subtitle for this section is based on the 1966 movie, *A Funny Thing Happened on the Way to the Forum*, a British-American musical-comedy based on the stage musical of the same name. The chapter title is also the title of an article I wrote that was accepted for publication by *Fate Magazine* in 2013.

[9.] Mircea Eliade. *Rites and Symbols of Initiation*. New York: HarperCollins College Division, 1980, pp. 127-128.

[10.] The data shows that the trend toward religious disaffiliation documented in the Pew Research Center's *2007 and 2014 Religious Landscape Studies*, and before that in major national studies like the *General Social Survey* (GSS), has continued to increase. "Americans may be getting less religious, but feelings of spirituality are on the rise," *FactTank: News in the Numbers,* January 21, 2016.

[11.] Pew Research Center: *Religion & Public Life*, Dec. 9, 2009. In addition, results from the *Chapman University Survey of American Fears* reports that paranormal beliefs, such as belief in ghosts, aliens, hauntings, and advanced civilizations (Atlantis) having once existed- have become the norm in the United States, with as many as ¾ of Americans believing in at least one paranormal phenomenon. While these qualitatively differ in many respects from spiritual or religious experiences (there is some overlap), these findings contribute to the understanding that Americans are opening to the idea of realities beyond the physical or material realm.

[12.] See books by Mary Rodwell, such as *Awakening: How ET Contact Can Transform Your Life*. New Mind Publishers, 2010.

[13.] *Refinery29* is an American multinational digital media and entertainment website focused on young women. The quotes are from an article written by Sara Coughlin, titled, "Spiritual Moments People Experienced Nowhere Near A Church," March 22. 2017.

[14.] See *MIT News*, "Mathematics Predicts a Sixth Mass Extinction," by Jennifer Chu, September 20, 2017 (online). See also, "What are mass extinctions, and what causes them?" in *National*

*Geographic Science News* by Michael Greshko and NG Staff, September 16, 2019. https://news.mit.edu/2017/mathematics-predicts-sixth-mass-extinction-0920

[15.] Brian Greene. "A Physicist Explains Why Parallel Universes Exist," NPR, KPBS, Jan. 24, 2011. https://www.npr.org/2011/01/24/132932268/a-physicist-explains-why-parallel-universes-may-exist. Greene addresses the existence of multiple universes in his book, *The Hidden Reality: Parallel Universes and the Deep Laws of the Cosmos*. New York, New York: Vintage Books, 2011. Also read Michio Kaku, *The Future of Humanity*, New York, New York: Anchor Books, 2018.

[16.] I included the following information in the Endnotes of Ch.1, but it bears repeating here, with additional detail: A plane, as used in *Dancing the Labyrinth*, is a level of thought, existence or development; a region or dimension of reality. The two most popular number of initiatory planes are 7 and 12, but there are, in actuality, infinite numbers of planes/dimensions. The planes separated into distinct levels of consciousness, as I have done in this book, is simply a way to wrap our minds around spiritual growth. (Some claim that there are thousands of dimensions; see the paragraph below!)

As humans evolve in consciousness, they individually realize coarser to finer densities that affiliate them with certain planes. Human waking reality is considered Third Dimensional reality or 3D, because most humans share this consciousness; when most humans wake up to 4D (the astral dimension), then Earth will be a 4D planet. The $5^{th}$ Dimension (5D) is considered the realm of higher level thought forms. According to theorist Dr. Alan Lew, 1-5 Dimensions can be considered *Collective Dimensions*. See Alan Lew, *The One Most Complete Guide to the Spiritual Dimensions of Reality*," for further insights on this subject. Dec. 20, 2021. https://medium.com/new-earth-consciousness/explainer-what-are-the-different-spiritual-dimensions-of-reality-and-is-earth-moving-to-the-5th-2cd99d3dc319.

[17.] Interview with Lisa Randall in a discussion of her book, *Knocking on Heaven's Door*. Robert Irion, "Opening Strange Portals in Physics," *Smithsonian Magazine*, December, 2011. https://www.smithsonianmag.com/science-nature/opening-strange-portals-in-physics-92901090/

[18.] Christina Feldman and Jack Kornfield. *Stories of the Spirit, Stories of the Heart*, New York: HarperCollins, 1996, p. 263.

# CHAPTER THREE

# Mapping the Spiral Way: Five Stages of Initiation The Master and Stage 1

*Every positive change*
*—every jump to a level of higher energy and awareness—*
*involves a rite of passage.*
*Each time to ascend to a higher rung*
*on the ladder of personal evolution,*
*we must go through a period of discomfort, of initiation.*
*I have never found an exception.*
~ **Dan Millman**

## THE FIRST FIVE STAGES

*Every test successfully met is rewarded*
*by some growth in intuitive knowledge, strengthening of character,*
*or initiation into a higher consciousness.*
~ **Paul Brunton**

The descriptions of the first five Stages of Initiation in **Chapter 3** (Initiation 1), in **Chapter 4** (Initiations 2-3) and in **Chapter 5** (Initiations 4-5) are only meant to serve as a *general guide map* and not as a strictly regimented schedule of experiences or events. The initiation process is generally recognized as an advanced program of human spiritual unfoldment. It is a universal, non-denominational, and ancient system of profound experiential and transformational processes.[1] The delineations of the first five stages in *Dancing the Labyrinth* (and there are many more than five) serve as a broad-spectrum blueprint for the spiritual path of initiation toward Self-Realization at the Fifth Initiation. These stages are inexact and can flow into one another, and as philosopher Ken Wilbur has pointed out, each stage of realization is "transcended but included" in the next. Additionally, some spiritual paths do not offer an extensive or intensive system of initiation, which largely hinges on the level of mastership attained by the spiritual leader of an initiatory path. This factor is why, at certain levels of unfoldment, some spiritual students pass on to other teachers. (This chapter will include a brief overview of spiritual guides or masters).

Because every spiritual student is unique, an initiate may simultaneously work on tasks characteristic of two stages or more; or, in other cases, certain endeavors (such as becoming more honest with oneself and others) can for some continue throughout all stages. That being said, the tasks specified for each of the first five initiations are only loosely associated with these stages, but it *is* certain that, sooner or later, these challenges will be confronted by the initiate at some point along the Path. An additional consideration is that those on the Labyrinthine Path can stay a varying number of years at any one stage before passing on to another. Not every spiritual student goes persistently forward, finding it more comfortable to remain at a particular stage of growth, and perhaps choosing to pick up the Path in a future lifetime. These variations exist because everyone is distinctly different, yet humans are enough alike that common tests and tasks can be tentatively assigned to each stage.

It is important to point out that the Self (or Soul) as applied here, with a capital "S") spans *all* levels and stages of the Initiatory Ladder. At every rung of the Ladder, we become more of who we are (more closely aligned with the Self). This Ladder is not physical; it involves energies vibrating at different frequencies. These frequency bands represent the evolutionary progression of each and every human as well as of the planet Terra itself.

Climbing this Ladder with devotion and resolve allows for the reduction in the number of incarnations necessary to "graduate" from Earth School, which is why it is called a "forced path" in Theosophy and the "short path" in Tibetan Buddhism.

A good portion of humanity today includes humans operating at varying levels of free will (as many are largely acting out of a more or less programmed consciousness). For the masses of humans already on the Initiatory Path, most are at the First and Second Stages and are considered aspirants or "disciples" (also referred to as "novices" in this book). The First Initiation is primarily one of preparation and is focused on discipline and purification in everyday physical life. The disciple can turn back after the First Initiation. The Second Initiation, however, involves a commitment to the Labyrinthine Way. Most importantly, those deciding to go forward are linked at the Second Initiation to the Light and Sound (spiritual energies) of Spirit. They learn to no longer identify themselves only with their physical bodies, and recognize their true identity as spiritual beings. At this level, much work is done on refining the emotions. At these first two initiations, humans are waking up from their automatic, programmed, and unthinking states (much like Neo in the movie, *The Matrix*, 1999). The realization of a purpose and plan to life is of the greatest significance. The disciple is learning to no longer ask, *"Why did this happen to me?"* but instead to ponder, *"What meaning does this event have for me? What am I to learn from it?"* Finally, at these levels, humans are transitioning from "service to self" (or *me-consciousness*) to "service to others" (or *we-consciousness*).

We advance along the Ladder of Initiation from *animal-human* to ultimately become a *cosmic human* (variously named *The New Human, Homo Novis, Homo Noeticus, Homo Luminoso, Galactic Human* and more). It may take many lifetimes to advance on this Ladder; however, if someone has made progress in previous lifetimes as an initiate, these formerly achieved "rungs" are often accomplished more quickly than for those who are stepping onto the Ladder for the first time. Those who would enter upon the Labyrinthine

Way have been called *World Helpers, Children of the Light (and Sound), Light Workers,* and *Helpers of Humanity.* They are ushering in the Aquarian Age.

## THE JOURNEY BEGINS

> *The spiritual journey is the unlearning of fear*
> *and the acceptance of love.*
> ~ **Marianne Williamson**

In my mid-twenties, I was just beginning to embark on my journey of self-exploration. I was undergoing psychotherapy, reading everything I could get my hands on about various spiritual teachings, and attending a string of conferences—all the while searching for a spiritual path that was right for me. At this time, I had the following dream:

> *I was carefully preparing for a trip to the innermost regions of Africa. A mature woman who had already made the trip described her experiences while spreading out before her a sketch of a tree, so immense that only the sprawling root structure of the tree had fit on the drawing pad. The speaker advised all travelers to prepare for the trek with leather-soled shoes to protect our feet from the blistering hot springs along the way. It was a dangerous trip. Steve McQueen was the next speaker. He instructed us on further hazards as we sat at a round table, using a guidebook written by a man called Feasting to help us plan.*[2]

This dream illustrates the dangers of making ready to enter "into the secret interior" of myself. I recognized the mature woman in the dream as my Jungian analyst at this time, who, along with the hero, Steve McQueen (one aspect of my own single-minded inner masculinity), will guide me safely through Africa, the Motherland, to the very source ground of my being. This journey to the darkest heart, or unknown territory, of human existence, is fraught with dangers (hot springs). The dream tree, which is the mythical Tree of Life, is so all encompassing, that at the outset of this journey, I can only view the tree's roots. The guidebook by Feasting, studied at the round table, promises an abundance of life experience (feasting) to assimilate (digest) along the way, leading to the possibility of wholeness (round table).

In my practice as a psychotherapist, I have found, over the years, that many persons begin an initiatory journey via the psychotherapeutic process. In addition, every stage of initiation often begins with a dream journey. Just as I undertook a dream excursion into deepest Africa, a male client of mine dreamed of launching a dangerous ocean crossing:

> *A young man journeyed with a long line of people who were trekking through parts of the Indian Ocean, during the season when parts of it were dried up. The people were of a spiritual nature and were dressed similarly to the Amish or Mennonites. Dangers, such as whirlpools, were all around them.*
>
> *The young man had left his parents behind for this journey and was suffering for it. He carried an empty box or two for treasures that might be found along the way and used a white box as a pillow to rest his head on at night.*

This man had to symbolically leave his parents behind to embark on a spiritual pilgrimage. This means that he will suffer to leave his childhood behind (that is, the difficult shedding of his mechanical, programmed thinking and behaviors). He is required to do this in order to find out who he is as a mature and individuated (uniquely whole) person. Spiritual students will need to make their way through their own emotional seas (Indian Ocean) and will confront many perils along this trek (to drop down into a whirlpool is to be irretrievably lost in the unconscious). The dreamer will find treasures, too (valuable parts of himself will be recollected) which can be faithfully gathered up, purified, and integrated for greater wholeness during psychotherapy (saved in white boxes).

At the beginning of his sessions with me, another male client dreamed the following, which illustrates another of the many ways the daring initiatory journey begins. This man dreamed of entering a dark, unknown passage:

> *"I saw a dark, frightening cave or passageway leading from behind a chicken ranch. I knew that there were things to look at in the cave, but I was scared. I tried to ignore the tunnel or labyrinth, but I knew I would eventually have to summon up the courage to enter."*

The experience of going into the labyrinthine darkness of a cave or underground dwelling is a common theme at the beginning of self-exploration. This dream is indicating that the individual will need to go into the cave of his shadowy unconscious, where there are "things to look at." Entering the cave is frightening, but it holds out the potential (egg ranch) of significant personal growth. An investigation of this person's repressed past and its impact on the client's current life will be required.

Sometimes the process of making a descent within oneself is symbolized in a dream of going down into the basement of a house and finding something about oneself that was concealed there in the dark and frightening recesses. This theme is demonstrated in the following dream:

> *"I was in a strange castle, cautiously exploring its passages because I was unsure of its layout. I found myself going down a long flight of stone steps, brushing aside cobwebs and trying to see more clearly in the dim light. I came to a door and opened it, finding myself in a basement or dungeon. I knew that there were many ghosts or 'essences' of the past residing here."*

The dreamer knew that there were many things that he was going to discover about his own childhood (and maybe remnants of previous lifetimes) that would need to be faced and "cleaned up". It would take courage and determination (the true meaning behind the figure of the "warrior knight") to confront things hidden (in the unconscious) that can now be revealed to conscious awareness.

Entering into the unconscious can similarly be exemplified as a dream of a descent into the earth, also known as a *katabasis:* a trip to the underworld. In the following dream, the dreamer traveled to Iceland (symbolizing repressed or "frozen" memories in the unconscious) and found herself moving in a counterclockwise descent (which is how we "spiral down" into the unconscious):

> "My husband and I took a tour to Iceland. Just before we entered a large building to descend, the earth trembled. Our tour guide looked nervous. We looked up at the night sky at the stars. We decided to be at the last of the line in case we might need to make a hasty exit. (I later thought that being the last in line didn't guarantee our safety, since we were so far beneath the upper world). We sat in driverless cars and descended in great spirals going in a counterclockwise direction."

This dream shows that the dreamer will be shaken to her core (the earth trembling) by what she learns about herself. She takes one last look up at the stars because she knows she is journeying into the mysterious and unknown, which lies beneath the upper world, or the surface of daily life. Her husband symbolizes her inner masculinity which she will need to call upon to make this perilous downward journey.

In addition to a descent into the underworld, the theme of a "night sea crossing," or *nekyia,* can mark the onset of the spiritual voyage. Such a journey can be symbolized by the crossing of a great body of water—or can even be conveyed by being swallowed whole by a whale! During my first and most difficult Dark Night of the Soul experience, I dreamed:

> "Somebody lent me a boat. However, I am fearful of the open seas. How am I going to navigate, as there are no landmarks? (I think it was night, as it did occur to me that I could use the stars to guide me)."

In another example, a client once shared a dream that was strikingly similar to the Biblical "Jonah in the Whale" story:[3]

> "I was floating asleep on the ocean's surface. I awoke and noticed that a huge whale was approaching me. It had a great pile of kindling in its mouth. I started swimming as fast as I could toward the shore, but I knew the whale would swallow me."

To be swallowed up by the whale is to be enveloped by the unconscious. Through the initiate's conscious efforts of working through his problems in psychotherapy, he would light a fire (conscious awareness) inside the whale and eventually, be spewed up again (to everyday life) on a distant shore (a rebirth and renewal). His efforts to recover more of himself would ultimately reveal more of his truest nature, but not without the sacrifice of feeling lost for a time in a profound depression, which he associated with "sitting in the belly of the beast."

The start of the Initiatory Journey, whether a descent into the earth, a crossing of the seas, or being swallowed by a fearsome whale-leviathan, is to begin a trek through *The Heart of Darkness*. The Path is full of unknown dangers, vague directions, and indeterminate pathways. While we may begin this journey without a guide and master, we surely need one to help us along its entirety. Not only does the consummate master guide us through the perils of the process, but he or she acts as a transformer (converter) for the influx of energies we experience on The Labyrinthine Path and calibrates the transformative processes that occur within the initiate. The master, though never a substitute for God, can serve as a personal representative for the Divine, and is the recipient of the love and devotion that we wish to deliver to God.

## THE MASTER

*There is no teacher, living or past,*
*who can give us the actual understanding of truth.*
*A teacher can only put our feet upon the path and point the way.*
*That is all.*
*It is wholly dependent on the individual*
*to make his way to truth.*

**~ Paul Twitchell**

Once we have begun the Path of Initiation, we need a Wayshower. We need a guide who can point out possibilities and pitfalls. Someone must help us negotiate an unfamiliar and sometimes treacherous terrain, a forerunner who has walked this way before. This the true master.

## WHO IS THE MASTER?

*It is always beneficial to be near a spiritual teacher.*
*These masters are like gardens or medicinal plants,*
*sanctuaries of wisdom.*

**~ Dilgo Khywntse**

We have all heard the aphorism, "When the pupil is ready, the teacher will appear." We cannot go far on the Labyrinthine Path without guidance. In this book, the term *Master* (capitalized for the remainder of this section) applies to beings who have completed their human evolution, have been released from the cycle of reincarnation, and have elected to serve as a guide to other beings. The Master is a Wayshower, but not a savior. We never bow, worship or abjectly surrender to another human being, but always to God; if we practice surrendering to a Master, it is surrendering (our ego-selves) to the God within ourselves. We are to become, in time, our *own* Masters. As Paul Twitchell[4] states in the above quote, "A teacher can only put our feet upon the path and point the way." We must, through our own efforts, follow the Winding Way to Self-Realization (and beyond).

Importantly, it's beneficial if the Master is in a human body (although for many paths, this is not a requirement). The advantage of the Master being in the physical body is that this ensures that the spiritual teachings remain relevant to modern initiates. The Master also works with students on the inner planes as an Inner Master, communicating with students in dreams and contemplations or manifesting, when needed, on the physical plane at any time and in any place. In this way, there is both an *Outer Master* who works in the physical world—speaking at conferences, communicating via videos, and writing books and discourses—and there is an *Inner Master*, who can be with the initiate at all times without having to be physically present. The true Master also benefits the world at large, channeling the highest vibrational energies into the planet and bestowing blessings to many. As initiates, we are also distributors of positive spiritual energies; in this way we are Co-Workers with the Master, or as I was once told in a dream, we are serving as "fingers of God."

## WHY DO WE NEED A MASTER?

> *I believed in the oneness of spirituality*
> *—unconditional love for God,*
> *and unconditional compassion for the beings of this world—*
> *but I also understood that unless I chose a particular path,*
> *I couldn't focus and take blessings from teachers*
> *that would allow me to have deep realizations*
> *and spiritual experiences.*
> ~ **Radhanath Swami**

I remember at one time telling someone who was a member of a specific spiritual path that I was "spiritually eclectic" and was happy creating my *own* spirituality. He argued with me that not only would I not have the protection provided by a Teacher or Master, but it would be difficult for me to focus and advance through various stages of spiritual awareness. He was right. While a person can enjoy a solo spiritual life with simple faith and a personal relationship to God, the pitfalls of following the Labyrinthine Path are many. In this case, the spiritual journey is best undertaken with the help of a Teacher, a doctrine encompassing the Wisdom Teachings, and a community of like-minded spiritual students. The Initiatory Way is characterized by intense personal effort as well as the spiritual activation produced in us by the Master. As Harry Moody, the author of *The Five Stages of the Soul* explains:

> "The teachings of the great masters…always include an element of search, struggle, and overcoming. The stick needs the flint, say the Crow Indians, or there will be no flame. Without this search and struggle a journey is incomplete. Without them we can only go part of the way."[5]

What form that spiritual structure and guidance takes, however, is up to the spiritual seeker. The Sufis say: "There are many gates into the Garden, but to enter the Garden, you must pass through only one." **We would not be seeking God if God wasn't already within us to find.**

## HOW DO WE MEET UP WITH THE MASTER?

*How can one know who his spiritual teacher is?*
*When the heart sees a spiritual Master, if it is overwhelmed with joy,*
*then there is every probability that*
*that spiritual Master is the right one for the seeker.*
~ **Sri Chinmoy**

As we begin to advance in spirit (after many harrowing but refining incarnations), we begin to vibrate at a rate that produces an emanation and intensity of light. We are identified by this radiance, which those around us may not see so much as feel. Higher Spiritual Beings *do* see this light, however, as it marks us prepared to walk the Spiral Way. Our light signals that we are ready to find our way back to God.

We may be approached by a particular Master in a dream or in person, and it is often the case that we have previously known and worked with this being before. Our meeting then becomes a *recognition*. Finding the right Master for ourselves can be a mysterious and inexplicable process. For many years we might attend conferences, read spiritually-oriented books, and maintain spiritual practices such as meditation and dream work, all the while actively in search of a Spiritual Director of the Soul. We do so because we are unconsciously seeking initiation; our hearts thirst for spiritual immediacy, for a *living* religion; we want to *know* the Light and Sound of Spirit. During our search, we may be attracted to a speaker at a lecture or workshop; be referred to a spiritual teacher by a friend; read about a teacher in an autobiography or in a book written by another; visit spiritual centers, temples, and other places of worship; or even view a photo of a teacher which profoundly touches our heart or awakens long-buried spiritual longings. Coleman Barks, the poet and translator of several books of Rumi's poems, met his Master in a dream:

> *"In my dream I am sleeping on the bluff above the Tennessee River five miles north of Chattanooga, where I grew up. I wake up inside the dream, though still asleep. A ball of light rises off Williams Island and comes over me. It clarifies from the inside out and reveals a man sitting cross-legged with a white shawl over his head, which is bowed. He lifts his head and opens his eyes. 'I love you,' he says. 'I love you too,' I answer. The landscape, my first deep love, the curve of that river and the island, feels soaked with love…"*[6]

A year and a half later, Barks met his Master, Bawa Muhaiyaddeen, a Sufi Mystic from Tamil, in the physical world and was taught by him for many years until Bawa's death.

We may have one teacher for life or find many over time, each teacher contributing to our spiritual growth at a specific stage along the way. As an example of the former, Irina Tweedie was born in Russia, and was educated in Vienna and Paris before moving to England. When her husband died in 1954, Tweedie became involved in the Theosophy Society to study religion and philosophy. A friend of hers, Lilian Silburn, a specialist and translator in Indian studies, told her about her own spiritual guide, a Hindu Sufi sheikh living in Kanpur, India.[7] At the age of fifty-two, Tweedie traveled to India and sought out this Sufi Master, whom she later called Bhai Sahib (Elder Brother). Tweedie began writing a five-year diary (published as *Daughter of Fire*),[8] a recording of her spiritual transformation on the Sufi path of realization. Irina Tweedie was the first Western woman to be trained in this ancient Sufi lineage. In a contrasting example, anthropologist and Buddhist teacher, Joan Halifax,[9] talks of having had many teachers and spiritual guides at certain times in her life, including Dolo Ogobara, a teacher from the Dogon Tribe in Mali in central Africa, the Korean Zen Master Dae Soen sa Nim, the Huichol shaman Don Jose Rios, and the Buddhist teacher Thich Nhat Hanh. Now a Zen Roshi (teacher) herself, Halifax expresses how learning from various teachers from many world cultures has prepared her for the life of the spirit: "We go into the darkness, we seek initiation, in order to know directly how the roots of all beings are tied together…This understanding is expressed in the term *nonduality*."[10]

I found my own Teacher through an attraction to two people with whom I attended graduate school; it seemed to me, in some inexplicable way, that I already "knew" them—that we "were all swimming in the same sea." So, I was first drawn to a spiritual community and spiritual path through the *quality* of the people who were members there. When I had dreams of the teacher of this path, I knew somehow that I had been previously connected to this Soul, though it took some time for me to form an idea of what I was committing to and what lay ahead of me. It slowly dawned on me (I was not without doubts and defenses) that I was on the Initiatory Path, with its great lineage of Wisdom Teachers, the *Vairagi*, that I had been looking for most of my life.[11] When I was a child, it was *this* Master whose voice I had heard, cautioning me when to steer clear of certain harmful situations. *This* was the Spiritual Director of my heart that I had been seeking when as a child, I walked down the aisle of my church to be "welcomed home" by the Protestant minister, who beckoned his flock to "come forward" to recommit themselves to God.

## HOW CAN WE TELL A TRUE MASTER?

*I remember my first visit with my guru. He had shown that he read my mind.*
*So, I looked at the grass and I thought,*
*'My god, he's going to know all the things I don't want people to know.'*
*I was really embarrassed. Then I looked up and*
*he was looking directly at me with unconditional love.*

~ **Ram Dass**

While this list is by no means exhaustive, I have found that a true Master:

- **will never dominate or coerce**; your autonomy and sanctity as Soul is profoundly respected. You must *ask* for intervention and guidance before receiving it. However, if you do not receive the aid you requested, there may be a lesson to be learned that would have otherwise been lost.

- **will not always answer a question** (and I have, in the past, been a very tiresome spiritual student, with hundreds of questions). Often when we do not receive an answer, it is because we need *to live into the answers;* an important life experience may give us the answer we need in *the fullness of time.* Spirit always has its own timing!

- **has a sense of humor.** When we are too intense or too serious, we may hear with our "inner ear," experience in a dream, or see it play out in our physical life, something that makes us laugh out loud. The true Master often has a "light touch" when approaching life's complexities. A sense of perspective and objectivity is always encouraged.

- **will be gentle or strict, kind or formidable,** depending on the individual's temperament and the situation at hand.

- **will offer us a sacred space**—a protected, loving and accepting sense of beingness—that permits us to trust and to open our bruised hearts for healing. We have a safe harbor in which to unfold in our beauty as Soul.

- **will not ask you to give up all of your belongings and money** for the benefit of your spiritual organization. This does not mean that there won't be lessons around survival that present themselves to some spiritual students—but it's never a required policy for spiritual growth that an authentic spiritual organization, in the name of a Master, appropriates your property and money.

- ***will expect you to fulfill your role as a member of your family and to keep your employment*** as a means to support yourself. There may be difficult life lessons in this area, but even so, taking responsibility and "standing one one's own two feet" are emphasized on the Path.

- ***will assist you to grow as an independent, self-reliant, judicious*** and increasingly Soul-infused personality. Mass consciousness, herd mentality, and cultish "groupthink" are left behind as one unfolds in Soul. You are expected to grow, over time, into being your *own* Master.

- ***will be a model and ideal of temperance, humility, and love.*** There are stories of spiritual leaders using so-called "shock" tactics, such as sexual hedonism, indulgence in alcohol, displays of wealth, or demonstrations of humiliation and control of others, to awaken their students. Overall, the adage, "When someone shows you who they are, *believe* it" applies here. A true Master lives life as an example of impeccability and unassailability. Such a Master teaches through his very being and in the way he conducts his life. In illustration of this, when Gandhi was asked for a message to the world, he replied, "My life is my message."

- ***does not put the health and welfare of seekers at risk.*** Who can forget the cautionary tale of the New Age guru, James Arthur Ray, who was convicted of three counts of negligent homicide after three of his attendees died in a sweat lodge "challenge" during his 2009 "Spiritual Warrior" retreat in Sedona, Arizona? While Ray is not a spiritual master, this incident illustrates the care with which one needs to investigate a potential spiritual guide—and the absolute necessity of following one's inner intuition, guidance, and importantly, common sense!

- ***never ranks power over love.*** (In fact, they are opposites). If a spiritual organization is characterized by a great deal of jockeying for position or by struggles between members for the Master's attention, it pays to be cautious about joining. While a hierarchical structure is often part of any spiritual path, perpetual infighting or displays of power are danger signs. (Of course, spiritual organizations are made up of humans, so intermittent disagreements and fallouts are to be expected; it's best, however, to attempt to determine if these disputes are embedded in the path because of the quality of its leadership). The highest octave of *love* is always the ruling principle of a true Master.

- ***is both a human being and a channel for the highest consciousness.*** When the Master is in the physical body, the *Outer Master*, this often ensures that the Wisdom Teachings are transmitted in ways that modern persons can comprehend. The spiritual form of the Master (the *Inner Master*) appears in dreams and contemplations; for example, the Inner Master can take us on learning excursions and explorations during the dream state. The inner form of the Master is with us, always.

## WHAT ARE THE EFFECTS OF THE MASTER?

*One has to ascertain the right path for his activities*
*by following the footsteps of great saintly persons*
*and books of knowledge*
*under the guidance of a spiritual master.*
~ A. C. Bhaktivedanta

All I can truly share with absolute certainty is that on my Path I have radically *changed*, and much for the better! This is because the Path I follow has not spared me for a second; the lessons have been so difficult at times that I felt I had fallen into a chasm, never to be found, forgotten by friend and foe (and especially, by God). But the sense of freedom, the capacity to love, the desire to be of service, and the ability to see the beauty of life have increased a thousandfold. And though we say that we have changed, we have been solely becoming who we are as Soul, our immortal Self. Because the proof really *is* in the pudding, the following questions are ones you might want to ask yourself when working over time with a Master:

- *Are you interested in being admired for your spirituality, or are you able to work silently and unrecognized in the background?*

- *Conversely, are you able to overcome your fear in any situation, such as when you are pushed to the front to speak to a room full of people?*

- *Do you have a great and growing love for all beings?*

- *Have you developed greater compassion for others?*

- *Have you healed the split in yourself; do you suffer from less inner conflict due to integrating your "little selves"?*

- *Have you faced your own Shadow? Have you depotentiated (made less harmful) this part of your nature?*

- *Are you becoming more independent, more of an individual (identifying more with the uniqueness of Soul and less with the expectations or judgments of others)?*

- *Conversely, do you feel more universally connected to all others?*

- *Are you bent on service to others, to serve as a Spiritual Co-Worker (known by some today as a Lightworker) to bring greater blessings to the world?*

- *Are you more truly yourself? Have you healed the wounds of childhood and become more authentic and true to "the face you had before you were born"?*

- Can you accept and love yourself, knowing all too well your own imperfections and shortcomings?

- Are you able to give others the space to be themselves without impinging on them or sitting in judgment? This includes not trying to force your spiritual path or religion upon others.

- Are you becoming less attached to material things? Of course, we can enjoy beautiful things and surroundings. There is no spiritual gain in being unnaturally ascetic, denounced, or impoverished. But if material things define you, you are working on the ego level.

- Are you less attached even to those you love? Again, nonattachment in this sense does not mean turning your back on your loved ones or becoming any less loving. Having people in our lives that we love can teach us a great deal about opening our hearts. What you learn through spiritual unfoldment is that to love someone as one Soul to another is to offer them freedom of being (the opposite of a relationship built on enmeshment or codependency).

- Are you becoming quieter, both internally and externally?

- Do you find that you no longer need to be the center of attention or to take credit for your accomplishments?

- Are you better able to handle what life throws at you? Are you growing in flexibility, resilience, and confidence?

- Do you find more joy in the everyday things of life?

- Do you have and express gratitude for all that is given to you?

- *Are you able to surrender to Spirit? Remember, you must first assemble a self to surrender it! To surrender in this way is not about being subservient but being willing to voluntarily put the wants of the ego-self aside to serve others as a Lover of God.*

Our goal is never perfection, it should be emphasized, but *completion*. Wholeness contains everything, including the remaining foibles and flaws in our character. As long as we inhabit a physical body, we must express some negativity (as in the negative charge of a battery) in order to operate on the physical plane. It is the perfection of the purely spiritual part of us that we seek via initiation.

## WHICH ROLES DOES THE MASTER FULFILL?

> *The fact is that all Saints, all Prophets,*
> *belong to the same Religion:*
> *the Religion of the Lovers of God.*
> ~ Irina Tweedie

Again, I can only answer this on a personal level. For me, the Inner Master has taken on many roles, among them:

- **Companion.** There are times I think that I would have died of loneliness on this Path, but for the constant company of the Inner Master. It is as if there is a (usually invisible) presence with me at all times, and in all places. I find myself talking out loud to this Master, even about mundane things.

- **Guide.** I cannot walk the Initiatory Path by myself. I need the help of someone who has "been there" before me, just as a *facilitator* (as an experienced mountain guide is now called) shepherds climbers up the steep and treacherous incline of Mt. Everest.

- **Protector.** There are many situations on the physical as well as on the inner planes, where a student may need assistance. Not everything or everyone we meet along the way has our best interests at heart. Though I am learning to be independent and ultimately to be my *own* Master, I may still need someone to call on when the going gets rough and push comes to shove!

- **Teacher.** There is so much to learn on the Path, and much of it is acquired in the dream state at temples of learning on the inner planes. What we learn on the physical plane is largely experiential learning, but on the inner planes, there are classrooms that teach us things of a universal nature. The Master oversees our spiritual education in an individualized program of learning which may include, both on the physical and inner planes, our consumption of books and spiritual discourses as well as charts, records, and ancient writings of all sorts. In our dreams, the Master can also "mock-up" various training exercises, so that if analogous events are experienced in our physical lives, we are prepared for the challenge. (And sometimes our experiences on the inner planes actually *prevent* unfortunate events from manifesting in the physical life!)

- **Counselor.** The Master communicates with us in the ways we learn best: a whispered message in the ear; a song lyric that conveys a message; a visual appearance in our dreams; a meeting when, using the *anja* or Third Eye chakra, we contemplate upon the Master; a "waking dream;" an unusual or noteworthy event that occurs in our daily lives; when someone we need to meet is "sent" to us; or we are given a book with just the information we need at that moment. It is through these lines of communication that we are counseled and supported in our lives, such as when we ask: *What do I need to heal a medical condition? Is this person a good choice as a partner for me? How can I heal a difficult relationship with a sibling? What is the next step for growth on this Path?*

- ***Ideal.*** The True Master shows what you may become at some future stage of development (much like when people say, "You can only become what you can see"). The True Master models our ultimate perfection and is to be revered, *but not worshipped.*

- ***Inductor into the Mysteries.*** We are schooled in Wisdom Teachings in our dreams, led by the Inner Master to Temples of Wisdom appropriate to our spiritual development. In addition, the true Master is able to conduct energies into our multiple bodies at certain junctures (most particularly at initiations) to quicken our spiritual unfoldment into the Mysteries. This is the Master as Initiator, a conductor of highly-spiritual vibrational frequencies that bring complete and utter change to the initiate at each stage of initiation. The True Master links us with Spirit (the Light and Sound) in ever-increasing degrees. The Master manages the flow and amplitude of these energies for the spiritual initiate.[12] This makes it possible to have direct experiences with Spirit: we *live* the Path because we *are* the Path.

## THE FIRST INITIATION: PURIFICATION

*I had always known that I would take this path,*
*but yesterday I did not know that it would be today.*
~ Narihira

## THE BIRTH

*Here we must ask: Have I any religious experience.*
*and immediate relation to God,*
*and hence that certainty which will keep me, as an individual,*
*from dissolving in the crowd?*
~ C. G. Jung

To take up the Spiritual Path, the beginner (Disciple) must be willing to walk, as the poet Robert Frost phrased it, "the road less traveled." This means that the novice must part ways with the "collective," and remain committed to becoming a truly individuated (uniquely authentic) person. This process does not require that you leave all friends and family behind; it does demand that you no longer *identify* with many of the same developmental and social patterns—and sometimes the interests of—those you know. You begin to objectively regard your life as a story, a narrative in which you are no longer entirely enmeshed. As your life circumstances and choices increasingly change, others may not always understand or support you; in fact, you are sometimes at a loss to articulate your experiences or the reasons for them—and you may sound defensive or confused when you try. You yourself may not fully understand what you are experiencing. This can bring loneliness and suffering, but this despondency is offset by the secret knowledge in your heart of hearts that, at some profound level, you have pledged yourself to God.

## THE MULADHARA CHAKRA

> *Maybe you are searching among the branches,*
> *for what only appears in the roots.*
> ~ **Rumi**

The First Initiation is focused on managing, balancing, and purifying the physical life. This Initiation could be correlated somewhat to the first chakra (*Muladhara*), located at the base of the spine. This is the chakra of physical matter. A balanced "root chakra," as it is also known, lays a foundation for all the chakras above it. It lends stability to your life, helping you to secure your basic needs (food, water, shelter) so that you feel grounded and safe. Additionally, a well-balanced root chakra helps you to worry less and to let go of fears. In addition to the root chakra, *multiple chakra centers are activated or stimulated at every initiation.* The sacral chakra and the heart chakra, for example, are identified as additional energy centers that are vivified at this initiatory stage.

## THE PHYSICAL PLANE

> *As we enter the physical plane,*
> *we are love temporarily hidden from itself.*
> *When we remember who we really are,*
> *our inner light, our love, shines forth for all to see.*
> *That, I believe, is why we are here.*
> ~ **Robert Schwartz**

The First Initiation is related to the Physical Plane of existence, which is identified by the sound of thunder and colors that range from brown to green. Before walking onto the Wisdom Path, you likely spent thousands of lifetimes fully entrenched on the physical plane and its materiality. You chased money, amassed power, pursued sex, destroyed others, and never questioned these goals and ambitions. During these past lifetimes, you may have wholly agreed with Gordon Gekko in the movie, *Wall Street* (1987), who famously declared that "Greed is good;" or you may have completely embodied the truism pronounced by the Oracle in *Matrix Reloaded* (2003), "What do all men with power want? More power!" The sorrow, regret, dissatisfaction, and disappointment that were inevitably accrued by you over such a long and wearisome time are ultimately responsible for your decision to spiritually fill the "God-shaped" hole that exists within yourself. You now know, without a doubt, that the physical world does not hold what you need.

If you are taking your first probationary steps as an aspirant or disciple on the Serpentine Path, you will need to successfully persevere to experience "The Second Birth." Your first birth was the day you were born into the world as a physical being, and the second birth is when you are born into

Spirit. You are then opened to an influx of spiritual energies and awakened to revelations, teachings, and an expanded consciousness. You learn at this stage to rely less on the physical senses and more on your *intuition*, which connects you to your higher guidance. In a spiritual sense, you are truly *born again*.

## LISTENING TO THE VOICE OF GUIDANCE

*The word, LISTEN, contains the same letters
as the word, SILENT.*
**~ Alfred Brendel**

The Religious Science of Friends (or Quakers) have their roots in Christianity, but modern Quaker meetings often include a variety of spiritual practices and beliefs that include Paganism, Buddhism, Baha'i philosophy, agnosticism, and others. In their worship Quakers practice "centering," keeping an expectant attitude while "focusing in" and waiting for the "still small voice" of God to speak to them. They believe that God is within every person, so that when a Friend quietly stands and briefly relates a message he or she received during the meeting, all worshipers present may benefit. Mostly, however, meetings are experienced in silent prayer and meditation, practices that are honed and deepened over time.

The practice of learning to mute the noisy clamor of our minds so that we can fan "the tiny ember" of our connection with Spirit—to isolate the still, small voice of our guidance—is very much part of the First Initiation. Developing the habit of "inner listening," or "cultivating the inner ear," can benefit us in our everyday lives, not only during periods of worship. One woman named DeeDee shared that to nurture a connection to inner guidance, "You have to believe in a higher power and you have to listen, feel, and believe that you are surrounded with love and a hand of protection." DeeDee shared a dramatic experience with trusting this inner voice:

*"I woke up at 3:00 am and drove from the East Bay into San Francisco to work a farmer's market. I began at 5:00 am and worked for about 3 1/2 hours straight. Once I loaded up the crates into the back end of the truck and said my good-byes, I got into my vehicle and headed back out of town and up north to Sacramento. Yes, I was tired, but also exhilarated to spend the rest of the day with a long-time friend. I was anxious to get down the road and get to my destination. I was going faster than the allotted speed limited, while remaining alert to the traffic, patrol cars, and my safety. Hurrying, but driving carefully, I was in the fast lane, doing 70+ MPH (in a 65 MPH posted speed). There was some construction on the far left side shoulder of the road. There were caution "SLOW" signs visible.*

*"I noticed another vehicle quickly coming up behind me. It was driven by a young man. I was very aware of him and wondering if I should move over and let him by. I heard a very distinctive, urgent voice in my head to "slow down." I listened to that voice and slowed way down. All of the sudden traffic came to a sudden halt. It did not slow down; it STOPPED! Because I had already slowed my speed, I was able to stop safely. My immediate attention went to my rearview mirror to see whether the young man behind me was going to be able to stop in time—or if my car was going to be rear-ended! The young man was able to miraculously veer to the next lane over. But due to his sudden maneuver, the car behind him was not prepared for an unexpected stop in the traffic. He went off on the shoulder of the road in order to avoid slamming into the back of my car. The car behind him was taking action to slow down. The car behind that vehicle was going too fast and plowed right into the car in front of it, unable to stop in time. I saw car parts flying across the freeway and smoke curling up from the scene. The traffic picked up again and we were off."*

> "I emphatically repeated to myself: Always pay attention to that "VOICE"! I call it my guardian angel(s). They have never let me down. It only works if you are aware of the message and most importantly...that you pay attention to the voice and follow your instincts. This event made a huge impression on me. I have never forgotten this experience, as the 'inner voice' saved my life on that day."

We may not actually hear a voice: We may have a strong intuition or an undeniable urge to do (or not to do!) something; we may hear a lyric on the car radio that is uncannily relevant; we may even see or read something (the voice does not have to be audible for truth to get through to you). The first thought of the day is called "the thought of truth" in the *Yoga Sutras*. Modern sleep science calls this transitional or threshold state between sleeping and waking up *hypnopompia. (Hypnogogia,* on the other hand, is the state a person enters into before falling asleep). It's helpful to have a means to write down these first thoughts, as they often contain messages that are both important and useful to us.

Learning to listen is difficult in our culture; college catalogs list courses such as speech classes, but there are no courses offered for the training of *listening* skills! If you practice listening during your quiet time, whether in prayer, contemplation, or meditation, it helps to begin with a sincere sense of gratitude, as this opens the heart to love. Ultimately, listening is an act of love. If we stop to listen, and we do it often, we will begin to hear the Divine within. As Mother Teresa reminded us, "God speaks in the silence of the heart. Listening is the beginning of prayer."

# TASKS

*There is a spiritual obligation,*
*there is a task to be done.*
*It is not, however, something as simple as*
*following a set of somebody else's rules.*
~ **Terence McKenna**

Between each of the major initiations, there are several tasks that must be successfully accomplished; they are connected to the three minor steps (some authors posit more) or achievements required between each major initiation. The tasks that are listed for each of the first five initiation stages are not necessarily in order nor are they always correctly matched or limited to the specific stage to which they are designated. A few tasks can continue throughout several stages of initiation, depending on the needs, proficiencies, and experiences of the individual initiate. At these first two stages of initiatory preparedness, the spiritual student may not even be consciously aware of undergoing a spiritual test related to a specific task. Such tasks, especially in the beginning, usually have to do with outer life experiences. The tasks set out for each of the first five stages of initiation in *Dancing the Labyrinth* are not all inclusive, but they are included as significant spiritual lessons on the Great Way of Initiation.

## IDENTIFYING YOUR HIDDEN SELVES

*People fear their inner selves, afraid they will break out.*
~ **Gregory Benford**

We learned to create secret selves when we were children so that we could cope with situations: the divorce of our parents, a death in the immediate family, moving away from school friends and familiar streets, or the loss of a first love. These selves are cobbled together and often they are not well made; however, they are "the forces that awaken us to the need to create ourselves out of the materials of life."[13] At some point, these personas, or fabricated selves, no longer work in our favor. Who are we, then, under the masks?

Our secret selves help us to cope until they become liabilities to what is most authentic in ourselves. We must search for these hidden selves, and after we identify them, transform them into a cooperative team within ourselves. One self, for example can be the belligerent and argumentative Renegade Rebel; another can be the compliant and servile People Pleaser with low self-esteem; yet another can be a Detached Dreamer, a self who is disconnected from everyday life. We start out on the Path by identifying these disparate parts of ourselves. (More on these hidden selves later in this chapter).

This process of getting to know the splintered, hidden parts of ourselves sometimes shows up in dreams of houses with many rooms, some of which are completely unknown to us. We may find that there is an unexpected attic to our house or a long and winding stairway to a dirt-floored basement. C. G. Jung wrote about a profound dream of this type:

> "I was in a house I did not know, which had two stories. It was 'my house.' I found myself in the upper story, where there was a kind of salon furnished with fine old pieces in Rococo style. On the walls hung a number of precious, old paintings...Descending the stairs, I reached the ground floor. There everything was much older, and I realized that this part of the house must date from about the fifteenth or sixteenth century. The furnishings were medieval, the floors were of red brick. Everywhere it was rather dark...I came upon a heavy door and opened it. Beyond it, I discovered a stone stairway that led down into a cellar. Descending again, I found myself in a beautifully vaulted room which looked exceedingly ancient. Examining the walls, I discovered layers of

> brick among the ordinary stone blocks, and chips of brick in the mortar. As soon as I saw this, I knew that the walls dated from Roman times...I looked more closely at the floor. It was of stone slabs and in one of these I discovered a ring. When I pulled it, the stone slab lifted and again I saw a stairway of narrow stone steps leading down to the depths. These, too, I descended and entered a low cave cut into rock. Thick dust lay on the floor and in the dust were scattered bones and broken pottery, like remains of a primitive culture. I discovered two human skulls, obviously very old, and half disintegrated. Then I awoke."[14]

Jung concluded that the house was a symbol of his psyche or personality. In the dream, he begins to explore his personal living space, and as he descends the various layers of his "house," he is descending the levels of his own consciousness. What he discovered was that each successive layer connects him with an earlier time in human history as well as his own earlier existences. Jung began the dream in his personal living space on the upper floor and ended it in a cave, where he uncovered his prehistoric origins, the roots shared with all humankind. (Jung leaned toward the idea of reincarnation in later life.)

If you are interested in exploring your own "inner house," or personality, you can do so by imagining that the *top floor* is your own personal narrative, the story that governs your everyday life (your autobiography). You can also decorate this floor in a manner that suits you, no matter how outlandish. The *ground floor* represents your family of birth and your immediate lineage, both on the spear (male) and distaff (female) sides (e.g., mother and father, grandparents, siblings, aunts and uncles, cousins). Think on and then write about how they have influenced your looks, character, and tendencies. How would you decorate this room? Would you use traditional furnishings, a nautical theme, or would you line the walls with shelves full of books or old music albums (LPs)? The *cellar*, or *bottom floor*, symbolizes the culture in which you grew up, taking into account any ethnic or racial groups that you belong to, as well as community influences such as school, church, athletics, etc. that have influenced your story. The *cave* under the house represents the raw materials, the deepest roots, of your ancestral line. Reflect on the archetype of the people from which you are descended (*Ancestry.com* and *23andMe* are useful sites for this type of work). Think about what implements, household items, or wall drawings might be in this cave.[15]

You are a complex being with many selves. Becoming conscious of these parts of yourselves and the influences that have shaped you is a first step on the Path of Initiation. You must sort yourself out. In the myth of *Cupid and Psyche* by Apuleius, Psyche is given four huge tasks by Aphrodite (Psyche's jealous mother-in-law) in order to win back her husband whom she has disobeyed. Psyche's first task was to sort the seeds—a jumble of corn, poppy seeds, and barley—into separate piles before the following morning. It was an impossible task until an army of ants came to her aid. Your own assistance is the help of Spirit; for once we are on the Road to Freedom, many unexpected factors show up to support us. This is because *you are now doing precisely the human work that you were sent into this life to do!* This work is your *true mission!* Rumi imagines this undertaking this way: "It would be as if a king sent you to a village on a specific mission. If you went and performed a hundred other tasks, but neglected to accomplish the task for which you were sent, it would be as though you had done nothing." Rather than becoming lost in the trivial "10,000 things" of our modern lives, we must remember that our purpose is to complete our task for the King.

## ENCOUNTERING THE SHADOW

> *Even on the spiritual path,*
> *we'll have things we tend to cover up*
> *or be in denial about.*
> ~ **Sharon Salzberg**

For both the First and the Second Initiations, the novice must be willing to look squarely at the little self, or ego. For example, in a dream, it might be pointed out that the spiritual student is vain or proud. Perhaps a confrontation in the workplace reveals a hidden reservoir of rage. In addition, the beginning initiate may discover a fondness for gossip or for clever or hurtful sarcasm or may recognize a judgmental attitude that is disparaging of others. Or sometimes a friend or family member will let us know that we are a poor listener, or that we are selfish or self-absorbed. These events and reminders can be seen as "uncovering the Shadow." The Shadow encompasses qualities people display in everyday life but seldom see in themselves (only in others).

Shadow work is painful, and sometimes even humiliating, but it is of incalculable importance. Facing the Shadow includes confronting negative traits that separate us from others, which are always fear driven: racism, intolerance, self-righteousness, bigotry, hatred, and greed to name a few. These are the destructive qualities that lead us to bully, oppress, judge, persecute, and terrorize others, and ultimately, they steer countries into war. These traits need to be cleansed in a significant number of humans before mass initiation can occur on a societal level. Hopefully, many of these divisionary attitudes and behaviors have surfaced over the last few years so that their poisonous effects can be acknowledged and then largely purged.

Doing shadow work could be called *sin-eating*. In medieval times an individual who was willing to take on the bleak role of sin-eater would be paid to consume food—an apple or piece of bread—that was believed to carry the sins of a recently-deceased person. This ritual absolved the dead and made the sin-eater forever damned and a social outcast. Today's meaning of sin-eating sometimes extends to those journalists who are witness, for example, to wartime atrocities as well as to psychotherapists who bear witness to the "confessions" of those they report on or see in treatment. For our purposes, "sin-eating" refers to the objective observance of our *own* negative thoughts and behaviors or shadow qualities as they occur. We can no longer pay someone else to take on our sins (although this is similar to what we are doing when we project our own shortcomings onto others), but must "eat" them ourselves. Think of the idioms "I'll have to swallow this" or "I'll eat my hat." A part of our consciousness (variously called the *witness* or *watcher*) remains detached and impartial, observing our own undesirable acts and words without intervention or judgment. Somehow, this act of attentive self-awareness in and of itself serves to bring about positive transformation. The first thing we need to do, then, is to become *conscious* of those parts of ourselves that have been repressed, suppressed, ignored, discounted, and worst of all, projected onto others.

On the Labyrinthine Path, the Shadow, or what is esoterically called the *Dweller on the Threshold,* is not just the representation of this life's misdeeds, but is the accumulation of our darkness over many millennia. During her process of initiation onto the Andean Path, the spiritual teachings and practices of the ancient Inca, Elizabeth Jenkins found herself face to face with the Shadow:

> "...during one of my morning meditations, my skin began to crawl and the hair on my arms stood straight up as an image appeared in my mind's eye. I found myself staring into the face of the most horrific creature I had ever seen. On sight the creature produced an abysmal feeling of dread. Its facial features were large and thick. The creature had charcoal-gray skin that covered its hairless poll. Its eyes were glaring yellow. A putrid ocher light bathed its head and shoulders, and its torso was covered in a thick gray leather armor. Around its neck was a collar of huge iron spikes. A sadistic expression moved across the twisted features of the creature's face as it spoke to me in a tone that broadcast imminent danger."

The monster announced itself as "intelligent, organized evil." Elizabeth knew that, "This was a creature that consciously and intentionally perpetrated acts of cruelty and violence and gained energy by harming others."

> "I tried to protect myself. I imagined pushing the creature away or putting a barrier between me and it. Nothing worked. Then all at once, I realized that I wouldn't be able to see it at all unless there was some part of me that corresponded to it. Suddenly memories came flooding through me of times when I had intentionally done things to hurt others, from small, silly things to larger, more important events in my life, which now made me blush in embarrassment."[16]

Elizabeth realized that if this creature had shown that it was some aspect of herself, she could surrender to this fact, and instead of feeling afraid, she could embrace the creature, taking into herself that part of her own darkness, completely and tenderly. With this realization, the shadow creature, as an energetic structure, began to break apart and dissolve.

On her particular initiatory Path, she had been instructed by her Master to "eat" heavy energy; for our purposes, this refers to facing and then taking into ourselves our negative energies for transmutation. These energies are not destroyed, but the energy is used for further development of the individual (this is what we do when we take our projections onto others back into ourselves). In this way, a new center—the Self—is eventually established, an altogether different level of consciousness than ego-consciousness.

Beginning at the First Initiation, our job is to take responsibility for ourselves, as only we can transmute our own negative qualities into tolerance, acceptance, unity, harmony, and love. The more we allow ourselves to see our "backsides" (or shadow selves), so to speak, the more we can take accountability for our attitudes and behaviors. We can then modify and transmute our own negativity so that we bring more harmony into a chaotic and contentious world. Then we are ready to advance on the Path.

## CONFRONTING YOUR FEARS

> *I have accepted fear as part of life*
> *—specifically, the fear of change—*
> *I have gone ahead, despite the pounding in the heart*
> *that says, "Turn back…"*
>
> ~ **Erica Jong**

Another task of the First Initiation is to face one's fears. One of the greatest fears that people have (besides public speaking!) is the dread of approaching the unconscious. In fact, most people go out of their way to avoid confronting the truths that the unconscious brings to their attention. This is the cause of neuroticism. Contents long hidden from conscious awareness surface through dreams, reveries, visualizations, sudden insights, or psychotherapeutic work. It is by plumbing unconscious depths that repressed and suppressed memories and experiences come into view. (*Repression* is an automatic, unconscious mechanism that serves to protect the ego structure from a shocking blow; *suppression* is a conscious decision to forget something). Childhood wounds rise to the surface for processing and healing. Relationships with one's parents are explored, including early parental attitudes that were unconsciously adopted by the novice and no longer "fit" or serve the best interests of the spiritual student. To do this psychological excavation work, the Disciple must have courage. Before the ghosts of the past can be healed, they must be fully admitted into consciousness, processed, accepted (loved), and then released. There are no shortcuts.

Similarly, the fear of death must be confronted. In fact, as a person interacts with the tasks of initiation, they may have many dreams of death. These dreams usually symbolize the "death" or dissolution of old ego-personality aspects rather than actual physical death. These dreams are often followed by pregnancy dreams, which herald parts of the person's psyche that are ready to be "birthed" into conscious awareness. The new initiate begins to understand that physical death, just as death in a dream, is only the threshold to more life, but lived differently and more fully.

## MODERATION AND DISCRIMINATION

> *Anyone can get angry—that is easy—or give or spend money;*
> *but to do this to the right person, to the right extent, at the right time,*
> *with the right motive, and in the right way,*
> *that is not for everyone, nor is it easy.*
>
> ~ **Aristotle**

When confronted with such words as "moderation" and "discrimination," it may be easy for some of you to understand why St. Augustine, a fourth-century theologian, philosopher, and Catholic bishop, once famously prayed to God, "Grant me chastity—but not yet."[17] But at the level of the First Initiation, mastery of the physical life is paramount. Overindulgence in food, drink, drugs or sex is scrutinized for its use as a substitution, usually for love, or for its application as an anesthetic to numb emotional pain. To regulate physical appetites of all kinds is to become a clearer vessel for spiritual energies. The first or physical world initiation includes improving the ability to appropriately *discriminate,* exemplified in the following ways:

- *What activities in my current life are good for me and which are not?*

- *Which of my old friends should I continue to see—and who no longer resonates with me?*

- *In making a decision, am I following the highest calling of Soul (going a direction that will help me grow spiritually) or is this a decision made to benefit my ego (adding to my own self-importance)?*

- *Which of my thoughts and beliefs support me and which do I actively need to reject and deny? (Many thoughts influence us from outside sources such as media, advertising, and other types of negative programming.)*

- *Do I recognize when I am reacting to situations rather than responding to them (which requires discernment)?*

- *Is what I am about to say true, kind, or necessary?*

At the First Initiation, we are required to make *conscious* decisions about how we lead our lives; no longer can we continue to live life unconsciously with a lack of awareness and self-control. Gary Zukav addresses making "responsible choices" when we consider the consequences of our actions when making decisions:

> "Only through responsible choice can you choose consciously to cultivate and nourish the needs of your soul, and to challenge and release the wants of your personality…It is the choice to follow the voice of your higher self {and a} decision to open yourself to the guidance and assistance of your guides and Teachers."[18]

When you have made a decision to heal an addiction, to release anger, or to relinquish the hold of power or greed in your life, everything comes to assist: your dreams, your relationships, the situations you meet in everyday life. But be aware that there may also be an eleventh-hour flare up of the very behaviors you are attempting to change; some old patterns mightily resist change! In this way things may become worse before becoming better. Fortunately, when you want to grow and are determined to do so, the Self (Soul) wants to support that resolution; auspicious energies flow in to help you to ultimately succeed in your decision.

## SUMMARY: CLEANING UP

> *I think a spiritual journey is not so much a journey of discovery.*
> *It's a journey of recovery.*
> *It's a journey of uncovering your own inner nature.*
> *It's already there.*
>
> ~ **Billy Corgan**

To summarize, the great undertakings of the First Initiation are to purify our physical lives, to begin shadow work, and to start the healing process of the wounds of the past. These labors may be understood as a "cleaning up" enterprise, which can be depicted in dreams as the scrubbing down of a house, building, or other structure, such as one individual dreamed:

> "I am cleaning up a house with many rooms. I am painting the walls white and washing down the floors. There is a lot of piled-up trash to throw out. The toilet and tub are especially nasty and take a lot of time to scour clean. I am exhausted by this work but also elated by it. I want the house to be sparkling."

The purification of the physical world extends to our daily routines. To this end, one person dreamed of an unkempt zoo, with listless and passive animals languishing in cages. He interpreted this to mean that he had to tidy up his instinctual or animal (physical) life. He surveyed his poor nutritional and sleep habits and his tendency toward lethargy and procrastination. He also looked at the hours he spent on the computer as a gamer—far too many, he surmised, to lead a balanced existence. He concluded that to function more competently in his daily life, he needed to make efforts to become better disciplined to achieve his goals.

People who are making efforts to clean up their lives often incorporate their occupations into their dreams. For example, a client who taught school dreamed that she had a classroom full of children, which represented her "inner throng" or crowd (all the separate little selves that are mentioned earlier in this chapter). In her dream, one child was a holy terror; another was a priggish know-it-all; one student showed himself as exceptionally helpful; and another routinely thumped students on the head with a textbook. At the beginning of the client's work on herself, her "dream classroom" of children presented themselves as a chaotic and unruly bunch. With hard work and effort over time, the classroom began to operate in harmony as she integrated parts of herself into a smoothly working whole.[19]

Another client, who counseled at-risk youths, dreamt that he was in Juvenile Hall, visiting young people who were variously angry, rebellious, distrustful, dominating, and slyly mischievous. Their strengths were also apparent, as many youths in his dream were resilient, tough, and had leadership potential. Once these dream-selves were addressed and worked with, he found that he had less inner conflict and anxiety, while experiencing better focus and increased energy for daily activities. He could more easily access the strengths of his "inner crowd" and apply these qualities to his physical life.

The First Initiation is a stage where persons learn to identify less with physical and sensual pleasures. This does not mean that an aspirant on the Path needs to become an ascetic or to engage in extreme self-denial. The novice must find a happy balance, something that in life, the man in the following parable had failed to do:

> A man died and woke to find himself in a place of incredible beauty; he was surrounded with luxurious comfort. A neatly uniformed attendant walked over to him and announced that he could have any food, pleasure or entertainment that he desired.

*Naturally, the man was delighted! He sampled everything—all the delicacies and delights of the flesh that he had only previously dreamed of while alive on earth. But one day, he grew bored with the routine; the very things he had once hungered for were now tedious and dull. He asked for the attendant, declaring, "I am really weary of all this! What work do you have for me? I need to do something!"*

*The attendant looked at him and sadly shook his head. "Sir, we can only provide what you have before you. There are no jobs here; I cannot give you work." The horrified man heatedly replied, "Well, I might as well be in hell!" The attendant, arching one eyebrow, quietly responded, "Sir, where do you think you are?"*

So it is with all of us: After hundreds of lifetimes seeking to sate ourselves with all the pleasures provided by the physical world, we find that we want something more, a purpose that will give us a sense of meaning. We begin our long, winding search for the true significance of life. We seek a sense of transcendence, a state of being that has overcome the limitations of our worldly existence.

# CHAPTER THREE EXERCISES

## Who or What Runs Your Life?

To help us to learn how *discrimination* (what does and does not promote our well-being?) and *moderation* (how much is enough?) operate in our lives, it is useful to ask the following questions of ourselves: (Use a journal to discuss each of these items).

What part of your physical self is out of control: gambling, eating, drinking, substance abuse, sex, pornography, shopping, or social media use?

- How much of your day does this part of yourself take up?

- How does this out-of-control part of yourself make you feel?

- Does this part of your physical self help you express your emotions or serve to avoid them?

- What is the reason that you tell yourself to excuse this behavior (e.g., childhood abuse, parental alcoholism, etc.)?

- Has this part of your ego-self ever satisfied you for long, even when you've given it in to its demands?

- Relax, close your eyes, and imagine that you are talking to something, perhaps a symbol, that represents this part of yourself (for example, too much drinking symbolized by a bottle/can of alcohol). Ask this symbol what need it substitutes for? Make sure that the symbol responds to you using the personal pronoun "I." The response might be, "I shop too much because I am unhappy in my marriage." This is the *true* demand that is hiding behind the out-of-control part of yourself. The next step is for you to determine how you can resolve your situation in a way that is beneficial to you instead of self-damaging.

- Use "The Figure Eight" technique in Phyllis Krystal's *Cutting the Ties that Bind*, to separate from and release this behavior.[20]

# CHAPTER THREE ENDNOTES

1. The descriptions of the first five initiations in this book are partially derived from the personal initiatory experiences of the author who is currently a sixth initiate of many years. The author relied on her interpretations and studies related to those experiences over 40 years of being on an initiatory path. In addition, extensive research was utilized, including various books in theosophy, anthroposophy, modern psychology (C. G. Jung), parallel paths of initiation in other systems and cultures, interview material, and spiritual autobiographies.

2. This dream was recounted in *Drinking the Dragon: Stories of the Dark Night of the Soul.* Sothis Press: Encinitas, CA: 2021: p.40.

3. "Jonah and the Whale" is a story in the Old Testament that relates how Jonah (or Jonas) was called by God to be a prophet. When Jonah refused and left on a sea voyage instead, God raised a great storm. The beleaguered sailors drew lots to see who would be thrown into the sea to prevent the ship from capsizing. Jonah lost. While in the sea, he was swallowed by a whale and stayed "in the belly of the beast" for three days. Finally, he was washed up onto a far-away shore.

4. Paul Twitchell is the modern-day founder of ECKANKAR, The Path of Spiritual Freedom (ECKANKAR translates to "Co-Worker with God"). Twitchell brought out the ancient teachings of ECK ("Spirit") to the public in 1965.

5. Harry Moody. *The Five Stages of the Soul.* New York: Anchor Books, 1997: 168.

6. Coleman Barks. *Rumi: The Book of Love: Poems of Ecstasy and Longing.* New York: HarperCollins Publishers, Inc., 2003: p.140.

7. The Sufi master Radha Mohan Lal Adhauliya, a Kayasth Hindu, was of the Naqshbandiyya-Mujadiddiya Sufi Order (currently working through the Golden Sufis) lived in the city of Kanpur, India.

8. Irina Tweedie. *Daughter of Fire: A Diary of a Spiritual Training* with a Sufi Master. Nevada City, CA: Blue Dolphin Publishing, Inc., 1989.

9. Roshi Joan Halifax, Ph.D., is a Buddhist teacher, Zen priest, anthropologist (cultural ecologist), pioneer in end-of-life care, and the founder of Upaya Institute and Zen Center in Santa Fe, New Mexico. She is the author of several books, among them, *The Human Encounter with Death* (with Stanislav Grof); *The Fruitful Darkness; Simplicity in the Complex: A Buddhist Life in America; Being with Dying: Cultivating Compassion and Wisdom in the Presence of Death; and Standing at the Edge: Finding Freedom Where Fear and Courage Meet.*

10. Joan Halifax. *The Fruitful Darkness.* New York: HarperCollins Publishers, 1994: p. 137.

11. For over 40 years, the author has been a member (and clergy since 2004) of ECKANKAR, *The Path of Spiritual Freedom*. The word ECKANKAR means "Co-Worker with God." The current spiritual leader of ECKANKAR is Sri Harold Klemp. The unbroken lineage of spiritual masters in ECKANKAR is the *Order of Vairagi Adepts*, a line that stretches back into the far reaches of time. See https://www.eckankar.org

12. On the inner planes, the Master will sometimes use a Staff of Power as an electrical conductor to galvanize certain chakras and calibrate certain spiritual energies within the Initiate. From this fact there arose the belief of Osiris as the life force of creation, with his backbone the *Djed*, or the sleeping, dormant potential of consciousness (or kundalini) in humans. The Djed was both the means of ascension and the symbol (Rod of Power) that activated this process. (Think of the *Jedi* Knights of *Star Wars* (1977), advanced defenders of the universe, who wield light sabers). Later, wizards were shown to use staffs of power (as in the *Middle Earth Trilogy*, 2001). Today, the idea has degenerated to the notion of magicians employing a wand to perform tricks on stage.

13. Don Webb. *Overthrowing the Old God*. Rochester: Vermont: Inner Traditions, 2013.

14. C. G. Jung. *Memories, Dreams, Reflections*. New York: Vintage Books, 1989, pp.158-159.

15. Credit goes to Stephen Farah for the basis of this adapted exercise. See *Applied Centre of Jungian Studies*, "Jung's dream house and discovering your own archetypal home." June, 2014. https://appliedjung.com

16. Elizabeth B. Jenkins. *Initiation: A Woman's Spiritual Adventure in the Heart of the Andes*. New York, New York: G.P. Putnam's Sons, 1997, pp.122-23.

17. The actual words of this prayer are said to be: "Grant me chastity and continence, but not yet. "

18. Gary Zukav. *The Seat of the Soul*. New York, NY, Simon and Schuster, 1989, p. 131.

19. Author, marketing expert, and expressive arts facilitator, Judith Balian conducts interactive classes/workshops on Secret Selves® which she describes as "those voices in your head which pull you one way when you know it's in your best interests to follow a different path." Secret Selves also represent the "positive sides of you that would, if unleashed, take you forward to fulfill your highest dreams." Find out more about Judith's work at excoveries.com.

20. Phyllis Krystal. *Cutting the Ties That Bind*. Boston, MA: Weiser Books, 1986., pp.14-16.

# CHAPTER FOUR

# Mapping the Spiral Way: Five Stages of Initiation Stages 2 and 3

*Spiritual life is like living water*
*that springs up from the very depths of our own spiritual experience.*
*In spiritual life everyone has to drink from his or her own well.*
*~ Bernard of Clairvaux*

## THE SECOND INITIATION: COMMITMENT

*Incredible things can be done simply*
*if we are committed to making them happen.*
*~ Sadhguru*

*The spiritual path is not always going to be smooth and easy,*
*There are going to be difficult situations, hardships, losses, and lessons.*
*Don't lose faith along the way.*
*You are exactly where you need to be.*
*~ Jennifer Young*

The Second Initiation will challenge you until your teeth rattle. Are you truly dedicated? This stage will test that! Faced with the tests of the Second Initiation (the Initiation of Commitment), you may decide to "roll up your mat and go home." (Dilettantes need not apply!) At this point, you can commit to continuing on the Spiritual Path or decide to turn back. During this Initiation, a person is linked to the Light and Sound, or Spirit. The influx of Spirit into a person's psyche, with its refinement and purity, brings tremendous changes in its wake. It may have been with the Second Initiation in mind that the Tibetan Buddhist teacher Chogyam Trungpa flatly warned those who were not absolutely dedicated "not to undertake the spiritual path." He cautioned that the Spiritual Path was "too difficult, too long, and…too demanding" and would "ask everything of you." Trungpa insisted that "it is best not to begin" the Path at all unless once begun, the spiritual student was willing to take it to the *finish line*.[1]

You may be wondering at this point why anyone would choose to undergo such rigorous tests and trials—why continue the Initiatory Path at all? By the time you reach the Second Initiation, you have gained in spiritual strength and resolve. You are set on discovering your purpose in life and of being of greater service to humanity. Finding God is everything. In addition, initiates at this stage have not only been challenged by difficulties; along the way, they have been encouraged by dreams and visions of beauty and promise, illuminating insights and realizations, and experiences of an all-encompassing love. Fundamentally, many follow the Path because, as the psychiatrist Carl Jung stated, it is imperative to the seeker of authenticity to express "loyalty to the law of one's own being."

## THE SVADHISTHANA CHAKRA

> *Let's not forget that the little emotions*
> *are the great captains of our lives, and*
> *we obey them without realizing it.*
> ~ **Vincent Van Gogh**

Many humans today are taking the First and Second Initiations. Sometimes called "The Baptism" initiation, the Second Initiation centers on the initiate's emotional life (remember that our emotions are symbolically represented in dreams as bodies of water). In some ways, this Initiation is equivalent to cleansing and balancing the sacral (*Svadhisthana*) chakra, located just below your belly button. The Svadhisthana Chakra, which relates to the water element, controls versatility, freedom, and flexibility, especially in regard to the sexual, emotional, or creative areas of your life. This chakra is connected to how well you are able to relate to your emotions as well as to the emotions of others. In some esoteric traditions, the initiate who learns to control the emotions is characterized as a *Walker of the Seas* or as someone able to "walk on the surface of the seas."[2] This is a metaphorical way of saying that a person is no longer drowning (overwhelmed) by the volatile and stormy emotions that still characterize a large percentage of humans. Pleasure and creativity are hallmarks of a balanced sacral chakra; emotional instability, sexual dysfunction, and creative blocks are typical of a sacral chakra that is unbalanced. Other chakras are stimulated at this initiation as well, particularly the solar plexus and throat energy centers.

## THE ASTRAL PLANE

> *The astral world is not the ultimate liberating experience...*
> *nevertheless, soul progress begins with the effort to disengage*
> *from the delusion of material bondage*
> *into the higher awareness of one's finer astral existence.*
> ~ Paramahansa Yogananda

> **Fascination with the psychic**
> **can be a dangerous sidetrack on any spiritual path.**
> ~ Starhawk

The Second Initiation relates to the Astral Plane, the plane of existence that is "above" the physical (if, for the sake of understanding, we imagine planes, or realms of being, vertically stacked one on top of another; they actually enfold or interpenetrate one another). The identifying sound of the

Astral plane is the roar of the ocean; its colors span from red to pink. As an artifact of general human evolution, the physical and astral planes are intersecting or blending into one another more and more: This is why we are so fascinated, especially in our books and movies, with ghosts, vampires, witchcraft, demons, telepathy, comic book superheroes, young people with enhanced abilities, clowns and carnivals, extrasensory perception, some alien phenomena, and more. These topics are largely related to the lower regions of the Astral Plane.

Las Vegas is an astral-type locale on the physical realm, a city characterized by glamour, fantasy, exaggeration, and illusion. The movies, *What Dreams May Come* (1998) and *Astral City: A Spiritual Journey* (2010) depict the astral plane, which for the most part, is made up of much finer energies than the physical level. The upper regions of the Astral Plane, which are colorful and pleasant, are where many humans transition to after their physical deaths on Earth. The lower levels can be grayer, drearier, and less pleasant, a more or less "hellish" region created over time by human thought forms—and *not* by a punishing God. We are attracted to those regions that we most resonate with; our own vibrational levels compel us to seek that level of consciousness which agrees with our own.

Most dreams are astral level in origin as human dreams deal primarily with the processing of emotional material. Currently, many persons are waylaid or distracted by lower-astral psychic phenomena, which do not necessarily equate to spiritual advancement. Spiritual progress involves applied effort and profound transformative processes, though many psychic experiences—while initially entertaining—are unreliable, illusory, and deceptive.[3] To this point, television personality and author Iyanla Vanzant humorously quips, "I think most people think that a spiritual path or growing spiritually means that all of a sudden you'll be able to forecast the six lotto numbers, and all your bills will be paid." The Path of Initiation, for those who remain committed to it, is all encompassing and never ending, and indeed, "asks everything of you." There is always one more step to spiritual perfection, even for the Great Masters and Guides.

## INTO THE ABYSS

*There can be no rebirth without a dark night of the soul,
a total annihilation of all that you believed in
and thought that you were.*
~ **Vilayat Inayat Khan**

*If a person wishes to be sure of the road they tread upon,
they must close their eyes and walk in the dark.*
~ **St. John of the Cross**

Within an 18-month period in my early thirties, I divorced, moved, completed my graduate work, joined a spiritual path, and was bitterly disappointed in a romantic relationship. A hoped-for job unexpectedly came to nothing, and I was close to running out of money. In the midst of these complications, I had the following dream:

> "I was nervous and jumpy. Unseen forces were shaking my bed from one end to the other. My bed covers were ripped off of me, and I shouted, 'Give them back!' while trying to grab the corner of one of the blankets to retrieve it. Outside, the weather was raging; the wind was howling and bold lightning flashes lit up the night sky. I was leaning partially out of my bedroom's window, high up from the ground, and I had the feeling that I might be pushed out. I yelled, 'I suppose this is going to burn me!' thinking of the lightning strikes all around. I had so much anxiety and fear in this dream that I woke up as I was calling out. Instantly, I thought of the Tarot Tower Card."[4]

I immediately set an appointment with a psychotherapist. The Tower Tarot Card represents chaos, sudden upheaval, change, and destruction. It foretells a change that is unavoidable and life altering. Often such a sweeping and transformative change brings with it serious issues of survival, as the foundations of one's life (if built on unrealistic goals or false beliefs) are dramatically swept away. I knew I was in for it!

I sold my furniture, boxed up my remaining belongings, and moved into the back room of a friend's condominium. Here, I began a two-year "underground" ordeal during which I was changed in every atom and cell. And though I was reassured in occasional dreams that I was in a "hospital" for renovation and healing, I was often scared, despondent, and disoriented. In addition, I was coping with intermittent bouts of anxiety, depression, and physical exhaustion. I was not able to explain what had happened to me to others, and when I tried, I sounded defensive and cryptic. I was able to find only sporadic work, so I spent much of my time researching books to better understand what I was experiencing. I was simultaneously fascinated and fearful of my experiences. I had no idea that I was entering into a long and dismal Dark Night of the Soul, a life-altering ordeal that would forever influence every single thing in my life.[5]

I was having vivid, tumultuous dreams, many displaying the four basic elements in momentous upheaval: *water (the emotions), earth (instincts), fire (intuition)* and *air (intellect)*. In dreams, the four elements of nature make up the outer world as well as the constitution of the personality. When there is a renovation of the psyche on a fundamental level, these dream themes act as replications of the creation myths. Disruptive elements in my dreams included massive earthquakes, volcanic eruptions, tidal waves, toxic air, raging fires, ferocious storms, wild whirlpools, vast floods, and turbulent tornadoes. This disordered activity usually indicates purification, modification, and reorganization of the personality. For example, over-dominant, negative fire traits—such as arrogance, obsession, jealousy, irritability, and egocentrism—are cleansed, refined, and balanced. On the flip side, traits that are weak are intensified and strengthened. The result of this process is that, when the individual's fire element is well balanced, the individual is better able to express the characteristics of passion, creativity, determination, and leadership.[6]

The chaos of my dreams was not only an indication of inner conflict and devastation; it reflected my ongoing shadow[7] work and the withdrawing of my projections onto others. Shadow work, which I mentioned earlier in this book, is an irrevocable step when individuals want to grow spiritually. When I tried to resist laying claim to the darkness within myself, I would have dreams, for example, of a cold, angry, witch-like woman trying to fight her way through my screen door. The more I ignored or turned away from her, the more incensed she became. She was trying to break into my conscious awareness for acknowledgement and acceptance. To be clear, shadow work is not undertaken for the purpose of making us feel disproportionately worse about ourselves; recognizing and integrating our own negativity over time makes us steadier and more centered. We become persons "to be reckoned with" (persons of substance) who will not be easily taken advantage of because we know what we ourselves are capable of—even if we choose not to do it. We more readily see the manipulations of others. I heard once that "naivety invites the wolves," which translates to: Anchor yourself in reality and claim your inner power. Shadow work accomplishes this so that, when you need to, you can stand your ground and hold your own.

Part of shadow work includes reclaiming the projections made onto others. In this regard, Jung stated, "Projections change the world into the replica of one's unknown face." This exercise is painstaking and painful; it involves looking at the very people we are most irked by and examining ourselves for the same faults. The reason this process is important is we are reclaiming parts of ourselves to make ourselves whole. These parts are collected, "washed," and reintegrated. When we become conscious of our negative qualities, we can transmute them and, at the very least, keep them reined in. This process is our necessary contribution to establishing a less destructive and violent world.

The first year of my underground cycle was full of inner conflict and turmoil. In some ways, the second year was even harder because it seemed that I was wandering in a desert without sign posts or markers. Only my dreams and the few books I could find that addressed my inner process, were oases in a barren landscape. My inner turmoil was calming down, so that the upheavals in the first year could be carefully integrated and reconstructed into a more authentic and harmonious personality. But I was incredibly frustrated because I wanted to be in the world again, making a living, and demonstrating to others that I was making my way into "the land of the living" once more. I felt deserted and lonely. I sold my car because I needed the money and walked to out-of-the-way cafes, sitting at outdoor tables to pour over books, make notes, work with my dreams, and fervently hoped not to be recognized. This "wandering in the wilderness" abruptly ended when I was finally offered a job and moved out of my hideaway, but not one day before I was ready—the timing was always in the hands of God.

An acquaintance named Kelsey described her Dark Night of the Soul as the culmination of a lifetime of events beginning with her adoption into a dysfunctional family:

> *"I always knew that my beginning in this world was different. I spent my early formative years in foster care until at about age five, I was adopted into a family with mental illness. I found myself in the middle of a chaotic existence in which I felt out of place, sometimes fighting for survival in a world that made no sense. My daily life was turbulent and unpredictable. As a teen, I became distant and rebellious to protect myself from the manipulative and sometimes violent interactions of this family.*

> "Both adopted parents were drug addicts, which added an additional spin on trying to deal with the mental illness in the family. They leaned on me to provide a sense of normalcy, and their neediness exhausted me. When I was 16, my adoptive mother confided in her doctor that she wanted to kill me. This doctor immediately called my father and told him to get me out of the house ASAP. I came home from school to find a suitcase along with a wad of cash waiting for me. My adoptive father told me to stay away for my own safety as I was escorted out the door. I walked the dark, cold streets all night because I was too afraid to lie under a tree and sleep. After a few days I found an all-night gas station with a heater! There were other teens there in similar situations, so we developed a kind of camaraderie.
>
> "Through the years, life has had its challenges and sometimes I found myself fragile and unable to deal with life's blows. As an adult, I was ill prepared for some situations, becoming easily depressed, drinking way too much, and sleeping the day away. After a boyfriend jilted me and I lost my dog of 16 years, I fell into a dark place. I cried endlessly, unable to recover from my losses. I cried for a whole winter, even missing work while lying on the couch with a bottle of vodka! I felt a hopelessness that I couldn't shake."

Kelsey related that the only thing that kept her from total desolation was her exceptional connection to nature and to animals. A backpacker, she often hiked the Tahoe wilderness trails where she lived and found periods of grace and peace. Then on a trip to Hawaii, she turned a corner:

> "I was attending a formal work event where the grand raffle prize was a trip to Hawaii. I bought several tickets but I didn't win. Those days It didn't take much to send me into a spiral of despair since I had been counting on that trip to heal my broken spirit.

*Luckily, I was able to go with another person. It was a great trip, but I still felt that pang of hopelessness that I couldn't shake.*

*"On our last day, we signed up for a whale-watching trip on a 50-foot schooner. Upon boarding, the captain announced that we would not be seeing any whales since it was May, and whale watching season had concluded at the end of February. After a few hours most of the other passengers were hanging over the bow with seasickness. Unaffected, I enjoyed feeling the trade winds blowing through my hair as I secretly scanned the waters in search of a whale.*

*"Suddenly the captain announced, 'Whale starboard!' And there she was, a lovely, graceful humpback who had calved late and had stayed in local waters, wanting her baby to gain strength before migrating to Alaska. This incredibly intelligent whale swam right up to me, lifted herself out of the water and made direct eye contact, looking right through me and seemingly into my soul. She knew I needed healing from a variety of events from which I couldn't seem to bounce back. She chose me out there in the vast Pacific Ocean, and through her eyes, she let me know everything was going to work out. We stared at each other for a long while, as though we had a million things to say to each other. Then she gracefully swam away to tend to her calf. This was a life changing moment. And I knew I was going to be OK."*

A Dark Night of the Soul experience occurs most commonly to those who are between the First and the end of the Second Initiations; but it is an experience, sooner or later, that most initiates will face again, in varying degrees of length and severity, along the Labyrinthine Road. Such work requires a very large heart and a generous broad mindedness in order to deal with the sometimes-overwhelming contents of the unconscious. Many today have been thrown into a Dark Night as a result of the extreme turmoil of recent years during which health, political, family, social unrest, and global crises have touched everyone in dramatic, and sometimes traumatic, ways. As difficult as these experiences have been, they have provided an opportunity for personal self-assessment and the reprioritization of life values. When we are up against a wall, we are forced to face certain realities and to realize our starvation for meaning, or for what the author Louise Mahdi calls "initiation-hunger." This is the craving for our own essence, the life-giving nourishment at the spiritual core of ourselves. It is during the bleakest hour of the Dark Night that the new individuality is born; we have endured a meaningful process, and we are now becoming who we were meant to be.

## TASKS

*Man learns through experience and the spiritual path*
*is full of different kinds of experiences.*
*He will encounter many kinds of difficulties and obstacles,*
*and they are the very experiences he needs*
*to encourage and complete*
*the cleansing process.*
~ **Sai Baba**

*To meditate on a quality and then to live it,*
*that is the way of definite progress.*
~ **Annie Besant**

By now you have learned that the Second Initiation is not merely about adding something new to your personality to make you whole. Rather, it is a process (and not just at this particular initiation) of cleansing, releasing, or transmuting those existing qualities that do not align with your truest Self. Spirit breaks up what is hardened or too extreme in your personality—stubbornness, a judgmental attitude, anger—and hardens or strengthens what is weak—willpower, low self-worth; or an inadequate sense of self-responsibility. As one example, the Theosophist Annie Besant wrote of how she curbed her own willful nature and a "natural imperiousness."[8] She stated that these innate qualities were a result of having lived other lifetimes of "struggle and storm." For a set period of time, she decided to make it a practice never to refuse a single thing she was asked to do by others, no matter how trivial or time consuming, She made it an exaggerated practice to say yes to everything so that she could more quickly learn to yield, not to another human, but to the promptings of spiritual guidance. Annie went to the opposite extreme of her natural tendencies so that these inherent qualities would become more moderate and evenly calibrated, ultimately finding a balanced place in the middle.

## TRANSMUTATION OF ENERGIES

> *Become an alchemist.*
> *Transmute base metal into gold,*
> *suffering into consciousness,*
> *disaster into enlightenment.*
> ~ **Eckhart Tolle**

This initiation level also brings about the transmutation of emotional and sexual energies. Transmutation means to change from one state into another. Sexual energies are not eliminated but are balanced. People living in the modern world are not expected to withdraw into a cave to live a celibate life. Instead, sexual and emotional forces are regulated and moderated, so that a portion of these energies become available to us in the very real efforts necessary for psychological wholeness. Emotions remain an important component of our psychological makeup, but we find that the lower range of emotions such as rage, jealousy, bitterness, fear, cruelty (which, ultimately, are "crimes against love") eventually transmute into the higher emotions of compassion, understanding, trust, acceptance, and most of all, love. How is this alchemical change activated? Usually when our greatest fantasies and most ambitious plans for ourselves are thwarted! We suffer: We are despondent when someone we love does not love us back; we feel defeated when the job we wanted so badly goes to another; we experience bereavement over the loss of an irreplaceable friend; we are frustrated and frightened as we struggle with aging and ill health. Through suffering, our emotions are refined in the fires, then "washed" by our tears. Our hearts are broken open. By the end of the Second Initiation, we better understand what Eckhart Tolle means by transmuting the gray lead of suffering into the gold of consciousness.

There are very real sacrifices and difficult renunciations required on The Path, and often these profound experiences cannot be articulated or shared. This process of true initiation can only be collaborated with—and never controlled, exploited, or counterfeited. The initiation process eventually demands your entire life. Because the Initiatory Path is a transmutational process, a person is completely changed in every muscle, bone, nerve and cell. Over many years of dedicated effort, a person's heart is opened and spiritual energies pour in; these energies should never be appropriated by the ego—but be quietly directed to the benefit of the entire world.

## SEEING THROUGH GLAMOUR

*There is the world of Maya (physical), the world of glamour (emotions) and the world of illusion (mental).*
~ **Alice Bailey**

One of the issues at this Initiation is to recognize and detach from *glamour*. This refers to our emotions and desires. Glamour is astral in character and is far more potent and prevalent at this time than illusion, which is mental in character, owing to the enormous majority of people who are primarily functioning on an emotional level. We are in glamour when we want to see the results of our own work, to win the admiration of others, to be recognized as "shiny" and special, or to show off our knowledge at every opportunity. I am reminded here of the spiritual parable of the student who had left his Master to teach on his own. When he next met up with his Master, the student-turned-teacher boasted of his popularity and the many followers he had attracted. After a long pause, his former Master said quietly, "I am so sorry to hear that."

We want to be famous, glorified, and emulated. Charisma is a glamour: Initiates can easily attribute their powers of attraction to their alluring ego-personality rather than to the spiritual energies that, at each level of initiation, increasingly flow through them. In this regard, glamour includes the "cult of the personality," which occurs in many groups, including spiritual communities. There are many stories of spiritual teachers who have succumbed to this type of vanity, and in doing so, have inflicted a lot of damage on their followers. Glamour is essentially self-deception, vanity, delusion, and self-importance. On the Spiral Way, we learn, sometimes through very hard lessons, to become humble, democratic (non-elitist), and detached from what others think of us or project onto us. In today's media-conscious world, we see what fascination glamour has for us in the idolization of movie stars, television personalities, sports heroes, some politicians, and social media influencers.

Glamour is so enticing because it is something constructed, and therefore easier to achieve than authentic beauty; glamour sells. My young college students over the years have often given me the feedback that they feel insecure and inferior when they scroll through social media sites and watch life style and fashion influencers. Even though most know that everything is staged, airbrushed, and Photoshopped, they compare themselves and find themselves lacking. This often results in depression, anxiety, body image issues, and eating disorders. In their book, *Social Media and Its Effects on Beauty*[9], authors Mavis Henriques and Debasus Patnaik reviewed research on the impact of social networking sites in regard to their promotion of unrealistic standards of beauty and their effects on the body image and self-esteem of young people. They concluded that the greatest proportion of these messages lead to body dysmorphia (obsession with perceived flaws in physical appearance), depression, anxiety, and fear of not being accepted by their peers. It's important to learn how to see through glamour at an early age, as this ability offers a greater sense of well-being, a more realistic outlook on life, and the ability to discern the motives of others.

Learning to leave glamour behind is part of the process of becoming detached. What are some of the ways that we succumb to glamour?

- We are under the astral power of glamour when we *devote ourselves* to only one person, one idea, one authority, one side of the truth; this leads to fanaticism and worship of the personality, such as the idolization of Hitler.

- Related to the above item, we are under the control of glamour when we emphasize those who represent for us the *power of the mind* as the miraculous solver of all ills. For example, we often worship scientists as modern-day wizards, such as Albert Einstein and Michio Kaku. Unthinking, slavish adoration is a glamour. (As mentioned elsewhere in this book, the mind is necessary, important, and useful, but ultimately, it exists to show you its own limitations. We need the analytic properties of the mind, especially when irrationality and unchecked emotions hold sway. However, it's important to remember that today, we are transitioning into the development of the *intuition*, which is beyond the mind. *Illusions*, rather than glamours, are mental; they are mistaken and misinterpreted ideas that govern our daily lives and are more often dealt with at the Third and Fourth Initiations).

- When we set *ourselves up as someone special,* glamour is at work. We might promote ourselves as being on a singular mission, that we are the sole "appointed ambassador" for a famous dead person or for an off-world entity or group; or that we know something that others do not know, and so others must recognize that we are exceptional and out of the ordinary. It's important to remember that we are only one among many who serve humankind. To prepare to do this, we have own inner psychospiritual work to do. If we do not complete a life task or mission, there is always someone else lined up who will bring necessary ideas, concepts, or inventions into manifestation. We are not the only individual who can complete a particular purpose. To think so promotes a type of glamour that creates vanity and separateness.

An effective dispeller of the glamour of vanity in ourselves is to regularly declare ourselves as a conduit or channel for Spirit, with the heart intention of doing the highest good for the greatest number. **To keep in mind that our inspirations come through us rather than from us is the most effective approach to maintaining our humility and gratitude as initiates.** We each have but a role in the greater whole, as there are many instruments ("fingers") of the Divine who are incarnate at this time; we are part of the wave.

## FALLING INTO THE VOID

> *Fear of loss, fear of failure, fear of being hurt, and so on,*
> *but ultimately all fear is the ego's fear of death, of annihilation…*
> *fear of death affects every aspect of your life.*
> **~ Eckhart Tolle**

At the Second Initiation, the confrontation of our greatest fears is intensified. Humans are very fear based, which leads to much of our aggression. To counter these fears, some have dreams in which they are learning to pitch themselves off of cliffs, knowing they might die. Some of you may have read something similar to this in one of Carlos Castaneda's books,

*Tales of Power*, when, under the tutelage of a Yaqui native, the author purportedly leapt off of a cliff into the void. "Jumping into the abyss" is a theme found in almost every spiritual belief system in the world, from Shamanism and Sufism to Christianity and Buddhism. On the Initiatory Path spoken of here, it has nothing to do with physical risk and everything to do with learning to psychospiritually jump into the unknown. A fall into vast nothingness—and our survival of it—induces an awakening or a new beginning and enables us to leave old patterns and tired routines behind us. We overcome doubt and fear by learning how to *surrender* and *trust*. Those of us who had a difficult childhood may especially find it very challenging to trust Spirit. To leap into the void is really *a leap of faith*. To illustrate, a male client had the following dream:

> "I was driving in the dark. It seemed familiar to me that I would be driving in the dark hoping all would be well, in spite of all evidence to the contrary. Suddenly, I began to drive off the road and soon was endlessly falling into a pitch-black void. It was like diving down an elevator shaft. I was yelling out as I plunged into the darkness, hoping that I would be helped. But as I fell, despite the almost overwhelming instinctual fear, some deep part of myself knew that I would be all right, even when I finally hit bottom."

If not dreaming of plunging into a chasm, we may suffer the void as a limbo state in everyday life. When we are in limbo—twisting in the wind, hanging in the air, out on a limb—we don't seem to be going either forward or backward in life; something old has left, but nothing new has arrived. This is generally a very difficult space for humans to occupy. But a lot of underground psychospiritual activity—a type of hidden germination—is fomenting during these latent periods which comprise the middle phase of transitions. For example, when we have recently divorced and left our spouse behind, we have also forfeited a former personal and social identity, a socio-economic level, perhaps a house, maybe even a geographical area. This is the first phase of a transition—losses, endings, and the passing away of life as you knew it. The middle phase (the void experience) usually follows; there has been the death of the old life, but the next life has yet to be been born. Rather than rushing into another relationship or shifting one's immediate attention to all things new, this middle time is best spent in reflection, self-evaluation, and reassessment. This phase offers a unique potential for inner growth and self-awareness. The fear of facing the void sometimes propels people into truncating this stage; they short circuit the transition process to hurriedly fill the emptiness. The third or last phase is one of beginnings, and if we have given the void phase its due, new prospects, people, and perspectives will naturally occur in our lives.

**The existential experience of "falling into the void" allows us to confront our fear of death—and ironically, our fear of life!** When we leap into the unknown, we "make death an advisor." We allow the certainty and unpredictability of death to shift our attention away from external things and more onto what's most important. By being continually conscious of the fleeting nature of time and the inevitability of physical death, we can allow death to propel us forward. The experience of dramatically facing the immediacy of annihilation—whether in dreams, participating in extreme sports, or engaging in combat—shifts our assemblage points so that we perceive things in a new and vibrant way. Facing death makes us feel more alive.

## LONELINESS

*Don't surrender your loneliness so quickly. Let it cut you more deep.*
*Let it ferment and season you as few humans*
*and even divine ingredients can.*
*Something missing in my heart tonight has made my eyes so soft,*
*my voice so tender,*
*my need for God absolutely clear.*

~ **Hafiz**

After the chaotic process of the death and dissolution during the first part of our journey, we are often tasked with wandering in the vast, unmarked hinterlands or on the empty seas. This is a waiting period which can be likened to *the doldrums*, a nautical term that refers to the encircling band near the Earth's equator where sailing ships sometimes become trapped for days on windless waters.

In my own experience, I came to understand that this flat and arid quality of my life during the latter part of my first Dark Night of the Soul was an opportunity for the integration and stabilization of what I had previously experienced. Knowing this gave me comfort. But this time of Wandering in the Wasteland is saturated with loneliness. Such loneliness (which has elements in common with homesickness and alienation, two tasks discussed later) can haunt the spiritual student at any time on the Path of Initiation. It is more acutely felt at certain junctures along the Way but can remain in the background as a chronic, dull throb. Some of this loneliness can be attributed to the call to a life direction that is different and unfamiliar to others and cannot be easily explained or defended.

Spiritual loneliness can set in, for example, if family and friends feel that you have turned your back on them or have even gone off the deep end upon some nonsensical quest. In Somerset Maugham's book, *The Cutting Edge*, a young man named Larry Darrell leaves his friends and his fiancé on a search for meaning. The American pilot has returned from war a different man. Having witnessed the death of a close friend, he is no longer interested in conventional life. Larry puzzles his friends and fiancé by bypassing an opportunity to become well positioned and prosperous. The book follows Larry from Chicago to Paris, where he spends his time studying philosophy and religion, and then as he travels throughout Europe, working at menial jobs. He studies for a time at a Benedictine Monastery in Alsace, France, and then continues his quest by traveling to southern India. There Larry trains in an ashram with the venerated Maharshi, Shri Ganesha, and after experiencing a measure of spiritual enlightenment, returns to America. His goal is to live, as far as possible, a life of spiritual simplicity, renunciation, and anonymous service to others. Throughout the book, Larry's life is contrasted with those of his friends. His fiancé, though she loves Larry, marries a man who will give her the affluent lifestyle she craves; her American uncle, while generous and loyal, is a snob and social climber living in Paris. Though loved by others, Larry is a mystery to them. He is a lonely figure who has chosen the Winding Path, and he must walk it alone.

Being set apart is always difficult and often leads to loneliness. A 2017 documentary, *Becoming Who I Was*, follows a Buddhist boy named Padma Angdu who at age six is identified by a high-ranking lama as the reincarnation of a revered Tibetan monk, or Rinpoche, who was once head of a monastery in Kham, Tibet. Padma lives and studies in a monastery in the mountainous region of Ladakh in northern India, where he was born, but when his former disciples fail to arrive to claim him, he is expelled. Padma is forced to live with his godfather, an elderly lama and the village's only doctor. Padma was filmed over eight years, part of that time while living with his godfather, Rigzin Urgyan. There is great affection and devotion demonstrated between Padma and Rigzin, but there are film sequences that clearly depict Padma's growing loneliness and disappointment. He is occasionally called a "fake Rinpoche" by a few villagers who do not understand why he has not been contacted by the monastery in Kham. Padma is by nature cheerful and playful, but he is increasingly disheartened by not being able to fulfill his purpose. When Padma is twelve, he and his godfather decide to set out on a long journey to his former monastery in Tibet. The way is arduous, the weather conditions are treacherous, and the travelers are warned that the Chinese do not allow anyone to cross the borders into Tibet.

The two-month trek becomes harrowing as they travel by bus, train, hitchhiking, and on foot, wearing inadequate clothing and suffering from frostbite. Disappointed, they are not able to cross into Kham because of the dangers of being detained or imprisoned, but they make the best of their situation. We are shown at film's end that Padma elects to continue his education in a monastery bordering Tibet, and his ailing godfather returns to his home near Ladakh. The journey did not end the way that they had wished, but love—and loneliness—remain.

So what is the spiritual function of loneliness? When we are "thrown back on ourselves," we find spiritual reserves and resources we might never have realized otherwise. It is when we are in deep and solitary silence that we are open to insights and revelations. Our solitariness helps us to listen to our interior selves; we focus on the "still small voice" and know God. It is in profound loneliness that we cultivate the relationship with the "Inner Companion." It is in our aloneness that we can "practice the presence" of the Divine, just as Brother Lawrence,[10] while working in the Carmelite Monastery's kitchen, found God in the simplest and most menial of tasks.

## SUMMARY: COMING INTO BEING

*To undertake a genuine spiritual path*
*is not to avoid difficulties*
*but to learn the art of making mistakes wakefully,*
*to bring them to the transformative power of our heart.*
*~ Jack Kornfield*

The Second Initiation is a tough one. But if you have committed to the Path, you are given tools to better weather the emotional storms of this level of initiation. You find yourself gaining in resilience, strength, resolve, and perspective. You know (although at times you may be quaking with doubt) that you are involved in a sacred process. This Initiation primarily focuses on the Astral Plane and the sacral chakra and deals with the transmutation of the emotions and sexual instincts. Experiences during this initiation are tumultuous, as the spiritual energies you are now channeling come into unsettling contact with the accumulated detritus (karma) of lifetimes. Old wounds and repressed memories come into view for processing and healing. You are continuing to deal with your shadow qualities, all those characteristics that demand your complete honesty and humility to face. The issues of glamour, detachment, and fear (especially fear of death) are confronted. You may even find yourself in a long and arduous Dark Night of the Soul, an ordeal triggered at times by inner conditions, such as disappointment, desolation, and futility, or by difficult outer crises, such as a divorce or death in the family. As you deal with these issues, your heart is opening to more love and compassion. And as you increasingly align your ego-personality with Soul, you are less dominated by your life story and more identified with your God-being.

You will eventually leave all behind you, even your personal life narrative. A Sufi Master explained the process this way:

> "How do you swim? You throw water behind and behind you, that's how you propel yourself. Spiritual life is the same; you keep throwing everything behind, as you go on. This is the only way; there is no other."[11]

Finally, all that's left is your true identity as Soul. The Path of Initiation, with its multiple experiences of psychospiritual death and rebirth, assures the Initiate that life does not end with physical death, and that there is a life force within us that is unconquerable, unassailable, and immortal. This is the part of us that is taking in every experience and extracting the meaning from it. Being connected to Soul (or Self) allows us to stand back to more clearly observe the glorious and manifold life stories we have written for ourselves. It's sometimes a shock to me that books and movies can deeply involve us in their plot lines, but *leave out* the reason why people are experiencing these stories in the first place! Where is the spiritual perspective, the core spiritual aspects of ourselves, the very purpose *for* our rich experiences, life themes, and tropes? We need to recover awareness of the lost root of ourselves, the very source of our existence. **For this reason, it is important to recognize that the Labyrinthine Path of Initiation is not actually a path at all: It is a** *coming into being.*

## THE THIRD INITIATION: INTEGRATION

*What is Truth?*
*Truth is the attribute of when the human heart*
*marries the love of God,*
*and the result is passion for your spiritual path.*
~ Lee Carroll

## TO KNOW YOUR NARRATIVE

*If you ask me; 'Is there a next life after death? Can you show it to me?'*
*I will ask you; 'Is there a tomorrow? If yes, can you show it to me?'*
~ Ajahn Chah

In one life, I was a sturdy, buxom German woman living in the Black Forest with my husband and sons. One day while I was alone, my house was ransacked, and I was assaulted by nomadic invaders on horseback. In another life, I was a Greek male, a beautiful youth who was pampered with a leisurely lifestyle until bored, sought to study under a philosopher in Alexandria, Egypt. In this lifetime I tragically learned that to attract another out of vanity carries with it grave consequences. Once, I was an abbess who defied a government functionary opposed to the Church. By doing so, I had made a relentless and powerful enemy, one who ultimately paved the way for my being put to the stake. In yet another life, *I* was the persecutor, a cold and calculating member of the king's royal advisors, plotting with three other men to bring down a court favorite.

Soon after beginning my spiritual journey on the Initiatory Path, I entered psychotherapy with a psychologist who was highly trained in past-life therapy.[12] In tandem with her doctoral work in psychology, she had undergone an intensive program that provided her with a way for me to bring to consciousness and then resolve unconscious patterns from earlier lives, traumas that continued to negatively impact my current life. We did not look for lifetimes of success and splendor but were drawn instead to past situations of pain, trauma, or confusion. These negatively-charged memories had programmed my unconscious to react to situations and people in ways that no longer served me. Someone does not have to even believe in previous lives for this process to work; you can still experience more autonomy and ease in your life without believing in reincarnation. Once the unconscious releases negative memories through a specific process of reconciliation, your life structure is freed of past influences, allowing you to respond to situations instead of merely reacting to them.

One of the favorable outcomes of undergoing this process is that you do not only see yourself only as a victim, but you also experience yourself as a perpetrator. This is an important factor because once you are ready to step onto the Labyrinthine Path, you have had everything done to you—and you have done everything to others. It's part of growing into psychospiritual wholeness to know your own power for both good and evil. Soul gathers up these experiences and perceptions from each lifetime. **For Soul, no experience is ever wasted or worthless!**

Initiates today who reach the Third Initiation are often introduced to their past lives in their dreams. Your dreams may depict you as a different gender and race, living in a faraway country in a long-ago time. You may dream of yourself as a wealthy cloth merchant in Anatolia (now Turkey); a courtesan in France during the Age of Enlightenment; a poor tenant-farmer tilling the soil for a feudal lord in old England; or a monastic nun (or monk) in 14th century Germany. (By the way, it may surprise you to learn that a prostitute's life experience is just as valuable to Soul as that of a nun's!)

The emphasis in these dreams is usually on what in your past lives needs healing in order to release fears and reactions that hinder your spiritual growth and happiness *in the present*. If you feel an affinity for a particular region of the world or are attracted to the clothing or furniture from a particular place, then you can almost be sure that, in another lifetime, you have lived there! Small children, usually between the ages of two and five, frequently share memories with their parents of when they used to be "big." Sometimes these children show unusual behaviors, such as phobias (for instance, aquaphobia, an irrational fear of water, perhaps originating from a past-life experience of drowning). They may also show strange preferences, such as when the spiritual teacher Elizabeth Haich compulsively contorted her body into certain poses as a child, later learning that these positions were yoga asanas practiced in a previous lifetime in the temples of ancient Egypt.[13] These actions or reactions cannot be explained in the context of the child's particular family or by any current life events. We find that we are now, at this moment, the sum total of every life we have ever lived. *It is our work as an Initiate (with the help of Spirit) to sift through, synthesize, and integrate our experiences—our own unique narrative — into an undivided, high-functioning wholeness of being.*

## THE MANIPURA CHAKRA

*Always do what you are afraid to do.*
            ~ **Ralph Waldo Emerson**

The Third Initiation centers on the Solar Plexus, or *Manipura*, which is located in the area of the abdomen, from just above the belly button to the breastbone. *Manipura* means "lustrous gem" in Sanskrit. The Manipura chakra provides a source of personal power and relates to self-esteem, warrior energy, and the power of transformation. When the *manipura,* or navel chakra is blocked, you can experience difficulty in self-expression, exhibit aggressive or controlling behavior, feel irritation, and anger, succumb to feelings of neediness and victimhood, be excessively fearful, experience stagnation, and have poor self-esteem. On the other hand, a balanced and aligned navel chakra lends itself to energy moving freely through the body, feeling a sense of purpose, clearly articulating your needs and desires, and enjoying a better understanding of your personal identity. The careful discrimination of the initiate's development of inner, personal power versus the misuse of power by attempting to control others is one of the challenges of the Third Initiation. Other chakra centers that are vivified at this initiation are the *ajna* or brow center and the crown chakra.

## THE CAUSAL PLANE

> *The common thread which connects the Akashic Records*
> *with most spiritual traditions around the world*
> *is the memory of God.*
> ~ **Cheryl Marlene**

The Third Initiation relates to the Causal Plane, where the color orange dominates and the primary sound is the tinkling of bells. The Causal Plane is where memories, karmic patterns, and Akashic Records are stored. These records are detailed accounts of our past, present, parallel, and future lives. The records (sometimes seen as file cards or as holograms that activate with your attention) are a chronicle of Soul's spiritual progress, including lessons we have learned as well as those we have yet to realize. The Causal Body is also another name for the Higher Self or more esoterically, the Solar Angel. This is the intermediary that has been the channel of communication between the ego-self and Soul over eons of time. (We will touch on this again in the section on the Fourth Initiation).

The seeds (or "ideas") of lifetimes are housed on the Third, or Causal, Plane. The reality of our life experiences are only latent events or energies—pure cause—on the Causal Plane. These potentialities (or dream pictures), which are lying latent in the depths of the unconscious, are manifested on the material plane as real events during physical incarnations. In ancient Egypt, initiates who qualified for advancement were enclosed inside a stone sarcophagus in the Great Pyramid to undergo, in an altered state, the "seed" possibilities of all lifetimes specific to each initiate. During this process, the initiates were tested in every possible way; if they forgot themselves and were "lost" inside any experience as a "reality," or if they succumbed to any of the distinct temptations associated with a particular plane, they failed. Some initiates would fail, instead, in their outer lives, giving way, for example, to pleasure or pride. And so, failed initiates would reincarnate on the physical plane to tediously live out, life after life, what were once only the "germs" of these lifetimes.

Today, we often experience the tests once lived by initiates in an altered state in our everyday, physical lives as well as in our dreams. The Path of Initiation can shorten the number of the physical lifetimes that we must endure; in fact, we can live out cycles of experience during which we live several compressed lifetimes into one. Working with a Master, we can "uncoil" certain tensions within ourselves, resolving the energies that become cause and create our future. During the long initiation process, all unconscious parts of the psyche are brought to the surface into consciousness.

Each move to a new level of initiation (or consciousness) entails a death and rebirth—a death of an old framework of consciousness and a birth of a new way of being in the world. With each progression on the Ladder of Initiation, we are coming closer to freeing ourselves from the "cycle of necessity," or physical reincarnation. Initiation has been called *forced growth*, but I prefer to see it as a *fast track*! When a certain level of progress has been achieved on the Path, many initiates are able to graduate from Earth School, only opting to return when they are on a mission of service.

# CLIMBING THE MOUNTAIN

> *Lions and Lambs, love and force, light and fire, good and evil:*
> *all things climb the same mountain, the mountain of God.*
> ~ Nikos Kazantzakis

Imagine that you are one of the select few planning to climb Mt. Everest which stands at over 29,000 feet, the highest point on the planet. Most prospective climbers spend a year or more physically conditioning with climbing, strength, cardiovascular, and flexibility training. Part of your physical conditioning might include running several miles per day as well as climbing other less formidable mountains. Just as important would be your mental preparation; patience, endurance, focus, and self-sufficiency are essential qualities for the prospective climber. Once at the Mt. Everest base camp, you would spend long periods at ever-higher camp sites to acclimate your body to higher altitudes before finally beginning the expedition to the summit. The trek to the top of the mountain is arduous and hazardous. You will need a guide (today called a facilitator), an experienced climber who has made the trip many times before.

Mountains represent divine inspiration and have long been the focus of religious pilgrimages. Mountains symbolize spiritual elevation, eternity, and constancy. The Nepali name for Mt. Everest is Sagarmatha, which means "Peak of Heaven." Such mountains serve as a cosmic axis or connection between heaven and earth. The Third Initiation is the initiation during which we climb the Mountain of God (a dream theme common at this stage) to be illuminated by Spirit. Sometimes called "The Transfiguration," the Third Initiation is a benchmark that a certain level of spiritual evolution has been achieved. By this time, we have gone through rigorous training in preparation for the trek and have become spiritually fit. We have modified our appetites and faced those aspects of ourselves we least want to claim. We have worked hard to integrate the multiple selves that formerly made up our psyche, ultimately producing greater unity and synthesis within ourselves. We have risen from one stage or level to the next, acclimatizing to ever rarer and refined vibrational energies. We have demonstrated endurance, focus, determination, patience, and compassion. We are ready to surrender ourselves to something higher (we needed to create a unified self before we can surrender it). We are focused on becoming effective conduits of spiritual energies in greater service to the world. Importantly, we have found a Guide (Master) to lead us to the summit. Now the divine in our nature can be revealed. On the mountaintop, we realize the truth in the phrase, "God is a consuming fire."

Considered the first of the major initiations (with the first two being regarded as largely preparatory), the Third Initiation demonstrates that what is human in us has been purified and transformed, and can now be blended with the divinity within us. This results in illumination or an expansion of consciousness.[14] There is now a synthesis of our higher and lower natures (both described under "Integration" below). We no longer function in a "split" or divided way but as a functioning whole. At the Third Initiation, initiates have transcended their physical and emotional natures, and there is now the possibility of synthesizing their physical, emotional, and mental aspects. At this stage, initiates merge both God and human, or Soul (Self)[15] and the personality within themselves. How does this True Individuality appear to us in our dreams? It often presents itself as the Mystical or Divine Child.

## THE DIVINE CHILD

> *The realization of the Divine, the birth of the spirit-child into matter, is the biggest miracle humanity can ever behold.*
> ~ **Asa Kleveland**

During this stage, we may have many wedding and pregnancy dreams. We may dream of the birth of a special child (men often dream that the anima, or the divine woman within, is pregnant or giving birth). This newborn is clearly precocious. Sometimes, the baby is born able to speak and to impart divine wisdom or can walk at birth and also perform miracles. (At this stage, I once dreamed of having a baby with the head of a rose). At the Third Initiation, the baby symbolizes a change of one's essential nature, a transmutation. Jung described this Divine Infant as "the transformation of a mortal into an immortal being, of a corporeal into a spiritual being, and of a human into a divine being."[16]

Everything in life is on a continuum and has its polar opposite: love-hate, masculine-feminine, diabolical-divine, yin-yang. These dualities are responsible for creating duality within your psyche, which is then turned outward into the conflicts of daily life. The Divine Child is the product of integrating these polar opposites: the Alchemical Child represents *the union of opposites.* We have long held within us the tension of the opposites.[17] Jung posited that there is no consciousness without first being aware of the opposites within yourself. We grow in consciousness by first purifying and then uniting two conflicting opposites into an integrated third. By this initiation, we have resolved many of these opposites to create a constant, steady Center of Gravity or Being, symbolized by the Imperishable Child. This shows up in our outer lives as a relative independent ego endowed with free will. We have achieved what is sometimes called a Soul-infused personality.

## THE CYCLE OF THREES

> *The symbol of the triad or trinity...*
> *can be understood as a key*
> *to the integrity and interdependence of all existence.*
> ~ The Book of Threes

The number three is universally recognized as sacred. The Triad, for example, contains the Holy Trinities of many world religions; it is the unity of body, soul, and spirit. In its cosmic reference it includes heaven, earth, and the waters. As a human reference point, it refers to the beginning, middle, and end of a cycle, and we know that everything in the physical world has a past, present, and future. The number three is also related to the laws of manifestation which use the principles of positive, negative, and neutral energies. The number three is especially prominent at this stage of initiation. Your dreams will reflect this by presenting three of everything: three eggs, three people, three houses, three roads to follow. (Actually, the middle path, or the "Middle Way," is the true spiritual path[18]). You may dream of three crosses, as one young client did. She was just starting to explore her spiritual journey and was not affiliated with any particular religion.

> *"My friend's baby had come early. While she was at the hospital, I took care of the baby. The baby and I got along very well together. The newborn seemed old in his understanding. I dedicated the baby to three narrow wooden crosses by placing him directly on top of them as they lay horizontally. The dedication did not seem particularly 'Christian' in its emphasis, even though there were three wooden crosses involved."*

Even though this dream is emblematic of the Mount of Golgotha, or Calvary, where three crosses stood (and where Jesus was crucified), the ancient meaning of the cross symbolizes the sacrifice of the ego-self for the sake of the Self (Consciousness). Ultimately, the physical, emotional and mental bodies of the lower self are being consecrated to God; the hard work of the purification of these bodies lies ahead. It often involves a radical embrace of suffering in order to evolve and change.

At this initiation, as explained earlier, the number three represents the integration of two opposites into a third, symbolizing something higher and finer than before, a new level altogether. It is also important to note that there are three smaller initiations that occur before a major one: We are challenged and tested—many times unknowingly—to apply what we are learning, as the Initiatory Path does not merely fill our heads with knowledge. There is much esoteric study associated with the Third Initiation: There may be many dreams of scanning ancient records, learning arcane languages, and memorizing cosmic charts (tasks we are actually performing while our bodies are asleep). We must illustrate that we have taken this knowledge into our hearts by demonstrating it in our interactions at home, at work, or when we are running errands. Then it becomes wisdom.

## LOWER MENTAL THOUGHT PROCESSES

> *You don't have to control your thoughts.*
> *You just have to stop letting them control you.*
> ~ Dan Millman

Before and during the Third Initiation, a gradual shift has been taking place from the astral/emotional to the lower mental thought processes. A major challenge during this initiation is learning to regulate or master our thinking at least to some degree. This is made very difficult today, as we are not only victims of our own habitual lower-thought forms (which hang out in our aura), but we are also assaulted at every turn by the thought forms originating from sources outside ourselves. Our consciousness is filled with negative thoughts that were passed along to us by our parents, by social media, political propaganda, advertising, and peers. Many of these thoughts are part of a mass consciousness and are fear based, aggressive, and separative. Negative thinking pollutes the atmosphere with psychic debris which has negative effects on everyone.

Some research has shown that once people have made up their minds to think negatively about something, they seldom change their mindsets, even when they are shown evidence to the contrary. Sociologist Alison Ledgerwood claims that people get stuck in negative thinking; the results of her studies indicate that it is easier for participants to change from "gains to losses" than from "losses to gains." She states, "Our view of the world has a fundamental tendency to tilt toward the negative," adding, "You literally have to work harder to see the upside of things." Ledgerwood asserts that it is much more difficult to think in a positive way, but that with hard work and effort, it is possible. Keeping a gratitude journal helps, and so does recounting the positive events of everyday life to friends and family. Repeating negative events to others keeps you stuck at the negative end of the attitude continuum.[19]

Unfortunately, many people today do not know the difference between feelings and thoughts; they imagine they are thinking when they are actually reacting emotionally. It helps to know that thoughts are *things* and can be *refused* as they come into your awareness. If these negative thoughts are repeatedly rejected and replaced with positive thoughts, these lower-level thought forms will no longer have the power to intrude or affect you. The spiritual initiate at this stage recognizes and nullifies mental illusions which are distortions of reality, just as the emotional glamours associated with the astral plane were confronted and curbed at the second initiation. On the global level, a hazy cloud of negativity—augmented by conflicts and wars of every kind—hangs over the world like a miasma. The initiate helps to cleanse this atmosphere by transcending lower-self thought patterns to send out positive and uplifting thought forms into the world. The controversial John Pope (who laid claim in the 70s and 80s to being a Native American Medicine Man known as Rolling Thunder) had these words to say, sage advice regardless of his debatable status:

> *"First of all, if we don't want to think certain things, we don't say them…we begin by watching our words and speaking with good purpose only. There are times when we must have clear and pure minds with no unwanted thoughts, and we have to train and prepare steadily for those times until we are ready. We don't have to say or think what we don't wish to. We have a choice in those*

*things, and we have to realize that and practice using that choice. There is no use condemning yourself for the thoughts and ideas and dreams that come into your mind; so, there's no use arguing with yourself or fighting your thoughts. Just realize that you can think what you choose. You don't have to pay any attention to those unwanted thoughts. If they keep coming into your head, just leave them alone and say, 'I don't choose to have such thoughts,' and they will soon go away. If you keep a steady determination and stick with that purpose you will know how to use that choice and control your consciousness so unwanted thoughts don't come to you anymore. Then you can experience purification…"*[20]

Once we differentiate our own thoughts from mass consciousness, we are no longer easily swayed by collective ideas. It is only when we have an undeveloped thinking process that we experience group think and herd mentality without real discrimination and judgment. It is concerning that some persons indulge in wholesale adoption of extremist ideology, for example, without vetting these ideas through necessary scientific research or analytic thinking processes. Just as troubling, however, is that so much of what the current New Age culture offers is a quasi-spiritual hodgepodge of practices which includes yoga, meditation, energy healing, psychic readers, dietary supplements, sound bathing, crystal practitioners, sweat lodges, and more—all of which are readily monetized and easily marketed to feed spiritual narcissism and self-indulgence.[21] Many people, of course, are sincere seekers, looking for true spiritual values while passing through a medley of promising but unfulfilling and sometimes damaging experiences. Even though many practitioners and adherents of the programs listed above are seriously devoted to their practices, the part of the New Age movement that promotes titillating and dilettantish explorations *cannot substitute for the hard and unglamorous work of the initiation process.*

# TASKS

# SEEING THROUGH ILLUSIONS

*You do not exist to serve the illusion.*
*The illusion exists to serve you.*
                              ~ **Lauren Zimmerman**

Seeing through illusions at the Third Initiation enables spiritual students on The Path to discern what is true and what is false, what is authentic and what is simulated. Becoming "clear-sighted" is part of becoming spiritually mature; it means that we *see* the illusion so that we can now become the "decider." We have the choice to work with it, live within it, or discard it. What are some of the common *illusions*[22] under which humans live?

- *That our outer, physical lives make up the true reality.* Once we realize that we are living out a narrative (which we helped to create prior to incarnation and continue to fashion with our daily decisions), we have taken a tremendous step in our understanding and perspective. We can now take the viewpoint of Soul: The ego-self is playing out a story so that we can learn necessary lessons for our spiritual unfoldment.

- *That what happens to us is the fault of others.* We believe that our circumstances are due to outer forces such as fate, bad luck, our parents, our government, and so on. On the Initiatory Path, we come to know that we planned on specific events taking place, such as in early life, so that we might grow in certain directions (for example, a young girl watches her mother die of cancer and decides to become a cancer researcher, or a person, abused when young, decides to become a child advocate in the Department of Social Services).

- *That those around us are negative.* Look closely at your circle of friends. If you have persons around you who are angry, vengeful, jealous, racist, homophobic, despairing, greedy, or self-pitying, then you may rest assured that you have attracted these people into your life by harboring these qualities in your own *unconscious.* You may be enacting these qualities in daily life circumstances while remaining unaware of this, seeing only the disagreeable behavior of those you meet at the grocery store, at the PTA meeting, or at a sporting event.

- ***That we do not have the power to change.*** Search for your real needs, your authentic needs, so that you won't feel the need to engage in false behaviors and dysfunctional life patterns. For example, if you put *all of your energy* into bodybuilding and cosmetic surgery (not that a measured amount of these physical modifications cannot be helpful) to fill the need to feel *loved, admired, and desired* by others, you will eventually, through inevitable aging, be disappointed. As another example, if you depend on feeling powerful by cleverly manipulating others so that you are always "one up" at work, what will you do when "new kids on the block," who have more updated skills or talents, are hired to replace you? What are your authentic needs (e.g., to feel unconditionally loved, to feel respected for your expertise, to engage in meaningful work, etc.)? What are the authentic ways to have these needs fulfilled? You have the power to change. If you are on the Path of Initiation, you have *signed up* to change, and that means clearing out the cobwebs of illusion.

- ***The biggest illusion of all is that we are alone in the universe.*** Some persons believe that they are alone because a Divine Source does not exist. A few of these individuals are actually protesting the teachings of their childhood religions; others think that any kind of spirituality is a crutch for weak-minded people. There is no way to convince others (and people's personal decisions regarding religion—when it relates to *themselves*—is always sacrosanct and should be treated as such). True spirituality is gained through experiences that are direct and immediate. When asked in a 1959 televised BBC interview if he believed in God, Jung strongly responded, "I don't need to believe, I *know*." Another aspect of the loneliness of humankind has to do with not knowing our place in the multiverse. The universes are teeming with lifeforms. Eventually this fact will make itself apparent to all of us, and many have already had experiences which confirm this. **Remarkably and beautifully, all the beings, creatures, and lifeforms that exist on every plane or dimension, planet, or star share the same end goal: to reach the Ocean of Love and Mercy, the True Home of all life.**

## INTEGRATION

> *Man becomes whole, integrated, calm, fertile, and happy when (and only when) the process of individuation is complete, when the conscious and the unconscious have learned to live at peace and to complement one another.*
>
> ~ C. G. Jung

Once the little selves of the ego-personality have been identified and sorted, the Third Initiation is a process of integrating those selves that are to be purified and to transmute those that are not supporting spiritual unfoldment. An even greater task of integration is to unify what are understood as the lower and the higher natures.

**The lower nature refers to the urges toward:**

- *survival* (fight or flight instincts, self-preservation at the expense of others, instability, fear)
- *pleasure* (promiscuity, self-indulgence or excess, mania, arrogance, aggressiveness, dependency)

- ***power*** (jealousy, domination over others, competitiveness, power-hunger, conceit, self-centeredness, and pride)

**The higher nature includes:**

- ***compassion*** (not sentimentality or conditional love, but real concern for the sufferings of others)
- ***submission*** (not a weak subjugation but a conscious surrender to the higher guidance of the Inner Master/Spirit)
- ***wisdom*** (knowledge is dealing with facts; wisdom is the ability to assimilate and understand knowledge; wisdom enables us to appropriately *apply knowledge* to make correct decisions)

As long as we are in a human body, some negativity will cling to us, which enables us to continue to live on the vibrationally-coarse physical plane. We are striving for wholeness or completeness—not perfection. In fact, we may be occasionally shocked at ourselves for something we feel we knew better not to have said or done. As the flow of spiritual energies gradually increases with every initiation, all of our qualities are amplified and intensified, including our negative traits. By the time we reach the Third Initiation, we have learned to take responsibility for our words and actions. When we hurt another, inadvertently or not, we are now more aware than ever that all beings are connected, since we keenly feel that person's pain. Our own self-evaluations cause us to suffer from our own shortcomings. We are still a work in progress.

# DETACHMENT

> *There is detachment when a person perceives things accurately.*
>
> ~ **Choa Kok Sui**

> *Detachment does not mean non-involvement.*
> *You can be deeply involved but not entangled.*
> ~ **Sadhguru**

Detachment is not coldness and lack of emotion. Nor does it mean to throw away your possessions and walk the way of a mendicant. To become detached is to enjoy the world around you, such as your material goods, while not becoming attached to these things. This is difficult to do in a culture that is based on consumerism, where we are exhorted to buy, buy, buy a hundred times a day. Whenever I hear the British rock group Queen's song, "I Want It All" with its lyrics, "I want it all, and I want it now," paired with a product that is being marketed, I think of how this "desire programming" is continually seeping into the minds of millions, keeping us attached to things that cannot love us back.

We must also detach from persons. Early on my own Initiatory Path, I was greatly captivated by a female therapist, not in a sexual way, but enchanted through what psychotherapy labels as the process of *transference*. I learned then that it is possible to not only project our shadow qualities onto another but to also project our *best* qualities onto someone else. We would not be so enthralled by another *if the magnetic qualities they exhibited did not somehow belong to us*. They only need to be reclaimed and painstakingly developed in ourselves. Much harder, however, is detaching from those who are especially close to us, such as family members. We can love them warmly, of course, and hold them close to us (for humans need companionship), but we learn as initiates to recognize the absolute autonomy and sovereignty of Soul. We can only walk our Spiritual Path ourselves, even if we are surrounded by loved ones. The Neoplatonist philosopher Plotinus spoke to this when he stated that "Life is the flight of the alone to the Alone."

One of the tests met by the initiate is dealing with and detaching ourselves from both public acclaim and public disdain. Many Americans idealize celebrity and fame. Riding the crest of the wave of success actually produces more opportunities to "forget God" than going down in flames or failing. When someone experiences failure, they may be depressed or self-pitying, but they are more apt to turn to Spirit. Success is far more beguiling; it is easy to forget that your lauded gifts come *through* you instead of *from* you. Vanity sometimes comes into play, even for advanced spiritual students.

Public popularity is also fickle; on the flipside of the coin of fame and material success is rejection and financial ruin. Success and failure in everyday life—and how to meet both with equanimity—is a spiritual test that is undergone in mainstream life by people today (and no longer only as an initiate under specialized training in a mystery school). This is a reflection of how general consciousness has slowly expanded over thousands of years. Modern persons in all walks of life face acceptance and rejection in their own lifetimes. For example, the last Major League baseball player to hit over .400, Ted Williams, won two MVP awards while playing for the Boston Red Sox (many say the outfielder should have won more) and twice won the Triple Crown (for leading the league in batting average, home runs and runs batted in). Despite his prowess as a ballplayer, Ted Williams was criticized for being a hot head. He constantly battled with the media and maintained a contentious relationship with the fans, refusing to acknowledge them with a tip of his hat after they had once booed him. All was later forgiven, however, and at the 1999 All-Star Game in Fenway Park, Williams was introduced as "the greatest hitter who ever lived."

Contending with both fame and defamation, Barbara Walters, the first female morning show cohost as well as first female co-anchor of a network nightly news program (and the first to ask—and get—a salary equal to male news anchors), was both reviled and praised for blurring the line between hard news and human interest or feature stories. Her interviews were often denigrated as "personality journalism," as Walters included celebrities among the political leaders she interviewed. Today Walters is recognized as a "glass ceiling breaker" for women in journalism as well as for women in general.

Muhammad Ali is a third example of those who have dealt with both public glory and notoriety. When Ali died in 2016, he was a beloved icon to many, but at one time the sports legend was widely detested. As early as 1964, when he fought Sonny Liston, sportswriters were critical of Ali, who was then known as Cassius Clay. When he changed his name to Muhammad Ali, reporters refused to recognize him by that name. In 1966, Ali became even more unpopular when he refused to be inducted into the U.S. Army during the Vietnam war, citing his religious affiliation as a Black Muslim. As a consequence, Ali was arrested for draft evasion and stripped of his boxing license for three years. His license once more reinstated, Ali went on to win his draft evasion case, clinch the world heavyweight title three times (the last against Leon Spinks in 1978), achieve popular acclaim as a great boxer, and earn general admiration for the grace and dignity with which he handled the diagnosis of Parkinson's disease at the age of 42.[23]

Whether the individual receives accolades or abuse, compliments or complaints, all must be handled with dispassion and objectivity. The Third Initiate is held to this standard of detachment, even though objectivity is made more difficult by the growing sensitivity of the initiate. The concept that the initiate "must be in the world but not of it" rings true at this stage. God increasingly becomes the center of our focus and the goal of our heart's highest yearnings. The following is a fable that illustrates the caprice of success and failure, the vagary of good fortune and misfortune:

> *A young man lived on the Northern frontier of China and one day, for no apparent reason, his horse ran away and was caught by the fierce nomads living across the border. The people in his village tried to reassure him, but his father said, "This could be a blessing." A few months later his horse returned on its own, bringing along with it a splendid stallion. The villagers congratulated him, but his father said, "This could be a curse." The son loved to ride the stallion. One day, however, he fell and broke his hip. The villagers tried to console him, but his father said, "This*

*could be a blessing."* Sometime later the nomads crossed the border to attack and pillage the small settlement, and all healthy men who could ride went into battle. There were mass casualties among the Chinese frontiersmen. The father and his son, who could not ride because of his lameness, survived to take care of each other. It is ever so that blessings turn into curses, and curses into blessings: These changes are eternal and cannot be fathomed.

## FLEXIBILITY

> *Ultimately, spiritual awareness unfolds when you are flexible,*
> *when you're detached, when you're spontaneous,*
> *when you are easy on yourself and easy on others.*
> ~ **Deepak Chopra**

Humans stubbornly resist change, even though ironically, it is woven into the very fabric of human life design. The ability to "dance on a moving rug" must be cultivated to flexibly and adroitly deal with change. One night I dreamed that I attended a class on pure process, or *flow*. At first, I wasn't sure I understood the class purpose or content, but then I began enjoying just flowing, without plan or structure. I continue to work, like many of you, so I do need organization and a schedule in my daily life. However, the dream is addressing how we need to set aside time to be in flow in order to clearly hear God. One of the tests along the Initiatory Path is to be able to respond to a situation in an instant, or "to turn on a dime" when conditions call for it. A few initiates I know have unquestioningly uprooted themselves to go whenever and wherever in order to do whatever Spirit impels them to do, sometimes without receiving any explanation as to why or how!

If you have ever felt completely absorbed in painting at an easel in art class, for example, or while engaging in a tennis game, then you are familiar with the state of flow.[24] We also know these states as being "in the zone," "riding the wave," "being present," or "living in the moment." Achieving this state can help people achieve better regulation of their emotions,[25] enjoy a higher level of creativity and motivation,[26] and more fulfillment and self-actualization.[27] Research has found that during flow states, there are interactions between at least five neurotransmitters that result in feelings of pleasure and well-being.[28]

Learning ways to introduce more flow into your life is related to flexibility, in that you have increased options to respond to different situations in various ways. Importantly, flow opens us up to clearer communication with our Inner Guide or Master, to more frequent dream recall, and even to the greater possibility of experiencing uplifting spiritual states. Transcendent experiences of the Spirit are similar to flow states, sharing commonalities with the states described by Julian of Norwich or St. Teresa of Avila, and more recently with the psychologist Abraham Maslow's definitions of "peak experiences."[29]

Becoming flexible reminds us that essentially, being an initiate is living a life of adventure! The Labyrinthine Path requires that you become the ultimate Spiritual Warrior. Flexibility is a sign of strength, not of weakness. The committed spiritual life brings incremental inner evolutions that eventually manifest as intermittent outer revolutions. Life is never dull and never stays the same. ***Finally, there dawns the certain realization that there is nothing else to do with your life but to walk the Path!***

## SUMMARY: THE LIGHT AND SOUND

*...when the initiate hears the Sound,*
*he leaves behind the desert life of physical incarnation,*
*the emotional life of the astral plane, seething and unstable as the sea,*
*and functions on the plane of the mind,*
*of which the symbol is fire.*
~ **Alice Bailey**

***Listen to the sound of waves within you.***
*~* **Rumi**

The Third Initiation is considered the first of the major initiations, largely due to the fact that by this time, the initiate has bridged the lower and higher natures (touched on earlier in this chapter). This does not detract, however, from the importance of the first two stages, where an immense amount of purification has been done. The first two stages laid the foundation for all the work to come. That being said, it is at the Third Initiation that the initiate may begin to focus on Spirit, not only as Light, but as Sound. Many traditional religions emphasize the Light of Spirit, but the Spiritual Sound is even more fundamental. Those religions who do recognize the spiritual aspect of Sound sometimes call it the "Voice" or the spoken "Word of God." The Sound travels out to the farthest reaches of creation, and it is on the return wave of the Sound that we hitch a ride back to Source. While there are various spiritual sounds that can be identified at earlier stages of initiation, it is during the Third Initiation that the initiate's inner ear is more sensitively awakened. The Sound can now be calibrated by the Master to work on the Initiate in concentrated ways to accelerate spiritual growth. At various stages of unfoldment, the Sound can be recognized in distinct ways, such as the roaring of the seas, the chiming of bells, the buzzing of bees, and more. Often, the inner sound is like the high, thin note of an electrical wire, the hearing of which can be of comfort to the spiritual student. (I wonder how many people have gone to a medical doctor with the complaint of tinnitus when the cause is possibly more spiritual than physical!)

At the Third Initiation, if not earlier, the initiate may also see the "Star," a guiding light seen with the inner eye (*ajna* center or brow chakra) in meditation or contemplation. Esoterically, the "Soul Star," when "switched on" by spiritual advancement, shows itself as a point of light situated a few inches above the head. The celestial "star" was used in many of the invocations of the early mystery religions, such as the Orphic "I am a child of Earth and Starry

Heaven, but my race is of Heaven (alone)." One of the earliest Christian theologians, Origen, wrote, "Understand that thou art a second little world, and that the sun and moon are within thee, and also the stars..." The Star, just as it has for millennia, symbolizes aspiration and guidance. And just as navigators on the seas have used Polaris, or the North Star, to guide them home, the vivid point of light that we see with our inner eyes during contemplation can represent the Master as Wayshower. You *yourself* are a star (even scientists claim that we are made of the stuff of stars).[30]

We are born on Earth, but as we awaken to the Light and Sound within us, these dual aspects of Spirit remind us that we are never alone on the Path. We are never without help. We are always loved. **Even in the darkest of nights, the Light guides our way and the Sound carries us forward.**

# CHAPTER FOUR EXERCISES

## Falling into Spiritual Darkness

The *Dark Night of the Soul* (DNS) is essentially a spiritual process. Its purpose is to break through the minutiae of everyday life, the hurry-up, self-absorbed, scattershot life that many of us live, so that we are compelled to face our own limitations. The DNS forces us to ask meaningful questions such as: ***Is there a plan for my life? Is there a purpose for my pain and suffering? What was I born to accomplish?*** During the DNS, our priorities begin to change: ***How to I spend my time? What is my primary motivation in life? Who are the people I keep around me?*** On the pages of this book or in your journal, respond to the questions below:[31]

1. How has the DNS affected your belief in God or in the harmony and beauty of the universe?

2. What purpose do you think the experience of the DNS serves? Why would God or life put us through these dark times?

3. What strengths or skills do you have that are helping (or have helped) you through this time?

4. How do you think the DNS will (or has) change you? How will it affect (or has affected) the way you move through life?

5. What spiritual practices and/or activities have you taken up since entering the DNS? (These can include dream work, journaling, expressive arts, dance, prayer, meditation, yoga, tai chi, reading of spiritual scriptures or books, etc.)

6. During the distress—and even the despair—of the DNS, how are you trusting in God, perhaps in a way or to an extent that you have never before? How is this newfound and enhanced trust expressed (e.g., more meditation or prayer, a greater love for all life, etc.)?

# CHAPTER FOUR ENDNOTES

1. The full quote by Chogyam Trungpa follows, which is attributed to Trungpa when he lectured in San Francisco, according to Jack Kornfield in *After the Ecstasy, the Laundry*. New York: Bantam Books, 2000, pp. 24-25.

> "My advice to you is not to undertake the spiritual path. It is too difficult, too long, and is too demanding. I suggest you ask for your money back, and go home. This is not a picnic. It is really going to ask everything of you. So, it is best not to begin. However, if you do begin, it is best to finish."

2. Alice A. Bailey. *The Rays and the Initiations*. New York, NY: Lucis Publishing Co., 1981, pp. 64, 65, 582.

3. I wish to interject here that some psychics are gifted and authentic. If their extrasensory abilities are used for the greater good, these individuals can genuinely help others. But to think that spirituality stops with the development of psychic abilities is mistaken; most psychic abilities equate to astral plane development, and there are many planes above this one on the Initiatory Path. A real pitfall for those on the Path of Initiation is the desire to have psychic powers to impress or control others.

4. I recount this dream and discuss this two-year "underground" period with more detail in my book *Drinking the Dragon: Stories of the Dark Night of the Soul*.

5. The Dark Night of the Soul experience can occur anywhere between the onset of the First Initiation and the end of the Second Initiation. Additionally, there may be other Dark Night episodes at other junctures on the Path, especially during the Fourth Initiation.

6. A balanced *fire* element symbolizes, for example, among other characteristics, passion, creativity, resolution, and leadership. Negative fire qualities (indicating not enough water) include arrogance, obsession, jealousy, irritability, domination, and egocentrism. The positive *water* element represents emotion, sensitivity, compassion, cooperation, adaptability, introspection and intuition. On the other hand, negative water traits (indicating not enough fire) include being over sensitive, over emotional, needy, sad, self-sacrificial, and having low self-esteem. *Earth* traits list as stability, reliability, caution, detail orientation, persistence, and practicality. With too much "earth," an individual is lacking in its opposite, "air," and would likely be stubborn, depressed, restrictive, and dull. *Air* represents intellectuality, logic, taking the broad perspective, inquisitive, communicative, adventurous, flexible, and unpredictable. Too much air (not enough earth), as you might guess, lends itself to someone being described as ungrounded, undependable, impractical, or what you might jokingly refer to as a "space cadet."

7. In esoteric psychology, the "Shadow" is called *The Dweller on the Threshold*.

⁸· Annie Besant in *Initiation: The Perfecting of Man*, Wheaton, Illinois: The Theosophical Press, 1912: p. 69-70.

⁹· Mavis Henriques and Debasis Patnaik. Social Media and Its Effects on Beauty, September 21, 2020. *Beauty-Cosmetic Science, Cultural Issues and Creative Developments*, Martha Peaslee Levine and Júlia Scherer Santos, IntechOpen, DOI: 10.5772/intechopen.93322. Available from: https://www.intechopen.com/chapters/73271

¹⁰· Brother Lawrence of the Resurrection served as a lay brother in a Carmelite monastery in 1600s Paris. The book, *The Practice of the Presence of God*, published after his death, recounted his intimate relationship with God, experienced even during the most mundane tasks of everyday life.

¹¹· Quote by Bhai Sahib in Irina Tweedie's *Daughter of Fire*, Nevada City, CA: Blue Dolphin Publishing, Inc., 1989, p. 19.

¹²· The psychologist was trained at the Morris Netherton Past Life Therapy Center in Los Angeles.

¹³· Elizabeth Haich. *Initiation*. Santa Fe, NM: Aurora Press, 2000, pp. 52-53.

¹⁴· The First, Third, and Fifth Initiations are connected in important ways: The First, or "Birth" Initiation, is when we are born into the new life of the Spirit; the Third or Initiation of "Transfiguration," is when we have purified our lower nature to such an extent that the divinity within us can be revealed (often this integration reveals itself as the dream birth of the Divine Child.) The Fifth or "Self-Realization" Initiation completes the integration begun at the Third Initiation; the initiate is now fully aligned with Soul. Discussing the connection between the First, Third, and Fifth initiations, Alice Bailey wrote in her book, *From Bethlehem to Calvary*: New York, NY: Lucis Publishing Company, 2015:

> *"[The First Initiation] Through orientation to new modes of living and of being, we pass through the necessary stages of adaptation of the vehicles of life, [The Third Initiation] up to the mountaintop where the divine in us is revealed in all its beauty. [The Fifth Initiation] Then we pass to a 'joyful Resurrection,' and to that eternal identification with God, which is the everlasting experience of all who are perfected."* (p. 137)

¹⁵· Somewhere between the beginning of the Third Initiation and the end of the Fourth, the Higher Self, which is a mediator between the ego-personality (lower self) and Soul (also called the Self but with a capital "S," a source of confusion), is no longer needed and is sloughed off.

¹⁶· C. G. Jung. *The Archetypes of the Collective Unconscious*. The Collected Works of C. G. Jung. Vol.9, Part 1, Bolligen, Switzerland: Bollingen Series XX, 1959, p.114: par. 204.

17. Examples of holding the tension of the opposites in everyday life:

- I am committed to my relationship, but, if I become consistently miserable, I might decide to leave.
- I am devoted to raising my children, but I need time to be alone and to share with my spouse.
- I heard from my spiritual teacher to commit to my spiritual practices as if my hair were on fire, yet, I know that spiritual unfoldment takes a lifetime or more.
- I am full of fear with this new challenge, but I will take the leap, anyway.

18. The Right-Hand Path is considered that of White Magic, which in modern definitions includes the inclusion of ritual and dogma as well as a belief in community, formal structure, and a higher power. The Left-Hand Path is associated with Black Magic groups that break social taboos and moral codes and is oriented toward personal power and service to self.

19. Alison Ledgerwood. "Getting Stuck in the Negatives—And How to Get Unstuck." TEDxUCDaivis, June 22, 2013. https://youtu.be/7XFLTDQ4JMk

20. Doug Boyd. *Rolling Thunder: A Personal Exploration into the Secret Healing Powers of an American Indian Medicine Man.* McHenry, IL: Delta Books, 1976, p. 99.

21. Examples of this are certain individuals who have adopted a "mishmash of pagan and Indigenous signifiers as a New Age aesthetic." Some of these same individuals are devotees of far-right extremist ideologies. In a March, 2021 *Washington Post* article, writer Marisa Meltzer posits that there is a "growing pipe-line between New Age male spirituality, new masculinity movements and Q-Anon." She adds, "This pipeline is one of unlikely connections and strange bedfellows, of mixed marital arts fighters and poets, evangelical Christians and yoga teachers."[6] This convergence of conspiracy culture and alternative spiritual beliefs (called "Conspirituality" by Matthew Remski, who co-hosts a podcast by that name) is also noted by the staff writer Laura Nelson in the *Los Angeles Times* in a June, 2021 article. She observes, "The health, wellness and spirituality world…though largely filled with well-meaning people seeking spiritual or physical comfort…can also be a hotbed for conspiracies, magical thinking, dietary supplements with dubious scientific claims and distrust of institutional healthcare, including vaccines." Marisa Meltzer. "QAnon's Unexpected Roots in New Age Spirituality," *The Washington Post*, March 29, 2021. Laura Nelson. "California's Yoga, Wellness and Spirituality Community has a QAnon problem." *The Los Angeles Times,* June, 2021.

22. While I am using illusion to include erroneous thinking, some define illusions as pertaining to unreal vision (a perceptual disturbance) and delusions as false beliefs (something perceived as the truth even after other information contradicts it).

23. Among the famous people who experienced both public criticism and praise in their lifetimes, primarily for their work, are the following artists: American author Kate Chopin (a forerunner of 20th century feminist writers) published some of her over one hundred short stories and novels in the *New York Times* and *The Atlantic*. She was generally well-reviewed until her second novel, *The Awakening*, was published. This work of fiction was universally disparaged, some critics claiming that Chopin's general treatment of female sexuality and her female protagonist's rebuke of societal gender norms were morally offensive. Considered the founder of French Impressionism, Claude Monet faced heavy criticism (his finished paintings were panned as mere "sketches") as well as acclaim and financial success during his lifetime. In 1919 when Russian composer and conductor, Igor Stravinsky, debuted his famous ballet, *Rite of Spring*, the audience was so shocked by the primitive style of dancing, irregular rhythms, strange instrumental sounds, and the unusual chords that they rioted, with some attendees breaking into fistfights. Critics called Stravinsky a "madman." However, just a year later, when the score was performed as a concert in Paris, Stravinsky received huge ovations and was carried in triumph on the shoulders of his fans.

24. Both flow and mindfulness focus on the present moment. However, while flow emphasizes focusing on the task at hand, mindfulness encourages people to widen their attention to include all present-moment experiences.

25. Kristen Salters-Pedneault, Ph.D. "How Emotional Regulation Skills Promote Stability," *verywellmind*, September 15, 2020. https://www.verywellmind.com/emotion-regulation-skills-training-425374

26. Kendra Cherry. *"What is Motivation?"* *verywellmind*, April 27, 2020 https://www.verywellmind.com/what-is-motivation-2795378

27. Kendra Cherry. "9 Characteristics of Self-Actualized People," *verywellmind*, July 17, 2019. https://www.verywellmind.com/characteristics-of-self-actualized-people-2795963

28. Martin Kuprianowicz. "The Brain Science Behind Flow States," *SnowBrains*, June 29, 2021. https://snowbrains.com/the-brain-science-behind-flow-states/

29. Abraham Maslow generally described "peak experiences" in 1964 as altered states of consciousness characterized by euphoria, most often achieved by self-actualizing individuals.

30. Kerry Lotzov. "Are We Really Made of Stardust?" *Natural History Museum*. (no date). https://www.nhm.ac.uk/discover/are-we-really-made-of-stardust.html

31. Exercises copied or adapted from my *Drinking the Dragon Reflections and Exercise Companion Workbook*. Encinitas, CA: Sothis Press, 2021.

# CHAPTER FIVE

# Mapping the Spiral Way: Five Stages of Initiation Stages 4-5

*The essence of the spiritual journey:*
*To diminish the vibrational difference*
*between the personally-asserted self and the*
*True Self, which lies timelessly at the core of who you are—*
*shining as beaming, infinite support, nanosecond by nanosecond.*
*~ Bentinho Massaro*

*We become a Co-Worker at every step of the spiritual path.*
*This is a universal law.*
*There is great hope here for those who are sincere in finding out*
*who and what they are:*
*becoming a Co-Worker with God, and realizing the Kingdom of Heaven*
*while still living in the body.*
*The key lies within you.*
*~ Harold Klemp*

# THE FOURTH INITIATION: ALIGNMENT WITH SELF

*A new type of thinking is essential
if mankind is to survive and move toward higher levels.*
~ **Albert Einstein**

*The spiritual experience isn't one of filling ourselves up
— with either religious or intellectual beliefs—
but of emptying ourselves so that
we can experience what is, directly unfiltered.*
~ **Kevin Griffin**

*Genuine spiritual knowledge lies not
in wonderful and mysterious thoughts
but in actual spiritual experience though union
of the believer's life with truth.*
~ **Watchman Nee**

# RENUNCIATION

*Renunciation is not rejecting the family
but accepting the whole world as family.
Renunciation is not changing the name or dress.
It is changing the attitude towards life.*
~ **Amit Ray**

What if you could (hypothetically) say to your family, now that your children are grown and you no longer need employment, that you are leaving the life you've known to live in a secluded cabin hidden within a dense and nearly impenetrable forest. You reassure everyone of your love, health, and soundness of mind. You are not taking a cell phone, television, or laptop, but you are available, on an emergency basis only, via snail mail (you've arranged for a disinterested third party to collect your mail, field cell phone calls in the event of an emergency, and to do an occasional wellness check). You explain that your retreat into the forest is not running away from life, but rather an attempt to become more in touch with it. You take spiritually-oriented books and world-class music. You stock enough food to last several months. You need very few clothes or possessions. You plan to take contemplative walks and to explore your dreams. You want to reintroduce yourself to God.

The spiritual retreat was once built into the lifespans of traditional Hindus. In the ancient Hindu system of four life stages, an Indian man (and sometimes a woman), would reach the end of life (around age 72) and enter *Sannyasa*, historically a stage of renunciation and a peaceful, simple life dedicated to spiritual pursuits and practices.[1] The withdrawal from the physical world began in the third life stage, when the *Vanaprastha* (forest dweller) inaugurated the process of discharging household responsibilities to the younger members of the family and retreating from community involvement. After transitioning to the fourth life stage, the *Sannyasi* (male) or *Sannyasini* (female) became ascetics, renouncing material possessions and emotional attachments and spending the remainder of life as itinerant wanderers with little more than a walking stick, a bowl for food and drink, and a holy book.[2]

Today we do not have to go into the forest, become a wanderer, or enter into monasteries, abbeys, convents, or ashrams to live the spiritual life. Nor are we required to give up all of our material possessions or retreat from those we love. In some ways, our modern lifestyle forces spiritually-dedicated persons to "live in two worlds." This fact often makes it *more* difficult to keep our focus on God than if we were living in a sheltered and sacred environment dedicated to that purpose. Yet, renunciation is an essential aspect of the Initiatory Path. So, just what is renounced? *Only everything we have ever identified with!* If the outer life is stripped away, it is only in the service of becoming detached from our entanglement with the lower worlds—physical, emotional, and mental. It is not that things, sentiments, and ideas are wrong in and of themselves; it is our continued blind (unconscious) allegiance to and enmeshment with these things that prevent us from moving ahead spiritually.

## THE ANAHATA CHAKRA

*The mind creates the abyss*
*and the heart crosses it.*
~ **Sri Nisargadatta**

The Fourth Initiation is related to the *Anahata* or Heart Chakra. In Sanskirt (one of the oldest languages in the world) anahata means "unhurt, unbeaten, unstruck." This refers to the "unstruck sound," or "music of the spheres" that is behind all existence. The anahata chakra center is associated with the air element as well as touch and hands-on action. The heart chakra is the individual's center of love, compassion, empathy, and forgiveness. If this chakra is blocked, it is usually due to a predominance of negativity, spite, mistrust, hatred, or ill will in your life. If these emotions are not effectively managed—going into therapy can help this process—then you may succumb to stress, worry, depression and low energy levels. The heart symbolizes the "core" of our being (*cor* means heart in Latin). The heart is our moral center, and a certain purity of heart has been attained by the fourth initiation. When this chakra is balanced, the spiritual student is able to make decisions, or to "follow one's heart," outside of the karmic limitations of the three lower chakras. Decisions can now be made based on the *intuited* guidance of Self (Soul) and not merely on the desires and emotions of the lower nature.

Interestingly, recent scientific research suggests that there exists "a little brain in the heart." The heart's nervous system is made up of about 40,000 neurons called sensory neurites which communicate with the brain. The heart is said to have its own nervous system with long and short term memory.[6] "Great ideas come from the heart," declared the French philosopher Blaise Pascal.[7]

Dr. J. Louis Armour, at the University of Montreal, states, "An understanding of the complex anatomy and function of the heart's nervous system contributes…to the newly emerging view of the heart as a sophisticated information processing center, functioning not only in concert with the brain but also independent of it."[8] In a videotaped interview,[9] author Gregg Braden shared that these neurites formulate a singular "language of the heart," learned from birth by the Kogi, an indigenous group living in the Sierra Nevada mountains of Colombia. Infants are kept in relative isolation with a minimum of external stimuli so that "they must first interpret the world through the heart," only later entering the outer world to learn via the logic of the brain. Braden remarks that these specialized cells in the heart think, feel, and remember independently of the cranial brain. This makes it imperative that we cultivate a harmonious relationship between the heart and brain to create an extended neural network. This relationship will assist us to build the resilience needed to navigate the tumultuous currents of personal and social change that we are presently facing.

Science is beginning to prove what many indigenous cultures, such as Native Americans, have said all along, that the heart organ is intelligent. In his autobiography, *Memories, Dreams and Reflections*, Carl Jung wrote about his 1932 encounter with the Native American Chief Ochwiay Biano ("Mountain Lake"), an elder of the Taos Pueblo Tribe in New Mexico. Jung quoted part of their conversation, including Mountain Lake's assessment of the white man:

> "…how cruel the whites are: their lips are thin, their noses sharp, their faces furrowed and distorted by folds. Their eyes have a staring expression; they are always seeking something. What are they seeking? The whites always want something; they are

*always uneasy and restless. We do not know what they want, we do not understand them, we think that they are mad."*

Jung asked him why he thought the whites were all mad. "They say they think with their heads," Chief Mountain Lake replied. Surprised, Jung asked, "Why, of course. What do you think with?" Mountain Lake responded, "We think here," indicating his heart.[10]

## THE FOURTH OR MENTAL PLANE

> *...a point of entrance into a new life for which all the past has been a preparation.*
> ~ Alice A. Bailey

> *The dualistic nature of thought is at the root of our suffering.*
> ~ Jack Kornfield

The Fourth, or Mental Plane, is the last of the "lower planes" encompassing polarity/duality. The planes above the Fourth are pure spiritual worlds of oneness (which begin with the Fifth Plane or Plane of Self-Realization). On the Fourth Plane, philosophy, ethics, moral teachings, and intellectual functions dominate. Great spiritual masters of orthodox or traditional religions (who have once been incarnate on Earth) have their residence on this plane. The "Om" or "Aum" sounds originates on this plane, and, along with the color blue, the sound of running water identifies this plane. Intuition is associated with the Etheric Plane, which is the highest level of the Mental Plane and is represented by the colors violet-purple and the sound similar to the buzzing of bees.

The Fourth Initiation emphasizes higher thought processes, illuminated by Spirit, and most particularly, the development of *intuition*. As perplexing as it might sound, the purpose of what is popularly known as the intellect is *to show you its own limits*. When I was young, I thought that when someone was gifted intellectually, that person was also closer to being a spiritually-awakened being. I came to realize that instead, the intellect can sometimes be a significant *block* to spiritual receptivity. "Intellectual pride" is frequently to blame. In Western culture, we have developed our thinking processes to a great degree, though they are still largely tied to the lower mind and are primarily influenced by the ego. (A great many of us continue to be ruled by the emotions.) The next evolution for Western society is to develop the higher mind or *intuition*. (One great way of cultivating the latter is to work with dreams, meditate, and engage in creative activities).

The brain is *not* the mind. The mind is often considered the center of human consciousness, which was once thought to only exist as a consequence of brain function. Scientific evidence now suggests that although the brain may be the primary hardware of our thought processes, the mind as software is not limited to the confines of our skulls. Dr. Dan Siegel of the UCLA School of Medicine, believes that the mind extends beyond our bodies and is both our perception of life *and* life itself. He defines mind as an "emergent self-organizing process, both embodied and relational, that regulates energy and information flow within and among us."[11]

This is literally outside of the box thinking! Dr. Siegel and others, through cutting-edge science, are shifting our perceptions of the mind and its capabilities. Practitioners and pundits of many spiritual paths, however, have argued for thousands of years that our thoughts are "things," and that they often intrude upon us from outside of ourselves (for example, wide-spread psychic waves of fear or anger, can "infect" us, especially during large disasters or wars, if we are not alert to their influence). We affect others with our thoughts (most of you have had the experience of thinking of someone just before you unexpectedly meet them at a restaurant or hear from them on your cell phone). Making an effort to monitor—and to purify—your own thought processes (you can self-correct as you go) is to make important progress on the spiritual path while helping the world at large.

Generally, the activity of the mind is governed by intentionality (thoughts, desires, beliefs, and hopes) which is directed by the ego. The ego wants to collect information or knowledge, in order to "conquer" and control the environment and others within it. The fourth initiation is a movement toward developing true wisdom (which is beyond mere knowledge). When we move into higher mind (or higher-order thinking), it requires that we do more than memorize information or facts. We must understand them, make inferences, connect these facts to other facts and concepts, put them together in novel ways, and then apply them to find new solutions to new problems. (Great mathematicians and scientists—as well as architects and artists—were once always initiates of some degree).

Along with higher-order thinking, we are learning to use our *intuition* to discern the guidance of Soul; we might suddenly just "know" the information or understand the inner meaning and significance of a situation without first having to follow a convoluted thinking process. Most of you know of scientists, inventors, musicians, and others who, after much research and effort, had a flash of intuition that gave them the solution for which they had been looking. (Or in some cases, they were gifted entire musical pieces, formulas, poems or stories—but in all cases, the material was related to their interests, skills, and vocations in some way.)[12]

When we center ourselves in the heart, looking for the deepest aspects of our being, we start to explore the "interior" of ourselves and to de-emphasize the "exterior" world. In this way, we bypass the usual "conquering" attitude of the ego-mind and become receptive, contemplative, and yielding. By the fourth initiation, the *quality* of our thinking has changed because now thinking has been *informed by the heart*.

# TASKS

## A SECOND DARK NIGHT

> *I am told God lives in me —*
> *and yet the reality of darkness and coldness and emptiness*
> *is so great that nothing touches my soul.*
> ~ **Mother Teresa of Calcutta**

Because we are making a clear break from the influence of the lower bodies at this stage of initiation, there is usually much suffering. Another long and troubling *Dark Night of the Soul* usually occurs at this stage. This second "trough of despond" may be made even more intense with, for instance, the stripping away of a steady job or secure housing. The initiate feels humiliated by his or her apparent failures; finances are uncertain; friends are lost; former supporters seem to vanish; family members seem disappointed or distant. Reverses seem the order of the day. It feels that all of our hard work on ourselves has come to nothing. These experiences intensify the initiate's renunciation of illusion, of the false ego, and selfishness (our *my-ness*). Renunciation is of the mind (Swami Vivekananda), as the real suffering at this stage is mental. As Jung pointed out, every step closer to the Self is a defeat for the ego.

During the Dark Night, the initiate enters into *The Great Separation*, where the individual is seemingly devoid of support without and feeling apart from God within. This is often experienced as being in a vast and arid desert. Feeling cut off from life or on its outlying fringes, initiates are desperately alone and lonely, often feeling isolated, defeated, weak, and betrayed. You may feel as if your life has withered and dried up, much as these clients have reported: A male client dreamed that the well-tended lawn in front of his house had yellowed and died; a woman recounted a dream in which she had returned to her once fully-furnished house to find it barren and empty; a third person dreamed that she was a ghost, wandering without hope, unseen and ignored by all she met. In my journal at this time, I wrote an entry that perfectly illustrates the type of suffering that can be experienced during this stage.

> "I have been distressed this weekend, primarily over my seemingly stalled and fruitless life. I have so much pent-up longing for a more meaningful life that it is actually physically painful. I am depressed and in limbo, wondering if I am dead or alive. Everything is barren, dried up, and lifeless. When I lay down to rest, I saw clearly with my inner vision the words, 'Blind faith.' This means that I must trust my process and particularly Spirit; that whatever happens is for my very best, although I do not see it now."

Mother Theresa of Calcutta experienced this type of Dark Night. She wrote, "When I try to raise my thoughts to heaven, there is such convicting emptiness that those very thoughts return like sharp knives and hurt my very soul." Mother Teresa lived a great deal of her spiritual life in what she described as a spiritual desert; the more she was publicly adulated, the more she felt abandoned and forgotten by God. Mother Teresa lamented, " …there is that separation, that terrible emptiness, that feeling of absence of God," which she summed up as a "continual longing."[13] We can surmise from the ache of longing we suffer as exiles in the wasteland that God is, in truth, pulling us ever closer; I read somewhere in Rumi's works that God *is* the longing.

# PRIDE

*If you want to touch the sky, better learn how to kneel.*
~ **Bono**

Pride is a quality of mind. It is closely linked to vanity. It is also related to trickster energy (think of the axiom, "Pride goeth before a fall"). Trickster energy teaches us not to take ourselves too seriously. Just when we think we are putting ourselves forward as a superior authority, expert, specialist, adept, or as a spokesperson, the trickster pops in. Trickster energy works to openly question, disrupt, mock, or humiliate us. It's interesting to note that the words, *humiliation* and *humble,* come from the same root word; both words are related to *humus*, or soil (being brought "back down to earth").

Trickster energy can seem something outside of ourselves, but it is actually working from within us! For example, when I was young and giving talks at conferences and putting on workshops, I would sometimes stumble over a word and mispronounce it. (I only *read* complex words in books as a child and rarely heard them spoken). During the events when I mispronounced a word, I would feel deep embarrassment, especially if I was publicly corrected. I am sure now that this "safety measure" of mispronunciation was pre-set to occur whenever intellectual pride reared its ugly head. The trickster energy (which was actually a part of *myself)* was at work to stem and chastise the quality of pride in my character.

In his spiritual autobiography, *Hidden Journey*, Andrew Harvey[14] recognized that the worst trait in his character was pride. A devotee of Mother Meera,[15] Harvey was cautioned, at a certain point in his spiritual work, not to discuss his spiritual process or progress with others. To share his experiences and insights might arouse in other devotees feelings of jealousy, scorn, or confusion. At first resentful and angry at being censured, Harvey later recognized that his "longing to enthuse others with the beauty of what I was being shown could mask a secret desire to impress, or even to humiliate them by the difference between the passion of my experience… and theirs." He realized that this could "veil a desire for spiritual power that was dangerous…"[16]

Pride is very subtle, and it slyly creeps up on you, sometimes without your noticing! When on the Initiatory Path, you are quickly alerted—via a dream, in a message from the Teacher, a comment made by someone you respect, or through an event in your outer life. In fact, the higher on the Ladder of Initiation you rise, the more promptly you are faced with the results of what you think, do, or say. I sometimes say that the Path of Initiation "thrashes" or beats these things out of us through numerous recurrences of humiliations and hardships over the years, but as long as we are in the physical body, some imperfections will remain. Be prepared, then, for the trickster spirit to occasionally present you with a "stone of stumbling" when you have gone astray in your attitude or approach, especially toward others!

## DISILLUSIONMENT

*Wisdom comes from disillusionment.*
~ **George Santayana**

Disillusionment is necessary to our psychological and spiritual maturity.[17] Disillusionment occurs when we have put our hopes on something to fulfill us that is *outside of ourselves*, and we are disappointed when it fails to do so. This can take the form of disappointment in love, betrayal by a close friend, or a letdown by the boss when a promotion we worked hard for is awarded to someone else. Disappointment can also be a loss or a perceived failure: loss of a job, money, prestige, or position. When we experience profound disillusionment, we see things more as they really are and less as we want them to be.

Disillusionment is incorporated into the rites of passage of indigenous peoples such as the Ndembu tribe in Africa, the Hopi Indians of North America, and the Wiradthuri tribe in Australia. In a ceremony of the Ndembu of Africa, novices were once inducted into the tribe's healing cult by being led into the jungle where they were brought before an intimidating shape, which was identified by the elders as Davula, the totem spirit of the cult. They were instructed to beat on the shape with sticks to kill it. Soon afterwards, the would-be healers were shown that the "spirit" was constructed out of a cloth and wooden form, under which certain spiritual adepts had been hiding.

Similarly, the Hopis unmasked kachinas during initiation rites to reveal to young novices that these "gods" were actually fellow members of their tribe. The Wiradthuri, an indigenous tribe in Australia, told their youth tales of the great spirit, Dhuramoolan, whose terrifying voice was later revealed to the frightened initiates as only a bull roarer, a ritual instrument made of wood and leather.[18] In this way, formerly naïve or childish views of reality were released so that the initiands were brought into a deeper, more thoughtful appreciation of the spiritual realities underlying all life. A one-dimensional literalism was destroyed by disenchantment so that individuals were stunned and shaken into seeking the mystery *behind* the things of the physical world.

Like the initiands in their tribal rites of passage, a modern person is sometimes shaken out of an easy complacency and gullibility by the experience of disenchantment. A disastrous disappointment can suddenly launch the individual toward seeking a spiritual life, to find something to believe in that is authentic and true. P. D. Ouspensky writes that his spiritual teacher Gurdjieff, before he enlisted new students, insisted that:

> *"...people must be disappointed, first of all in in themselves, that is to say, in their power, and secondly, in all the old ways...A man... if he is a scientist should be disappointed science. If he is a religious man, he should be disappointed in religion...and so on."*[19]

One of my young clients dreamed that in the sky above her, she witnessed a hawk swiftly dive to attack a pure white bird, dealing instant death by breaking the smaller bird's neck with its beak. In the days before this dream, she had been thinking of how hard the "real" world was now that she had finally begun working in her profession in the health field. She was hearing from her patients how much pain they were in and about the many difficulties they were facing in their daily lives. Her realization was that the world is often a dog-eat-dog (or bird-eat-bird) place, and that she could no longer live as naively (the white bird of innocence) as she once had.

With the Fourth Initiation, the illusions we have clung to for so long have loosened their grip. We now know that we want Truth at any cost. **At this stage, we are sure that the things of the physical world will never satisfy our deepest longing, which was always a yearning for God.**

# ALIENATION

> *All separation, every kind of estrangement*
> *and alienation is false. All is one.*
> ~ **Nisargadatta Maharaj**

At times (and not only during the fourth initiation), the Initiate feels alienated, apart, disgusted, or even cynical about national and world events and the people who create them. When we are chronically cynical, we are generally distrustful of others, and we have a lack of faith or hope in people, especially those who seem to be only motivated by ambition, greed, or materialism. During the early part of the 2020s, a feeling of cynicism was hard to escape in the face of disappointing politicians, unsatisfactory working conditions, sky-rocketing prices for basic needs, a worldwide pandemic, dangerous social divisions, global conflicts and wars, just to name a few challenges to our equilibrium. Becoming cynical, however, leads to feelings of being "a stranger in a strange land," and to the conviction that others, by their limited attitudes and opinions, are living in a prison of their own making. At a certain stage in her process, Irina Tweedie complained to her Teacher that "I seem to hate everything and everybody—hating them thoroughly and completely. Everyone seems to be disagreeable, ugly, even horrible. A constant irritation...I seem to have become barren and arid."[20] Tweedie's Teacher, Bhai Sahib, reassured her that this was a difficult stage, but one that would pass.

Once when Ram Dass was at the Kainchi Ashram with his guru, Neem Karoli Baba, or Maharaji-ji, he became irritated that he was sharing the guru's time with a group of young Americans who were getting on his nerves. He angrily thought to himself, "I have spent too much time outwardly pretending to love everyone. Inside, my mind is full of anger." The guru called him over and said, "Ram Dass, is something troubling you?" Ram Dass said, "Yes... I can't stand impurities. I can't stand all those people, and I can't stand myself. I only love you. I hate everybody else." Then he broke into sobs. Maharaji consoled Ram Dass and reminded him that he was to love everyone. Ram Dass knew he had to swallow his righteousness and pride. He sliced an apple into thin pieces, and sitting before each person, looked steadily and deeply into their eyes until he found a place within them that he could love. After feeding them all, there was no more anger. He realized that he could quickly release anger if he first relinquished the expectations of how he thought things (and people) were supposed to be.[21]

Feeling alienated is the opposite of feeling at-one-with, and these polar states often alternate along the Labyrinthine Way. Intermittent downloads of spiritual energies (illumination) sometimes bring us to a sense of the nearness with God; at these times, we have no doubt that God is on the field.²² When we no longer feel this close connection, however, we can feel estranged, lonely, and bereft. (If we experienced abandonment as a child, the suffering is felt even more intensely.)

It is important to remember that periods of purification and intervals of spiritual inspiration are complementary to each other; as we ascend the Path in spirals, we pass through a succession of these alternating states, but each time at a higher level. (The Teacher can purposely induce these states for our spiritual benefit, if necessary). During the disengagement phases, the initiate feels alienated from his or her *own* Beingness—and so, from life itself. In truth, *any* period of alienation stems from a primal feeling of being separated from (or abandoned by) God, not unlike being ejected from the Garden.²³ At some point, the spiritual student is rescued out of the wilderness (touched on earlier with Rick's "desert" experience). After a long and desolate period of aridity, a numinous spiritual experience may occur. Edward Edinger writes about this:

> *"The classic symbol for alienation is the image of the wilderness. And it is here, characteristically, that some manifestation of God is encountered. When the wanderer lost in the desert is about to perish, a source of divine nourishment appears."*²⁴

Sometimes this divine encounter is experienced through a powerful dream, one that catapults the initiate into greater consciousness and a new orientation toward life. An older woman client (who was postmenopausal) had the following dream:

> *"I was having painful and insistent birth contractions, with no doctor available and no medication. I could actually feel the sensation of the contractions in my physical body, even inside of my dream. The intensity of the contractions indicated to me that the time was near for giving birth. I could trace the outlines of*

*the baby's body underneath my skin A seeress told me that the baby would be a male, with a Leo astrological sign."*

The client had worked for many years to integrate conflicting parts of her inner landscape, resulting in the psychological birth of a new level of awareness. In modern persons, this is often symbolized in dreams by the birth of a baby, a baby born of Spirit. In Christian terms, this baby is the Christ Child; in the old art of alchemy, the babe was known as the Philosopher's Child; and in Sufism, this fruit of spiritual progress is called the Child of the Heart. This Child of Meaning is symbolic of God's manifestation in that form.

To give birth to the Self is to give birth to the King or the Sun (which is the ruler of the astrological sign of Leo), all synonyms for the Self. Leo equates to a strong will to persevere through any suffering when walking the Lion Path of the Heart. But instead of seeking to rule over others, the Fourth Initiate strives to rule over self (ego). At the Fourth Initiation, the personal will is given over to the will of God or Higher Purpose. The true Director of the Initiate's life is the Self or Soul, which now utilizes the mind for its own purposes (and communicates via *intuition*). At the Fourth Initiation, Leonine individuality has been fully developed, but rather than being used for selfish or self-centered reasons, the radiant consciousness is now consecrated to divine purpose.

The elevation of consciousness ushered in with the birth of the True Self can produce greater efficiency, direction, and focus to daily life and work. There is a heightened sense of being part of a greater plan and a desire to be of service to others. The heart has opened to compassion for all life, what Buddhists call the "quivering of the pure heart." And so, if the Initiate is patient, the overwhelming sense of alienation, a separative attitude, and cynicism eventually give way to a rapprochement with others. The initiate at this level is able to achieve one of the greater goals of initiation: to love and accept others without judgment or blame. This is a compassionate acceptance of the hidden beauty in others, even when they act counter to this secret magnificence or do not recognize it in themselves. Thomas Merton, the American Trappist monk, writer, and theologian, wrote about an experience that induced in him a greater recognition of his own humanity and connectedness to others:

> *"In Louisville, at the corner of Fourth and Walnut, in the center of the shopping district, I was suddenly overwhelmed with the realization that I loved all those people, that they were mine and I theirs, that we could not be alien to one another even though we were total strangers…The sense of liberation from the illusory difference was such a relief and such a joy to me that I almost laughed out loud…thank God, thank God that I am like other men, that I am only a man among others.…Then it was as if I suddenly saw the secret beauty of their hearts, the depths of their hearts…the core of their being, the person that each one is in God's eyes. If only they could see themselves as they really are. If only we could see each other that way all the time. There would be no more war, no more hatred, no more greed."*[25]

## SUMMARY: THE GREAT TRANSITION

*This is practical religion: Renounce the lower*
*so you may get the higher.*
~ **Swami Vivekananda**

The Fourth Stage of Initiation is called the *Renunciation* in the Eastern spiritual traditions, and in the West, it has been known as the *Crucifixion*. This initiation is so named because it is very difficult, as the initiate's whole being must become centered in Self or Soul. To point out once again, in this book, the Self (with a capital "S") is interchangeable with Soul, and represents the realized wholeness as well as the sacred center of the human being. Full consciousness of the Self is achieved at the Fifth Initiation, the stage of Self-Realization. From the Third to the Fourth Stage of Initiation, we begin to align ourselves directly with the Self, as the Causal Body is no longer needed and is sloughed off. The Causal Body is also known as the Higher Self or Solar Angel. The Higher Self has served us as an intermediary between the ego-self and Soul for eons of time. We subjectively experience the dissolution of the Causal Body as a loss, a suffering, and a defeat. We are now directly guided by the Self. Through suffering and "renunciation," the initiate has become free of the influence of the lower worlds while continuing to live within them. Succeeding in this initiation brings a great victory, as in some initiatory systems, it offers the individual freedom from the cycle of rebirth.

At the Fourth Initiation, we understand why this Initiation has been identified in the West as the Crucifixion. This stage marks a transition period, a limbo state following the death of a previous life orientation and preceding the birth of a new one. Irina Tweedie aptly describes the Crucifixion experience:

> *"...what is done is in reality a crucifixion—the burning away of the self, the supreme final sacrifice, mentioned in all the Myths, in all the Sagas...It is the story of the final giving up of the personality, the great drama of all the ages."* [3]

When we are nailed to the cross, so to speak, we accept the transforming power of suffering. For the ego, crucifixion is a paralyzing suspension as the divine and the ego-self are braced in a tension of the opposites. The four points of the cross equate to the four elements and psychologically, to the four functions (sensation, feeling, thinking, and intuition).[4] At every level of initiation, these aspects of our being have been differentiated, examined, and purified (usually through tears, tests, and trials).[5] This includes the lower self in regard to our physical, emotional, and lower mental bodies. The cross symbolizes the *sacrifice of the ego-self* for the sake of the Self. The Self or the Divine must become *conscious in the individual as life energy.*

We have died to the lower self (surrendered) so that Soul consciousness can incarnate. Once our lower nature is crucified, we are able to live the possibility of being in the world but not of the world. With time, we realize that our Cross of Crucifixion has become the Tree of Life.

## THE FIFTH INITIATION: SELF-REALIZATION

*Self-Realization. Soul recognition.*
*The entering of Soul into the Soul Plane*
*and there beholding itself as pure Spirit.*
*A state of seeing, knowing, and being.*
**~ Harold Klemp**

*In these five episodes the whole story of initiation is told:*
*birth; subsequent purification*
*in order that right manifestation of Deity may follow;*
*revelation of the nature of God through the medium of a transfigured personality;*
*and finally, the goal—life eternal and unending*
*because decentralized and freed*
*from the self-imposed limitations of form.*
**~ Alice Bailey**

## THE REVELATION

*One who explores and knows all aspects of his life,*
*is called Self-Realized.*
**~ Sadhguru**

At the Fifth Stage on the Path of Initiation, the mind is now under control. All opposites, all dualities are now unified. This Stage brings Self-Realization. It is a unity that is so all embracing that it has no opposite. The "revelation" at this level refers to the fact that the initiate is now polarized in the spiritual state and recognizes that all life below this level is an illusion. There is little that can occur that will unbalance the Initiate at this level; the Center of the Self-Realized individual has become something solid and unshakeable. That is why the Self has been long symbolized by the alchemist's Philosopher's Stone (or lapis) or as the Diamond Self. Soul or Self now illuminates and guides the personality.

> "Man consists only of Soul...He is Soul but has not yet recognized this. Soul is a spark of the divine ECK [Spirit]. It has... perception of eternity through inner sight, hearing, and knowing, but mainly knowingness...It recognizes or realizes Its relationship with God through God-Realization, Self-Realization, and Mind-Realization...It is the ECK Itself." [26]

The inner essence, the spark of divinity which is of God, is hidden (as it exists on a higher level) until the spiritual seeker begins to walk the Labyrinthine Path. The spiritual potential within all humans becomes Truth with the Birth of the Divine Self, which matures at the Fifth Initiation into Self-Realization (and later, at a higher initiation level, into God-Realization). The Fifth Initiate now lives in both the material and spiritual worlds and is able to coordinate a dual consciousness. The perspective has been reversed from a primary orientation in the material worlds to an absolute alignment with Soul; all things appear in a new light and perception. Everything can now be evaluated from the position of Soul consciousness so that the Initiate has access to inner truth, a plumbline by which to evaluate all things.

The Fifth Initiate knows his or her mission and purpose. At this level, there is no need to incarnate to gather additional Earth experience, which produces the awareness of ultimate freedom. This freedom also derives from an independence from the glamours, illusions, and delusions of the lower worlds. The unconscious has been made conscious, so that the individual is released from what were formerly unconscious emotional reactions as well as from psychological limitations. The following parable illustrates this sense of simplicity and ease with oneself:

> *After his enlightenment, the Buddha met a man on the road who was awestruck by his preternatural light and peaceful demeanor. The man asked Buddha, "Excuse me, but are you a celestial being or a god?" "No," calmly answered the Buddha. "Well then, the man sputtered, "Are you a great sage or saint?" Again, the Buddha answered, "No."*
>
> *"Are you a human being?" The man was really becoming a bit frightened. As before, the response was, "No." "Well, then," said the man in exasperation, "What are you?"*
>
> *The Buddha quietly replied, "I am awake."*

The Initiate may decide to volunteer at some point to execute an assignment within the lower planes. The Self-Realized person desires to work practically and systematically for the entire human race as well as other beings in the lower worlds. The Fifth Initiate has "won that most splendid of all rights, the right to help,"[27] whether in secret or in public. But there are other, higher planes of God to achieve, and the goal of *God*-Realization beckons ahead.

## THE THROAT CHAKRA

> *The throat chakra is the toll booth between the emotions and the mind.*
> **~ Kristen Leal**

As previously pointed out, more than one chakra is stimulated at the various initiations. The throat chakra (Vishuddha), is important at this stage, but the anja and crown chakras are activated as well. Throat chakra qualities include authenticity, purity, truthfulness, clarity, and idealism. When your throat chakra is blocked or unbalanced, you may have issues with creativity and communication. Fear of rejection and criticism can block the free expression of this chakra. (Some people remember being persecuted in previous lives for speaking their truth and are now reluctant to make their thoughts known). Inspiration and self-expression are enhanced via an open and balanced throat chakra, which is located at the center of the larynx. It symbolizes seeking and speaking the truth, not only outwardly but also our internal communication with our true Self. When this chakra is balanced, we are able to listen to our Inner Guide and we can also listen to and understand others.

# THE FIFTH PLANE

> *True knowledge is not attained by thinking.*
> *It is what you are; it is what you become.*
> ~ **Sri Aurobindo & The Mother**

The Fifth Plane is also known as the Soul Plane, and is the first plane that is of pure, positive spirit (no polarity or duality exists here). The Fifth Plane of Pure Spirit is the demarcation between the lower and the higher worlds, between the psychic and the spiritual regions. The factors of time and space do not exist on this Plane. Characteristics that distinguish this plane include its golden or light yellow color and the sound of a single note of a flute.

Most importantly, the Fifth Plane is the plane of Self-Realization. There are higher planes and additional initiations, but reaching Self-Realization is the current goal for all humanity. The achievement of the Self-Realized individual is really an accomplishment for all humans, as humanity as a whole is uplifted. The Path is made more accessible and the pilgrimage of each seeker is shortened. The Earth itself is helped to progress and advance in consciousness.

We know for certain at this initiation that we were *never* apart from God, even though we spent lifetimes crying in the wilderness as lost, prodigal daughters and sons. **Since we ourselves are part of the God-Matrix, we could never be separated.** The duality we imagined was never so; this is beautifully expressed by Irina Tweedie:

> "We think that the relationship to God and man is a duality. There is God and there is the man who will pray to God to ask for something, or who will worship, or love, or praise God. There are always two. But this is not so. I have found that the relationship to God is something quite different. It is a merging, without words, without thought even...into something. Something so tremendous, so endless, merging in infinite love...physical body and all, disappearing in it. And the physical body...is taut like a string in this process of annihilation. This is our experience of God and it cannot be otherwise." [28]

## SOUL RECOGNITION

> *Our own self-realization is the greatest service*
> *we can render the world.*
>
> ~ **Ramana Marharshi**

When I was in graduate school in psychology, I was captivated by the idea of becoming self-actualized. This is the word for Self-Realization that was popularized by psychologist Abraham Maslow and is frequently used in the humanistic-existential school of psychology. I remember one of my male professors, obviously besotted with the guest speaker he had invited for that night's class session, introducing her as a "truly self-actualized" person. I thought to myself, "If only I could develop Maslow's list of qualities, then *I* could be a self-actualized individual!" Some of these qualities include good judgment, tolerance and open mindedness, self-reliance and autonomy, comfort with solitude, profound relationships, and a sense of oneness with humanity.[29]

In many ways, Maslow was describing the Initiate at the Fifth Initiation of Self-Realization. But there is an important difference: While many persons can strive to develop the traits listed by Maslow, Self-Realization is never something that can be striven for by adding or subtracting certain behaviors via the lower self (or by simply being or doing "good").[30] Maslow is essentially describing growth and maturation merely on the psychological level, including the development of latent potentialities (even though he does point out that many self-actualized persons have had "peak experiences" of a spiritual nature). Self-Realization is the realization of the Self, and is only achieved by a long and difficult transformation of the individual in every way. Never perfect, the Fifth Initiate nevertheless expresses many of the qualities of an advanced personality, which *emanate naturally* out of the transformative evolution generated by the initiation process. There is no need to tell others how special they are as a Fifth Initiate, but rather to help *others* realize their own specialness. The personality at this stage is now built around the Self and not the ego; the Fifth Initiate has become a Self- or Soul-guided person.

Generally speaking, it's important to note that for all of the spiritual achievements attained at the Fifth Initiation, Self-Realized persons, though centered in Soul, sometimes continue to exhibit ego-related faults and frailties. They still suffer for their own shortcomings. However, when childhood issues rise to the surface, they usually recognize them at work and waylay them before damage is done. They are bent on "enlivening" others, to help people feel good about who they are and what they are doing in life. If anyone has been hurt by something that Fifth Initiates have said or done, they acutely feel the other's pain and try to make reparations. They strive to stay even-keeled. It's important to note that, unless their mission specifies otherwise, Self-Realized persons blend into everyday life and do not put themselves forward. There is always something new to learn and new spiritual horizons ahead—and there is never any doubt that the Fifth Initiate's sole (or Soul) purpose is to be a channel (conduit) for God in the everyday world.

## TASKS

## HOMESICKNESS

> *Spiritual yearning is the homesickness of the soul.*
> ~ Ma Jaya Sati Bhagavati

> *Destiny is what every human being creates for himself.*
> *Fate is when you fail to create your own destiny.*
> ~ Sadhguru

Rabbi Seymour Sigel declares that, "In everyone's heart stirs a great homesickness." This longing for home, especially on the Labyrinthine Path, creates a special kind of loneliness. Loneliness has been one of the most difficult existential issues that I've personally dealt with over the years. Once, I asked my Inner Master about this loneliness, and I was told that it's the "Eagle's Disease." I interpreted this to mean that as a person climbs higher on the Ladder of Initiation, the longing for one's true home intensifies. Many of us have experienced, "hiraeth," a Welsh word (pronounced *here-eyeth* with a rolling "r") that refers to a deep-felt spiritual longing, yearning, and wistfulness for a home beyond this plane of existence. It is the echo of something once known and lost somewhere in time, a bittersweet memory that is embedded in the wind, the rocks, the ocean—but primarily, in our hearts. This is the homesickness of Soul, which pines for its spiritual home.

While Irina Tweedie was in spiritual training with her Sufi Master, she experienced a longing in the "very depth" of her heart that was almost cruel in its intensity. She recognized the feeling of profound longing as identical to the yearning she had suffered since childhood. Irina professed that this endless sadness was "like a homesickness. A great yearning. Homesickness for our Real Home? For the Home of all of us, human beings, and the Home of everything else, as well, in this universe…"[31]

Currently, there is a quest to find a solitary whale that has been recorded singing at the pitch of 52 hertz, an anomaly, since whales commonly sing in the range of 10-40 hertz. The whale has been dubbed "The Loneliest Whale in the World" and "The 52 Hertz Whale." Its lonely cries were originally heard by an ocean-wide system of hydrophones once used by the U.S. military to detect Soviet submarines, which are currently being put to use by marine biologists. This whale's lonely song has been picked up in the Northern Pacific Ocean, but after nearly three decades of searching, the whale itself has not yet been located. No whale has ever responded to its call. Books, poems, music (such as the song, *Whalien 52*, by the K-pop band BTS) and a documentary film[32] have been created based on this unknown, wandering whale. People all over the globe are responding to the loneliness that they imagine must be the fate of a communal pod mammal whose call is never answered. They see their own loneliness and longing for their real home in the story of the loneliest whale in the world.

The day we were born, says Rumi, a ladder was set up to help us escape from this world. Some of us, in this lifetime, will make our way up this ladder to our Real Home, and others will climb the ladder on another turn of the Wheel of Fate during another cycle of life, death, and reincarnation. We're all captives of destiny until we become conscious that we are—and make the decision to earn our way to spiritual freedom. In India, a widespread belief is that at a child's birth, a deity visits to write the newborn's destiny upon its forehead. (There are many Indian folk tales that relate how individuals with courage and wit can outfox this fate). Similar beliefs are encountered in the Balkan countries, such as Greece, Bulgaria, and Albania. Some Sufis claim that the placement of certain moles or birthmarks on the body indicate whether the individual will grow to be spiritually-oriented or more worldly. Throughout the Christian Bible, there are passages that refer to the "seal" or "mark" of either good or evil, usually found on the forehead or the hand. Some Masters have a single letter marked on their foreheads, indicating a particular line of spiritual work. The Spiral Path of Initiation is the process of breaking free (psychologically) from family expectations, cultural traditions, religious dogma, social rules, and gender constraints; to live within these limitations are the fates commonly inscribed on human foreheads or etched into the lines of their hands. However, some are "marked" for a different destiny; they are called to become pilgrims on the Royal Road to Home, leaving their earth-bound histories and affiliations behind. Separating from a worldly destiny in order to find God brings with it the ultimate loneliness; but if, as Rumi says, this exceptional loneliness is more precious than life, then the loneliness of returning Home to the Ocean of Love and Mercy can be endured—and even celebrated.

## UNION

*The human body is the temple of God.*
*One who kindles the light of awareness within gets true light.*
*The sacred flame of your inner shrine is constantly bright.*
*The experience of unity is the fulfillment of human endeavors.*
*The mysteries of life are revealed.*
~ **The Rig Veda**

*Spiritual marriage consisted in the feminine force*
*or feeling uniting with the masculine force or reason*
*and thus, becoming whole in oneness with God.*
*The souls that went out of God were to be brought back to God*
*by the process of harmony in body, mind, and soul.*
~ **Paramahansa Yogananda**

One my clients, Marcy, a deeply spiritual woman in the last third of her life, had the following dream:

> "I was getting married to a man in dress white military uniform. I told him before the wedding ceremony that all the women guests had their eyes on him, as 'women love men who are in uniform!' We were marrying in an outdoor setting, and the trellis under which we would stand for the service was garlanded with white gardenias. I had loads of bridesmaids, so many that I planned to have them stretch across one side of the trellis down a long walkway. There had been much preparation, including the writing of our own vows. After the ceremony, we planned to sit with family and friends at a long table, laden with a feast. I noticed that there were many of my old boyfriends at the wedding (I did not remember inviting them)."

Marcy felt that the man in the uniform had two meanings: One was a reference to the love of her life, her only husband (she was a widow of 25 years), who had served in the Navy, with a white dress uniform as part of his military attire. Secondly, Marcy was focused on being of spiritual *service* in her life, and she derived this meaning from the fact that her dream-groom was a *serviceman*. He was *in white*, she concluded, because this symbolized the "purifying power" of the many physical/emotional/mental difficulties that she had endured over the years, which had "scoured her clean." *White gardenias* symbolize "the purity of a loved one," and the *arch* not only represents the future life of the couple, but in many cultures suggest initiations and rituals of renewal, a shedding of the past while moving into a new stage of life.

Marcy interpreted the many bridesmaids as herself as a woman in many past lives, and felt that her dream marriage would symbolize the sorting out, refinement, and integration of these varied feminine energies into a working whole. She extended this reasoning to the many old boyfriends in the dream; they represented her own male incarnations as well as various masculine qualities she had encountered in men over countless lifetimes. Furthermore, "The wedding vows are my spiritual commitment to offer my wholeness to the human family, as a Co-Worker with God," Marcy explained. "The feast represents to me," Marcy added, "the bounty of God, abundant creativity, and the true fulfillment of this union."

If you have come this far in the book, you may now have an understanding that the process of initiation includes the recurrent differentiation (or "sorting out") of parts of ourselves, followed by the dissolution of some of these aspects and the purification of others, and finally, the reintegration of these aspects at a higher level of being and functioning. Jung pointed out that every gain in higher consciousness first necessitates a separation of the opposites. Again and again, the opposite forces in our consciousness, the feminine and masculine energies, are redeemed and reunited. There is always a burning away, or *death,* of the old to make way (a *rebirth)* for a greater, or higher integration. The whole process is to make us consciously at-one-with ourselves. **We find the lover within us.**

The integration or unification process segment of this ongoing cycle is often represented, as has been previously mentioned, by inner liaisons, such as sexual unions and marriages. In fact, the *inner* union is the *true* union, rendering outer physical intercourse as only a shadow of the real thing. We pine for our "other halves," or "soul mates," while living in the physical world, but the true companion is the *inner partner* who resides on a high spiritual plane. We do not feel complete until we have unified with this energy being, who is part of our own greater wholeness! The male or female we are involved with in our physical lives can be an *approximation* of the "inner partner," but is never the one, true lover that we unconsciously seek in our outer-world relationships. Some women have shared that they cry after sex, and that, despite the intimacy that was just shared, they continue to feel a profound loss and longing. After experiencing sexual union with her husband, whom she greatly loved, author Elizabeth Haich wrote:

> *"One night, after I had experienced once again the greatest fulfillment of earthly love and unity, instead of falling peacefully*

*asleep, I sat on my side of the bed for a long time brooding over my problems in abject despair. I cried and I sobbed..."*

After a lengthy soul-searching, she realized that:

*"I was searching for fulfillment of an eternal nature, a real union which remains! I was searching for a union in which the identity of myself and that of my lover became one and the same thing. I desired to participate in his soul, his thoughts, his whole being! I wanted to become him!"*

Elizabeth recognized that she has been desiring this "complete accord" or "supreme union" all of her life. She now realized such wholeness can never be found by physical means:

**"… but only in a bodiless condition.** *I long for this lost unison. I knew it, somewhere and somehow, but I lost it. Could it be possible that I loved in an immaterial state a long time ago, and that, having been born into this body, I fell out of this spiritual harmony?"*[33]

To know that the true union is a *spiritual* Inner or Mystical Marriage is an important realization during the initiation process. This awareness, however, does not mean that you cannot enjoy intimacy with a loved one or find satisfaction and happiness in your primary relationship. It *does* mean that the inner and outer realms should not be confused: For example, many people today look for *soulmates*, which refers to two separate souls who are strongly linked (usually through past-life contacts) or for *twin flames* (thought to be one soul split between two bodies) as the perfect answer to their need for a sense of completion in their outer, physical lives.[34] These theories are romantic and appealing, but our "other half" remains in the spiritual world. We are wholly energy in spirit, but only a part of our Soul can descend to the physical world to be housed in the body; the vast amount of energy and awareness of Soul would be overwhelming to the physical vessel. A good part of what takes place in the initiation process has to do with the preparation of the body to accept incremental influxes of Soul energy. Soul is therefore a subset of the Greater Spirit that unites all beingness everywhere.

Lifetime after lifetime, what we are pursuing in our deepest relationships to one another is our *own* completion. Eventually, we come to realize that the "opposite" we have been seeking has always been inside ourselves. Even as recently as the 1950s, the relationship ideal was assigned to gender roles in which one half "completed" or complemented the other; today, the mandate is to become whole *within ourselves* and to bring that wholeness to bear in our quest to find another who has reached an equivalent stage of self-unification. Currently, so many of us are at so many varied levels of wholeness that finding a physical partner can be a difficult, and sometimes seemingly impossible, pursuit (but it can be done)!

It is important to remember that each initiation is the sum total of the previous initiations, with progressive unifications. This unification goes on at all levels—emotional, mental, intuitional, and spiritual. While this process of disintegration and reintegration is ongoing, there are three significant moments of unification during the first five initiations:

- The integration of the physical, emotional, and mental parts of the Lower Self or ego-personality.
- The integration of the Lower Self (ego-personality) with the Higher Self at the Third Initiation.
- The integration with Soul or Self at the Fifth Initiation.

The integration of masculine and feminine energies at the Fifth Initiation is a great task (Jung called it the *Magnum Opus*). It encompasses the identification, purification, and reintegration of all the life experiences you have ever lived and encountered as both male and female. This culminates in the Sacred Marriage within, an inner union of the Sacred Feminine and Masculine archetypes. Wholeness, or completeness, encompasses the conciliation of the opposites, the integration of polarities, and the union of masculine and feminine energies, all synergistically working together.

## SERVICE

> *I slept and dreamt that life was joy.*
> *I awoke and saw that life was service.*
> *I acted and behold, service was joy.*
> ~ **Rabindranath Tagore**

> *There is nothing to compare with the feeling*
> *of being of service to life.*
> *Once we get into the higher states of awareness,*
> *a dramatic change takes place:*
> *Never again are we satisfied to serve only ourselves.*
> *In one way or another, we must service all life.*
> ~ **Harold Klemp**

When I looked for people to interview for my previous book, *Drinking the Dragon: Stories of the Dark Night of the Soul*, I specified that prospective participants must have experienced life-changing events which propelled them into what I characterized as "going to the bottom of their own wells," or to great depths of despair and desolation. I was looking for interviewees who had survived a descent into emotional and psychological chaos by turning toward their own spiritual center and finding support and healing in spiritual literature, prayer, contemplation, meditation, spiritual counseling, and other methods of acquiring spiritual understanding and sustenance. (These spiritual methods and practices could be traditional, alternative, or non-denominational.) Finally, I asked that they share how they had learned to help themselves as well as find ways *to be of greater service to their fellow humans,* in large ways or small. One of my interviewees, after the murder of her young son in a country embroiled in long-standing conflict, eventually opened a foundation to help families recover from war-induced trauma and loss. After the death of his wife from a brain hemorrhage, one book participant worked with men who were preparing to be coaches for the Mankind Project's The New Warrior Training. Another interviewee, following her divorce and separation from family and friends and move to another state, decided to go into the field of health and wellness.

Service is a natural outpouring of the Self-Realized human. People often think of service as "servitude," which is the opposite of the type of service the initiate has to offer others. The capacity to serve humanity has steadily increased with every initiation, and it's a joyful, willing participation and recognized *privilege* in which that the initiate can now engage. Our destiny is to become Co-Workers in the multiverse, giving of ourselves in the name of God, Who, I once heard, especially loves to be called *The Servant of Servants.*

As part of his spiritual service to humanity, Ram Dass, whose name means "Servant of God," established the Hanuman Foundation, a nonprofit service organization that created the Prison-Ashram Project (Human Kindness Foundation). He also founded the Seva Foundation, a global nonprofit eyecare organization that builds self-sustaining eye clinics which provide critical eye care for children, women, and underserved communities. But as important as his service organizations, many books, workshops, and lectures, was the quiet service he rendered in the moment of their need to troubled individuals he met along the way. When he was approached by persons wanting to talk, he would gently encourage them to unburden themselves of their deepest fears and gravest secrets, and looking into their eyes, would listen with the greatest love and attention. While he listened, Ram Dass silently repeated a mantra to help himself to instantly neutralize and release these intimacies into Spirit. He knew that just by sharing these worries and concerns, they would feel a release and lightness of being.

Being of service begins with the simple things. Being kind to someone even if they're cranky (perhaps because they *are* cranky)! Being a good listener (deep listening, without judgment, is a true gift to others). Being tolerant and forgiving. Being generous. Doing an unexpected favor for a neighbor. Sending flowers to a work colleague. Picking up food for someone else when you make a grocery store run. Dr. Steven Southwick,[35] professor of psychiatry at Yale University School of Medicine, states that small acts are important, as they help us find meaning outside of ourselves. Adam Grant,[36] an organizational psychologist at Wharton, claims that there is evidence from studies that being generous is an effective antianxiety medication. Donating money, volunteering, or helping others release brain chemicals that activate the same part of the brain that is stimulated by pleasures such as food and sex. This phenomenon has been called the "helper's high." Persons who give to others in dime or time often enjoy lower levels of stress hormones. In an ongoing study on health and well-being, Emily Greenfield,[37] an associate professor of social work at Rutgers University, found that people who held orientation toward sacrificing for others coped better with their *own* life challenges.

The service that Initiates desire to offer is a necessity for their own well-being because they can do nothing *but* serve. The psychologist Erik Erikson named the seventh state in his Stages of Psychosocial Development *Generativity vs. Stagnation/Self-Absorption.* He characterized "generativity" as the desire to give back to life by contributing to society and doing things to benefit future generations. Failure to do so would lead, he posited, to poorer health, lower quality relationships, and decreased life satisfaction.[38] Generativity—the giving of oneself—at the level of the Higher Initiate includes "little things," but also embraces large-scale plans for the advancement of all humans everywhere. There comes a time when the only thing that gives life meaning and purpose *is* to give service.

# ORDINARINESS

> *Live in a way that you are everything and you are nothing.*
> ~ **Bhai Sahib**

> *When the faith is strong enough, it is sufficient just to be.*
> *It's a journey towards simplicity, towards quietness,*
> *towards a kind of joy that is not in time.*
> *It's a journey that has taken us from primary identification*
> *with our body and our psyche,*
> *on to an identification with God,*
> *and ultimately beyond identification.*
> ~ **Ram Dass**

At the level of Self-Realization, there are special hallmarks of spiritual maturity. An important indicator is that of *ordinariness*. "Don't try to be special. If you are simply ordinary, more ordinary than others, you will become extraordinary," Sadhguru advises. Also known as *post-enlightened practice,* this is a level of maturity denoted by simplicity, authenticity, and detachment. We do not have anything to prove nor anyone to impress. We only wish to be ourselves; others can see our light if they are attuned to it, but it does not matter to us either way. This type of ordinariness imbues a Self-Realized individual with a bearing that walks lightly upon the earth and an attitude toward life that is born of trust and gratitude. Our focus is not ourselves: **The truly spiritual person is not trying to convince others how spiritual he or she is, but is focused on awakening others to how spiritual THEY are.**

Becoming ordinary is not to belittle or minimize yourself; it's the recognition that one person is not less or more than another. You recognize that you are one among many, a unique vibration in the symphony of life. A famous quote by Pope John the 23$^{rd}$ illustrates this common humanity: "It often happens that I wake up at night and begin to think about a serious problem and decide I must tell the Pope about it. Then I wake up completely and remember that I *am* the Pope." It helps to know that we have lived many, many lives, and that for every Emperor, Pope, Queen, or King that we've been, we've lived hundreds of lives as farmers, indentured servants, and low-level functionaries—in other words, as everyday people. We actually go through a complete cycle during our total existence up to the Fifth Plane: We begin as simple, undeveloped, and dimly conscious individuals to becoming conscious, ego-centered individualities to evolving into fully conscious, Self-Realized spiritual beings.[39] At this latter stage, we are once again challenged to become simple, artless, and genuine, but in a completely conscious, detached, and Self-guided way.

## SUMMARY: THE OCEAN OF LOVE AND MERCY

*In the beginning there is struggle and a lot of work*
*for those who come near to God.*
*But after that, there is indescribable joy.*
*It is just like building a fire: at first, it's smoky and your eyes water,*
*but later, you get the desired results.*
*Thus, we ought to light the divine fire in ourselves with tears and effort.*
~ **Amma Syncletica**

There is always another step to take in the spiritual life. In some systems of initiation, the Inner Beloved is not fully married and merged with until the Seventh Initiation (and that two more initiations after the Fifth Stage are necessary to fully activate the ajna and crown chakra centers). It is only at the Seventh, some say, that we see our True Image face-to-face. Our "spark of God" has become star-like. Our own accomplishments on the Labyrinthine Path can now act as templates and accelerants for this eventual achievement by all humankind in the future. *All* beings on all planes, dimensions and planets are moving toward the Ocean of Love and Mercy where the Divine dwells. It is here that we find out who we truly are:

*There was a child made of salt who wandered the earth, trying to learn where he had come from. He traveled to many lands and listened to many persons, always hoping to better understand who he was. Finally, he arrived at the shore of a great ocean. "How beautiful!" he cried, and he ran to the water's edge and stuck one foot in the water. The ocean invited him further, reassuring him that "If you want to know who you are, do not be afraid." The child, hearing the ocean beckoning, "You must come," moved further and further into the water. As he did so, he began dissolving more and more with every step. "At last," said the salt child, "I know who I am."*

# CHAPTER FIVE EXERCISES

## "You Are Here"

Have you seen the photo (sometimes in poster form) of the swirling galaxy with the arrow pointing to where the Earth is located? Our planet is but a speck on one of the spiral arms of the Milky Way, called the Orion Arm, which is about two-thirds out from the center of the Galaxy. If nothing else humbles us, this photo should do the trick!

True humility is reverence for life. It's a recognition of our place in the scheme of things. It's also knowing what we do not know, an awareness that the ego-self is, in right relationship, a willing servant to the Divine. The greatest spiritual beings I know are exceedingly humble. Here are a few characteristics:

- *They act simply and have a wonderful sense of irony and humor.* It is a mistake to think that spiritual greatness is equivalent to brilliant intellect; one does not necessarily imply the other. In some persons, a lack of humility shuts down "spiritual knowing" in favor of the analytical mind.

- *Great spiritual beings do not need public relations firms, media professionals, or marketing experts to promote themselves.* Even if some sages may need to be in the public eye as part of their service, most go about accomplishing their work quietly and privately.

- *Humility is not servility.* Spiritually-accomplished individuals are powerful (and not to be trifled with), precisely because they do not only rely on themselves; everything is surrendered to the Source and achieved in Its name.

On this page or in your journal, respond to these questions:

1. What do you think the difference is between humility and low self-esteem?

2. When have you experienced a life limitation that taught you to honor a neglected quality or an aspect of life? (Example: financial difficulties which helped you to develop a greater respect for money). Explain.

3. Have you ever had a sense of entitlement or unreasonable expectations from life? How was this attitude changed? Was there an incident or experience that occurred that helped you realize greater humility?

4. As you realize greater surrender to God, how is it encouraging greater humility in your approach to life?

5. How would the practice of gratitude counter a sense of pride or privilege?

# CHAPTER FIVE ENDNOTES

1. *Sannyasa* is traditionally a time set apart for men or women in late years of their life, but young *brahmacharis* (ascetics or initiates on the spiritual path) have the choice to renounce the marriage and householder stages to dedicate themselves instead to spiritual pursuits.

2. The practice of devoting one's later years to spiritual contemplation and development extends to other cultures as well. For example, the Druze, a Lebanese religious sect, typically give up their belligerent, warlike behavior in later life for a more peaceful existence that includes community service and religious contemplation.

3. Irina Tweedie. *Daughter of Fire*. Nevada City, CA: Blue Dolphin Publishing, Inc. 1989, p. 204.

4. In his master's thesis, *On the Nature of Change in the Four Elements*, (Canterbury Christ Church University, December, 2015, p.49), Ben Rovers cited Jung's theory of psychic functions:

> "The answer to the question, whether Jung's theory of psychic functions can be seen as congruent with classical theories on elements, is undoubtedly affirmative. To see the parallels, we have to look beyond his writings on psychological types. In his later work on the quaternity and on alchemy, the four psychic functions take the place of the four elements of antiquity. The description of the dynamic between these functions and the way change takes place, is also deeply rooted in classical thinking. Jung argues that the real transformation (alchemy) takes place in psyche and not in matter." (Jung, *Aion*, 1959: ¶256, *Psychology and Alchemy*, 1968: ¶564).

5. The final synthesis of these purified elements have been reunited to create the quintessence, the fifth element, sometimes called aether (or Nothingness, Emptiness, or the Void). I prefer, like in the sci-fi movie, *The Fifth Element*, to call it love. This love, however, is not romantic love, but a love that radiates and transmutes, love that unifies all opposites into a perfected totality (symbolized by the Philosopher's Stone or Self).

6. "Second Brain Found in the Heart and Gut Neurons," by Jeanetter Kando Fi Chor, Owlcation, April 6, 2020 and "The First 3-D Map of the Heart's Neurons," Thomas Jefferson University, Phys.org, May 26, 2020. These articles indicate that just as the heart may be a "second brain," so might the "gut."

7. In regard to human fetal development, Pascal's conjecture may be more than poetic: In embryogenesis, the heart is the first organ to appear, beating by the fifth week after gestation. Also at the fifth week, the first synapses begin forming in a fetus's spinal cord; but the cerebral cortex, which we have conjectured as responsible for most of what we think of as

mental life—conscious experience, voluntary actions, thinking, remembering, feeling—is not mature until nearly the end of gestation.

8. J. Andrew Armour, M.D., Ph.D. "Neurocardiology: Anatomical and Functional Principles," Institute of Heartmath, 2003.

9. John L. Petersen, Interviewer, founder of the Arlington Institute. *PostScript*: "Gregg Braden: Fusion of Ancient Telomeres: We Don't Know WHY, but We Know HOW It Happened," Dec. 28, 2021. https://youtu.be/wntST_E6Chg

10. C. G. Jung, *Memories, Dreams, Reflections*. New York: Vintage Books, 1965, pp. 247-248.

11. "Your Mind Isn't Confined to the Inside of Your Skull," interview with Dr. Dan Siegel, Bigthink.com (Transcript), Vol. 90, March, 2017. Daniel J. Siegel, MD, is Clinical Professor of Psychiatry at the University of California–Los Angeles School of Medicine, and Executive Director of the Mindsight Institute. He is the founding editor of Norton's IPNB Series and best-selling author of *Mind, The Mindful Therapist*, and *The Mindful Brain*. Dr. Siegel's latest book, *Mind: A Journey to the Heart of Being Human*, was published by W. W. Norton & Co. in 2016.

12. Popular examples of intuitive problem-solving and creative inspiration are: In 1965, Paul McCartney heard the tune for "Yesterday" in a dream, a song later recorded by the Beatles. The famous golfer, Jack Nicklaus, learned how to improve his golf swing by dreaming of how to change his grip on his golf club to perfect his game. Stephen King's novel *Misery* was inspired by a dream, and so was Stephanie Meyer's Twilight series. The movie, *The Terminator*, created by James Cameron, was based on a dream he had while sick and feverish. Dr. James Watson came to understand the structure of DNA by dreaming of two snakes coiled around each other, with their heads at opposite ends.

13. Brian Kolodiejchuk, editor. *Mother Teresa: Come Be My Light (The Private Writings of the "Saint of Calcutta")*. New York: Doubleday, 2007: pp. 187, 210.

14. Andrew Harvey. *Hidden Journey*. New York: Henry Holt & Company, Inc., 1991, p. 208.

15. Mother Meera is believed by her devotees to be an embodiment (Avatar) of the Divine Mother (Shakti or Devi).

16. Andrew Harvey. op. cit., p. 208

17. The important role of disillusionment can be applied to any area of life: the phase, of the "Trough of Disillusionment," (following the stage, "Peak of Inflated Expectations") has even been formulated as a stage in the "hype cycle," a graphic representation of the breakthrough and development of new technology. The Gartner Hype Cycle is a graphical presentation

developed to provide a graphical and conceptual presentation of the maturity of emerging technologies through five phases. (It has been criticized for its lack of accurate applicability).

[18.] Reference to the Hopi experience of disenchantment can be found in "Disenchantment: A Religious Abduction," a chapter in book, *Native American Religious Action: A Performance Approach to Religion* by Sam Gill. Columbia: University of South Carolina Press, 1987. Reference to all three tribes can be found in the book, *Transitions Making Sense of Life's Changes* in the chapter, "Disenchantment" by William Bridges, Da Capo Lifelong Books, 2004, p 118 as well as in Ronald Grimes' book, *Readings in Ritual Studies*, Prentice Hall, 1996.

[19.] A quote by P.D. Ouspensky in his book, *In Search of the Miraculous*. Boston, Mass.: Houghton, Mifflin, Harcourt, 2001:pp. 249-250 formerly quoted in *Drinking the Dragon*, op. cit., p. 43.

[20.] Irina Tweedie. op. cit,. p. 324.

[21.] Ram Dass. *Polishing the Mirror*. Boulder, CO: Sounds True, 2014: pp. 53-55.

[22.] To stay in a constant state of identification with God can, for some, become an *inflation*. When an inflation occurs, the ego appropriates the God-energies, as is characteristic of pathological megalomania. In this case, the ego identifies with the Self, and may proclaim him- or herself as a Messiah, for example. The process of alternating states of separation and union can be understood in both psychological and spiritual terms: Edward Edinger. *Ego and Archetype*. Baltimore, MD; Penguin Books, 1973: p. 52

> "...it is impossible for the ego to experience the Self as something separate as long as the ego is unconsciously identified with the Self...The ego must first be dis-identified with the Self before the Self can be encountered as "the other." As long as one is unconsciously identified with God, he cannot experience His existence."

[23.] Our apparent lack of contact with the Divine, especially following a period of perceived intimacy with God, can feel like a *rejection*, and is reminiscent on the psychological level of being wholly undifferentiated, as innocent children in Eden. We feel as though we have been expelled from Eden and are experiencing a "fall."

[24.] Edward Edinger. *Ego and Archetype*. Boulder, CO: Shambhala; Reissue edition 1992, p. 50.

[25.] Thomas Merton. *Conjectures of a Guilty Bystander*. Dublin, Ireland: Image Publications; Reissue edition, 1968, pp 156-8.

[26.] *The Shariyat-ki-Sugmad*, Book One, Minneapolis, MN: ECKANKAR, 1987: p. 117.

[27.] Annie Besant. *Initiation: The Perfecting of Man*. Wheaton, Illinois, The Theosophical Press, 1912, p. 101.

28. Irina Tweedie. op. cit., p. 631.

29. Abraham Maslow. *Motivation and Personality*. London, England: Longman, 3rd Edition, 1987. Maslow's self-actualizing characteristics are (paraphrased):

- Efficient perceptions of reality. Ability to judge situations correctly. Ability to discern what is superficial or dishonest.
- Comfortable acceptance of self, others, and nature. Ability to accept one's own shortcomings and those of others.
- Reliant on one's own experiences and judgment.
- Spontaneous and natural. True to oneself.
- Task centered. A sense of a life mission that emphasizes the good of the whole.
- Autonomous. Not easily swayed by the opinions of others.
- Continued freshness of appreciation of life's beauty.
- Profound interpersonal relationships.
- Comfortable with solitude as well as being alone.
- Non-hostile sense of humor. This refers to the ability to laugh at oneself.
- Peak experiences, characterized by feelings of ecstasy, harmony, and deep meaning. Self-actualizers report feeling stronger and calmer, filled with light, beauty, and goodness, and at one with the universe.
- Socially compassionate.
- Few close intimate friends rather than many shallow relationships.
- Self-actualizers possess "social interest, community feeling, or a sense of oneness with all humanity."

30. Many persons have developed exceptional characters, such as the unselfishness and compassion of a nurse or the courage and discernment of an entrepreneur. These character traits are preparing many for the Path of Initiation. In this regard, Alice Bailey states, "Goodness and altruism grow out of realization and service, and holiness of character is the outcome of those expansions which a man brings about within himself through strenuous effort and endeavour." Alice Bailey. *Initiation: Human and Solar*. New York: Lucis Pub. Co., 1951: 93.

31. Irina Tweedie. op. cit., p. 27.

32. Documentary Movie: *The Loneliest Whale: The Search for 52*, Bleeker Street, 2021. Producers include Leonardo DiCaprio and Adrian Grenier.

33. Elizabeth Haich. op. cit., pp.77-78.

34. Some spiritual writers say that there is an Oversoul with many divisions, and that meeting on the physical plane with another "division" is sometimes akin to meeting a soulmate. There are many theories, but one of the more interesting books on this subject was written

by Dr. Joshua David Stone, *Ascension and Romantic Relationships* (Vol.VIII). Flagstaff, AZ: Light Technology Publishing, 2000.

[35.] Steven Southwick, M.D., *Resilience: The Science of Mastering life's Greatest Challenges.* UK: Cambridge University Press; 2nd edition, June 30, 2018.

[36.] Adam Grant. *Give and Take: A Revolutionary Approach to Success.* New York: Viking, April 9, 2013.

[37.] Emily Greenfield. "Felt Obligation to Help Others as a Protective Factor against Losses in Psychological Well-Being Following Functional Decline in Middle and Later Life." *The Journals of Gerontology Series B: Psychological Sciences and Social Sciences,* 2009 Nov; 64B(6): 723–732. Pub. online: Oct13,2009: doi: 10.1093/geronb/gbp074

[38.] Read more on Erikson's Psychosocial Theory in Kendra Cherry's article, "Generativity vs. Stagnation in Psychosocial Development," (Medically reviewed by David Susman, Ph.D.) verywellmind.com April 18, 2022. https://www.verywellmind.com/generativity-versus-stagnation-2795734

[39.] The philosopher and guru Sri Aurobindo wrote in *Letters on Yoga*, Vol. 1, on the distinction between the ordinary life, the religious life, and spiritual life:

> "The ordinary life is that of the average human consciousness separated from its own true self and from the Divine and led by the common habits of the mind, life, and body which are the Laws of Ignorance.
>
> The religious life is a movement of the same ignorant human consciousness, turning or trying to turn away from the earth towards the Divine, but as yet without knowledge and led by the dogmatic tenets and rules of some sect or creed which claims to have found the way out of the bonds of the earth-consciousness into some beatific Beyond. The religious life may be the first approach to the spiritual, but very often it is only a turning about in a round of rites, ceremonies and practices or set ideas and forms without any issue.
>
> The spiritual life, on the contrary, proceeds directly by a change of consciousness, a change from the ordinary consciousness, ignorant and separated from its true self and from God, to a greater consciousness in which one finds one's true being and comes first into direct and living contact and then into union with the Divine. For the spiritual seeker this change of consciousness is the one thing he seeks and nothing else matters."

# CHAPTER SIX

# Following the Thread: Initiation Patterns in the Arts

*In the case of someone who is spiritually receptive,*
*it is possible to talk of an analogy*
*between the impact made by a work of art*
*and that of a purely religious experience.*
*Art acts above all on the soul,*
*shaping its spiritual structure.*

~ Andrei Tarkovsky

## ART IS TRANSFORMATIONAL

*What is your best work for?*
*What it's for is to make change happen.*
*That's our best work... to change people.*

~ Seth Godin

Have you ever seen a movie or read a book that you considered life changing or transformational? Thinking back to your childhood, do you remember a special book of adventure, like the classic *The Call of the Wild* by Jack London or a book that touched your innermost self, such as *The Secret Garden* by Frances Hodgson Burnett? Or you may remember seeing the movie adaptations of these books, as they have each been made into movies several times.[1] More recently, you may have been fascinated by the seven fantasy novels (and movies) featuring the kid wizard, Harry Potter, loved the *Hobbit* and the *Lord of the Rings Trilogies*, or relished reading *The Hunger Games Trilogy* or watching the movie series.

Stories—whether represented in art, books, dance, opera, theater, or film—reflect life and conversely, life mirrors art. The poet Muriel Rukeyser expressed this by declaring, "The universe is made of stories, not atoms." All humans recognize the archetypal themes and motifs in art because life *itself* is structured by these prototypical designs and frameworks of experience. All life is made up of endings and beginnings (death and rebirth experiences), contests and challenges, defeats and victories, heroes and villains, tyrants and revolutionaries, and infinite states of hope and despair, fulfilment, and disappointment. Our lives are peopled by bullies, unfaithful lovers, outcasts, mentors, victims and survivors, the bold and the faint of heart.

I remember that as a child, I would often curl up in a corner to read the rather "grim" fairy tales collected by the Brothers Grimm, who published German folk tales that are unsentimental, violent, and sometimes dark, as well as tales by the Danish author Hans Christian Anderson. Fairy tales offer fundamental, if sometimes disturbing, morality lessons as well as deep insights into human psychology, precisely because they are based on archetypal characters and themes. Striking deep chords within us, fairy tales feature such archetypal figures such as the wise old woman (*The Goose-Girl at the Well*), the shadow (*The Bewitched Princess*), the helpful animal (*Hansel and Gretel*), the mother (*Mother Holle*), and the devil (*The Maiden Without Hands*). Later in life, my familiarity with fairy tales and myths helped me to recognize these same characters and themes replayed in the story lines in my own life and dreams as well as those of my clients in the therapy room.

Archetypal themes can also be found in contemporary movies, including, for example, stories of quests (the *Star Wars* series), star-crossed lovers (*The Titanic*), heroic self-sacrifice (*Terminator 2: Judgement Day*), coming of age stories (*Call Me by Your Name*), descents to the underworld (*What Dreams*

*May Come*), a fall due to pride or hubris (*The Wolf of Wall Street*), courtship and marriage (*The Notebook*), good versus evil (*The Fifth Element*), and preparation for death (*The Fault in Our Stars*). Archetypal themes comprise the framework upon which human lifecycles and experiences are overlain; the notion that all of life, including its spiritual aspect, can be found in art and literature is true. As British artist and author Nick Bantock asserts, "You cannot separate art from life or spirituality; they are bound together in a single unit."

One of the main themes in *Dancing the Labyrinth* is that we are often inducted into (or prepared for) the Initiatory Path by life events—through living our own stories and by vicariously experiencing the stories of others. We can look to these stories in books, art forms, and movies to find examples of certain attributes of initiation. Specific tasks that have been associated with stages of initiation in the previous chapters are found in books such as Cheryl Strayed's memoir, *Wild: From Lost to Found on the Pacific Coast Trail*, the autobiography of Abu al-Ghazzali, *Deliverance from Error*, Doris Lessing's novel, *The Golden Notebook*, and Karan Bajaj's novel, *The Yoga of Max's Discontent*. These initiatory tasks can also be observed in movies, including *Chasing Mavericks, Seven Years in Tibet, Whale Rider,* and *Dune*, each incorporating a human story that exemplifies a facet of the initiation process. Also included in this chapter are four women artists, Anna Halprin, Ann McCoy, Deena Metzger, and Carolee Schneemann, whose transformational art derives from their dreams and personal psychospiritual processes. Certain tasks related to initiation can be found in their works as well. While the following art works are presented in different media, they all represent aspects of the *archetype of initiation*. This is why we are profoundly moved and altered by certain types of art; such works draw us ever closer to the Divine.

# BOOKS OF STRUGGLE AND CHANGE

> *I read a book one day*
> *and my whole life was changed.*
> ~ **Orhan Pamuk**

Books can depict the struggles found on the Labyrinthine Path, whether these stories are fictional or based on real life. Books draw us in with character development and plot detail; they invite us to use the "theater of the imagination" to visualize settings or events. Because we control when we read and for how long, we are able to take the time to delve into characters' minds and motives, to identify with their struggles and strivings, and to savor their insights and perceptions. The following books highlight many facets of the spiritual unfoldment process, but I have chosen just one task of the initiation process to emphasize for each.

## *Wild: From Lost to Found on The Pacific Coast Trail:* Disillusionment

> *I have had to experience so much stupidity, so many vices,*
> *so much error, so much nausea, disillusionment, and sorrow,*
> *just in order to become a child again and begin anew.*
> *I had to experience despair, I had to sink to the greatest mental depths,*
> *to thoughts of suicide, in order to experience grace.*
> ~ **Hermann Hesse**

In 1995, carrying a backpack nearly half of her weight, Cheryl Strayed hiked the Pacific Coast Trail (PCT) as part of a transformative journey to deal with the grief of her mother's death at the age of 45 from lung cancer. Without experience or training, 26-year-old Cheryl trekked more than a thousand miles along the PCT, from the Mojave Desert in California to the Bridge of the Gods on the Oregon-Washington border. Alone, disillusioned, and with "a hole in her heart," she walked for a total of 94 days, encountering along the way an assortment of people, some of whom would profoundly touch her life. These individuals included a woman who had suffered profound loss; a trio of young men she named the "Three Young Bucks," and a community of people who accompanied her part way on the trail. Some of those she met on the trail, such as two potentially dangerous hunters, were threats from whom she felt fortunate to escape.

In her memoir, *Wild: From Lost to Found on the Pacific Coast Trail*,[2] Cheryl wrote that leading up to her trek, she was devastated by her mother's early death just seven weeks after her diagnosis. Cheryl was also estranged from her siblings, separated from her husband, and deeply disappointed that her stepfather had quickly moved on following her mother's death, leaving their family for another. Unable to adequately cope during the four-year period between her mother's passing and the beginning of her hike, Cheryl started using heroin and having promiscuous sex with random men. She was not only disillusioned by her current life, but was scarred by the sexual abuse she had experienced as a young child by her paternal grandfather. Cheryl also carried resentment for the domestic abuse inflicted on her family by her natural father, who left them when she was 12. Trudging day after day on the trail, she discovered that she was still full of unresolved grief. Now that her mother had died and her stepfather had defaulted, and with her last ties to her husband and siblings unraveling, she had nothing left to lose. Cheryl began to walk "to save her life."

Along the PCT, in sight of the "Range of Light," which is what John Muir called the Sierras, Cheryl faced hunger, thirst, fatigue, bloodied feet (with several lost toenails), injury, wild animals, and uncertain weather. She met people to whom she was instantly attracted and a couple of men who made her fear for her own safety. When she finally reached the beautifully-named Bridge of the Gods at the end of her trip, her heart had begun to reopen. Prior to the trek she had begun counseling and had chosen a new surname for herself, "Strayed." This new name represented for her how far afield she had strayed from a direct course in her life. "Strayed" also reflected the fact that she was without mother, father, husband, or home, and she was searching for connection. After surviving a rugged three-month hike without a radio, phone, credit cards, and very little cash, she felt that she had found her own direction, the lodestar within herself. Nine days after embarking on her hike, she realized that she had won a new-found sense of personal autonomy. It was then that she met the man who would be her second husband, the documentary filmmaker, Brian Lindstrom.

Disillusionment is an important feature of the initiation process. Cheryl was deeply dissatisfied in her marriage, disheartened that her siblings had become distant and had drifted apart, and disappointed that her stepfather had left the family. These letdowns are what drove her to make a pilgrim's journey, or, what in the book is called a "spirit walk," to seek a new perspective and a more fulfilling life. Without disillusionment, we would not grow discontented and feel compelled to search for something more meaningful in our lives. We first need to become disenchanted with what we thought would make us happy before we are driven to seek, like al-Ghazali in the next example, "the knowledge of the true meaning of things."

### *The Deliverance from Error:* Pride

*Pride and vanity, the opposites of humility, can destroy our spiritual health as surely as a debilitating disease can destroy our physical health.*
~ **Joseph B. Wirthlin**

In his autobiography, *The Deliverance from Error*,[3] Abu Hamid al-Ghazzali recounted how, at the age of 37, he was an esteemed and respected philosophy professor teaching at a prestigious university in Baghdad. He was at the height of his career: Celebrated and brilliant, his lectures were attended by students from foreign countries, his books were widely read, and his arguments during debates were considered triumphs of logic and reason. He lived a life of self-satisfaction and pride. He later wrote of his public lectures that they were "…motivated by a quest for fame and widespread prestige."[4] Then, suddenly and without warning, everything fell apart.

One day, al-Ghazzali stood up to deliver his prepared lecture to an auditorium full of admiring students—and not a word came out of his mouth. He tried several times to speak, but his voice was mysteriously frozen in paralysis. He wrote, "For God put a lock upon my tongue so that I was impeded from public teaching. I struggled with myself to teach for a single day…but my tongue would not utter a single word."[5] Mortified, al-Ghazzali fled the podium and later, the university. At first thought to be a medical ailment, this strange malady was later diagnosed as a psychospiritual crisis. Eventually suffering a complete physical and mental breakdown, al-Ghazzali recognized that his academic career was in ruins, and worse, he now questioned the very philosophy that he had spent his life writing and teaching. *Where were the answers to his deeper spiritual questions in the towering intellectual tomes he had written and in the dazzling lectures he had delivered?*

Abu Hamid al-Ghazzali was one of the most prominent and influential Persian philosophers, theologians, logicians, and mystics of Islam in the 11th century. His over 70 written works contributed to the sciences, Islamic reasoning, and to the inclusion of Sufism as an accepted part of orthodox Islam. Several of these books, most particularly his autobiography, *The Deliverance from Error,* recounted his own spiritual journey of initiation, and offer guidance—including the self-disciplines of moderation and discrimination—to those searching for spiritual development. Importantly, al-Ghazzali related in his later books that intellectual learning alone is not adequate to the spiritual student; *a seeker must also develop inwardness: an understanding and compassion via insight and immediate spiritual experience.*

Abu-Ghazalli only learned this truth after he resigned his teaching position, sold his personal belongings, said goodbye to his family (leaving them with a trust fund), and set out as a poor, wandering holy man, traveling alone across the burning Syrian desert on foot toward Damascus. For ten years, al-Ghazzali disappeared from the intellectual scene, living in various Sufi centers scattered over the Near East. While living in self-imposed exile, he fasted, studied, meditated, and learned from spiritual masters, some of whom called him to them via a mysterious inner voice. Al-Ghazzali came to know the *gnosis* of the heart, the wisdom and transformative potency of love and compassion. He encountered what he called the "fruitional experience"—the immediate spiritual contact of a *living* religion. No longer a conveyor of pure logic and rationalism, he began to pen writings that integrated theory with experience; pure reason with divine love. Once lionized for his intellectual superiority, Al-Ghazzali had been literally frozen in place and rendered speechless by his one sidedness. His life and works demonstrate that wholeness is not to be found in the outer world of success and acclaim but in the inner worlds of spiritual realities; intellectual pride must bend to the greater knowledge of the heart.

The theme of love gaining the upper hand over intellectual pride is not new to initiates on The Path. This does not mean that there is no room for intellectual discernment and analysis (or plain common sense). For the spiritual seeker, al-Ghazzali's personal story points out the spiritual emptiness and dissatisfaction of intellectual theorizing if the heart is not engaged and spiritual experience is lacking. Love trumps all.

## *The Golden Notebook:*
## Integration

*Wholeness is not achieved by cutting off*
*a portion of one's being,*
*but by integration of the contraries.*

~ C. G. Jung

*The Golden Notebook*[6] is a novel by the British author Doris Lessing, who at nearly 88 years was the oldest recipient and only the eleventh woman (out of 14 today) to have won the Nobel Prize for Literature in 2007. Described as part of Lessing's "inner space fiction" (stories that explore the human psychological terrain), *The Golden Notebook* is Lessing's best known and most influential novel. It examines the gradual psychological disintegration of the book's protagonist, Anna, and how her breakdown is emblematic of the chaos in the world. The book addresses many topics, including gender relations, love, marriage, parenting, suicide, and politics, but ultimately, the essence of the book, according to Lessing, is the message that "we must not divide things off, must not compartmentalise."[7]

Anna, the protagonist of the book, was a successful author. She kept four notebooks, each of which represented the divisions within herself: A black notebook chronicled her time in Africa; a red notebook detailed her former membership in the British Communist Party; a yellow notebook listed ideas for short stories, books, and included the partial manuscript of a novel; and a blue notebook written as a diary of her everyday life. Near the book's end, Anna struggled in a tumultuous relationship with an American screenwriter. This initiated her slow descent into psychic dissolution. Anna resolved to integrate the four notebooks into a fifth, a golden notebook, in an effort toward her own psychological wholeness.

At the beginning of the novel, Anna's sense of self was completely fragmented, and she felt like she harbored multiple people within her body (at one point, she rode on a train repeating, "Anna, Anna, I am Anna" to keep herself together). Anna's notebooks were disorderly and jumbled, a metaphor for her chaotic mind. She equated this to how society separates into contradictory and conflicting groups that no longer understand each other and are "blindly grasping out" for wholeness. She saw what she called her own "cracking up" as a symptom of global disorder. "Human beings are so divided, are becoming more and more divided, *and more subdivided in themselves*, reflecting the world, that they reach out desperately, not knowing they do it, for information about other groups…It is a blind grasping out for their own wholeness…"[8]

During her healing process, Anna reviewed her many inner contradictions, such as her resentment of the inequities of marriage while still longing for it, and her belief in communist theory but not the Communist Party. She was aware that her writer's block had everything to do with how she had "buttoned up" her fears, anger, and emotional pain, artificially compartmentalizing them within her four notebooks. Anna knew she could choose to continue to repress and deny her many inner inconsistencies or she could integrate them by embracing, and not rejecting, what was at odds in her own personality. She wondered if cracking up was precisely the key to achieving a sense of unity within herself: **Is it possible that breaking down is not the opposite of a totality but a means toward it?** To help consolidate her identity, she gave up keeping four separate journals and integrated them into a single golden notebook, deciding to consolidate her thoughts and to publish them in a new novel for all the world to see.

Even though Lessing's *The Golden Notebook* was first published in 1962, in many ways the book is more relevant now than ever. During the early years of the 2020s decade, political turmoil, a public health crisis, income, housing and food instabilities, and world conflicts as well as concerns about ecological collapse were factors in people experiencing escalating divisions both within themselves and between one another. In 2021, *Mental Health American* reported that 19%, or over 47 million,

Americans were suffering a mental illness. Add to those statistics the large numbers of people who were, and continue to be, suffering from some level of anxiety and depression or more serious mental disorders that have gone untreated or unreported. When so much is in upheaval and transition, the issues that are conveniently compartmentalized or "split off" from conscious awareness, rise to the surface for a reckoning, both for the individual and for society at large.

Lessing has Anna wonder whether a breakdown isn't somehow also a *breakthrough*. This reflection can also be considered in regard to recent American history. The outer crises that individuals undergo can trigger a *Dark Night of the Soul*, during which persons find it difficult if not impossible to cope. They may suffer such severe losses during these periods that they undergo psychological "breakdowns." But, surprisingly, these experiences of "falling apart" can, with grit and grace (and psycho-spiritual assistance), lead to higher functioning and greater wholeness. (I discuss this process in detail in my book *Drinking the Dragon*.) In a similar fashion, the breaking down of social institutions and systems is harrowing and dangerous, and there are societal stressors and conflicts that encourage us-against-them mentalities, pitting groups against one another. However, just as in individual cases, the eventual reconciliation of divisions in the culture and the rethinking of the structures of society can lead the way to a reorganization that better suits the needs of the people they serve.

There is a point along The Path when we begin the work of uncovering the many splintered parts of ourselves. We realize that far too often in our lives, we have been compartmentalizing instead of working as an integrated unit. Some of us need a psychotherapist to help us with this process; others can attend relevant workshops; a few can meditate or journal—all activities that can lend each of these secret selves a "voice." It requires courage to meet our many concealed aspects, which not only include the shadow characteristics of which we are ashamed (such as jealousy or envy), but the qualities of ourselves that need recognition and expression (such as musical talent). Integrating the lost and hidden parts of ourselves is a process that eventually affords us more energy and better functioning, and allows us to better regulate (through increased self-awareness) our reactions to situations and to others. Ultimately, the process of integrating these attributes of ourselves serves our spiritual quest for wholeness, and when our own consciousness has been raised, so has the world's.

## *The Yoga of Max's Discontent:* Alienation

> *Many people who are going through the early stages*
> *of the awakening process are no longer certain what their outer purpose is.*
> *What drives the world no longer drives them.*
> *Seeing the madness of our civilization so clearly,*
> *they feel somewhat alienated from the culture around them.*
> *Some feel that they inhabit a no-man's-land between two worlds.*
> *They are no longer run by the ego, yet the arising awareness*
> *has not yet become fully integrated into their lives.*
> *Inner and outer purpose have not merged.*
> ~ Eckart Tolle

Max did not feel at home in his city, his job, nor even in his own skin. He had succeeded where many fail; after growing up as the son of Greek immigrants in the Bronx housing projects, surrounded by drugs and violence, he made it to Harvard. Max eventually became a successful Wall Street analyst, but corporate America had begun to lose its luster. He was troubled by his mother's long illness and death from cancer, worried about his sister, concerned about a friend shot in gang violence and permanently injured, and haunted by the heartbreaking ending of a romantic relationship. In Karan Bajaj's contemporary novel, *The Yoga of Max's Discontent*,[9] the main character, Max, was alienated from his life, which seemed to serve no purpose: Most of his friends from the projects were dead or maimed; he worked for a corporation that bought up companies to exploit them; and his well-dressed business associates only talked about the best restaurants and the trendiest clubs.

It is while Max was feeling most alone and alienated that he had a chance encounter with the Indian food vendor, Viveka, on a chilly night on the streets of New York. The food cart owner told him that the beliefs of the Himalayan yogis encompassed the opposites, so that, "…if there is birth, age, suffering, sorrow, and death, then there must be something that is unborn, un-ailing, sorrowless, and deathless…" [10] In other words, there must exist something immortal. Max resolved to find the serenity and certainty that these yogis realized through their meditations in the icy cold solitudes of their mountain caves. In short order, Max was on a crowded Indian train in the dead of winter, heading to the foothills of the Himalayas.

Initially, Max was on a quest to find a Brazilian doctor-turned-holy-man, who was reported to be staying in a guesthouse high up in the Garhwal Himalayas. He nearly froze to death as he climbed through the snow (lost for most of the trek) until eventually finding the guesthouse, where he learned that the doctor no longer lived there. From the guesthouse, Max's journey took him on a circuitous path during which he located a mysterious Slovenian in Mumbai who directed him to the sage Ramakrishna. Max found his way to the saint's ashram-hovel in the dry, hot empty fields of South India where for three years he learned breathing exercises, yoga asanas, long stretches of silence, and during a summer drought, endured extreme hunger. This process, including the physical disciplines, was strangely familiar to him, and he dreamed of past lives when he had sought enlightenment and failed. Max learned to become more detached, realizing that "he felt more and more alienated from his life back home."[11] A fellow student reassured him as she left the dusty ashram, "Your discontent with the world as it is will lead you to your union."[12]

After leaving Ramakrishna, Max made the 60-hour trip back to the Himalayas. He once again climbed up a mountain, but this time he was looking for a suitable cave in which to live and continue his meditations. He planned to stay on the mountain with his meager supplies until he was enlightened, becoming the *Tathagatha*, the one "who has gone, whose body remains in the world but whose mind has become the universal, complete."[13] Max lived in his snow-covered cave until an avalanche forced him down the mountain, where he ended up at the very guesthouse he had stayed in at the beginning of his journey. It was still run by the same old woman, Nani Maa, who nursed him back to health. In return, Max helped to repair the guesthouse, and later, he cared for Nani Maa until her frail body failed and she died. Believing that he had failed in his quest for total union with God, Max stayed on at the guesthouse, giving of himself in detached but loving service to the guests who came for rest and supplies. At the end of the novel, he rescued a lost mountain climber, warming him back to life with his own energy and bringing him back to the guesthouse where he tended to the hiker's needs. Max was no longer alienated, loving everyone and everything, a part of the wholeness of life without inner division or attachment. He had become One in union with the Divine.

*The Yoga of Max's Discontent* shows one path to wholeness, a method characteristic of some Eastern paths to Self-Realization, which involve intense isolation combined with the extreme self-mortification and chastisement of the body. This is not The Way presented in *Dancing the Labyrinth*, which describes a path that is walked while maintaining the responsibilities of everyday life. It is a *Middle Way*, a slower but less severe mode of living in the world without being caught up in it. However, the factor of alienation is often part of the Path of Initiation, regardless of the method. Especially at the beginning of our spiritual journeys, we often feel out of step with those around us and dissatisfied with the goals that motivate others. Alienation in this context prompts our quest for deeper meaning. Along the *Labyrinthine Way*, we must discover how to become more detached from others without repudiating them; we must learn to love them in a new way. Max abruptly left all ties behind in New York and eventually, while living in his cave, completely separated himself from others. Only when he believed that he had failed in his desire for oneness did he become a channel for the expression of universal love in service to others. At last, Max was everyone and everyone was Max.

## DREAM-INSPIRED ART: IMAGES THAT TRANSFORM

*Making art is a rite of initiation.*
*People change their souls.*
~ Robin Lim

*My hand is entirely the implement of a distant sphere.*
*It is not my head that functions but something else,*
*something higher, something somewhere remote.*
*I must have great friends there, dark as well as bright...*
*They are all very kind to me.*
~ Paul Klee

Imagine creating art based on your dream images or themes, pieces of art that are inspired by intuitions from your deepest unconscious stirrings, as the following artworks demonstrate:

- A killer is caught after a community group, led by an acclaimed dancer and choreographer, performs dream-based dance rituals to clear the negative energy on Mt. Tamalpais where a number of murders have occurred.[14]

- A child repeatedly dreams that a king is dismembered and ground up with a mortar and pestle, an illustration commonly reproduced in books on the ancient science of alchemy. As an adult, she creates mural art pieces with colored pencils, depicting alchemical images and motifs to demonstrate the various stages of psychospiritual growth.[15]

- A writer dreams of a woman who holds a hand up, and the writer sees that there are no lines on her palm. Then, a string of words trails across the dreamer's vision, displaying the title for her next book, *The Woman Who Slept with Men to Take the War Out of Them*.[16]

- One artist—nude, harnessed and suspended—swings from a rope attached to the ceiling while scrawling with a marker on the floors and walls of her environment. Oscillating in a semi-dream state, the artist allows the unconscious to use her "as a pencil" in the creation of "automatic writings or trance markings."[17]

The above scenarios delineate a few of the dream-based and -inspired artworks created by several well-known artists interviewed for my book, *Women Dreaming-into-Art*,[18] first published in 2006. The interviewees in the book are **Ann McCoy, Deena Metzger, Carolee Schneemann, Anna Halprin, Christine Downing, MaryBeth Edelson, and Pauline Oliveros,** some of whom are no longer living.[19] While the seven artists vary in their choice of media, which includes visual and performance art, sculpture, dance, poetry, literature and music, they *all* express in their art the processes, themes, and imagery of the unconscious. These artists and their productions affirm filmmaker Jean Cocteau's conviction that "Art is a marriage of the conscious and the unconscious."

Nearly all the interviewees in *Women Dreaming* experienced The Dark Night of the Soul at least once in their lives, an initiatory experience that impacted every aspect of their lives, profoundly altering their relationship to themselves, to their art, and to Spirit. (Long ago, all artists were initiates, and accordingly, art was considered sacred). The artists in *Women Dreaming* have produced art that powerfully portrays their labyrinthine journeys of personal transformation. Artists, and most particularly, those who are closest to the dynamic forces of their own inner processes, are more vulnerable to periodic eruptions and outbreaks of the unconscious. The advantage that artists have is that they can channel and express these turbulent energies into their art, rendering these underlying processes not only visible, but evocative to the viewer. As these women represent in tangible art forms their personal ordeals—the depths of their despair and the triumphs of their rebirths—they delineate for us the various stations and labors along the Serpentine Way. Furthermore, in *making the unconscious conscious* in their artworks, these cutting-edge artists reveal hidden and emergent social trends and ideas of which the public is only dimly aware, among them, *the modern recovery of the ancient spiritual process of initiation.*

Initiatory themes, motifs, and images are demonstrated in the sculpture, dance, visual and performance art, novels, and film featured in *Women Dreaming*. Certain artworks and their relationship to selected tasks of the initiation process are introduced below, using art processes/pieces from four of the seven artists (though all seven artists have woven patterns of initiation into their art). As these artists-of-the-dream translate their own processes of psychospiritual transmutation into outer forms of art, they both inform and induct their viewers into sacred, unseen worlds of profound metamorphosis.

## Anna Halprin: Shadow Work

*I think of dance as a constant transformation of life itself.*
~ **Merce Cunningham**

For a number of years, Anna Halprin, a pioneer in modern dance and choreography who died in 2021 at the age of 100, led "Circle the Earth" ceremonial peace dances and other community dance rituals, many of which were based on her dreams. "My dances are my dreams, and my dreams are in the form of dance," she has stated. Anna and her daughter, Daria, founded the Tamalpa Institute in 1978, where she created "Life/Art Process" workshops dedicated to using dance for inspiring therapeutic, transformational, and psychological healing. During one of these workshops, Anna had participants draw individual, life-sized portraits. As her own contribution, Anna drew a self-portrait with a dark spot the size of a tennis ball in her pelvic area. Afterwards, Anna found that she had a malignant tumor in her pelvic region, the exact size, shape, and location of the dark, circular area in her drawing. As a result of this remarkable event, Anna began to focus on dance as a *transformer* of unresolved emotions and as a vehicle for somatic and psychological healing.

When she began having recurring physical problems three years after cancer surgery, Anna again drew her own portrait. She was uncomfortable when she saw that she had depicted a beautiful, fantasy-ideal version of herself. Turning the portrait over, she drew herself as a violent, bloodied warrior and then "danced her portrait," expressing in her movements her unconscious, unresolved rage, grief, and aggression. Later, when Anna had further medical tests done, her physical issues had disappeared. Anna explained that, during her warrior dance, "I was dancing my own killer, the killer in the backside of the portrait. I was dancing my personal death." One could say that this is an artist's way of using an artform to work with shadow qualities—not to hide from them behind an idealization of oneself, nor to destroy these qualities—but to recognize, honor, and transmute the energies of one's shadow side. This is part of the work of an initiate—to come to terms with the darker aspects of oneself as a way of self-healing as well as a means to affect the restoration of the planet.

In 1981, in response to the murder of seven women on the slopes of Mt. Tamalpais in Marin County, California, Anna Halprin created her dream-inspired "In and On the Mountain" community dance performance. This ritual was performed by 80 community members as they walked, chanted, made offerings, and prayed the entire seven and one-half miles down the trails of Mount Tamalpais. The murderer was caught only a few days later. In order to collectively reclaim and purify the mountain, considered one of the continent's oldest and most sacred, the ritual was repeated annually over the next five years.

Banishing the darkness on Mt. Tamalpais through a form that embodies community, art, and spirit was a means of rehumanizing and healing both society and nature. When a single individual, such as the murderer on the mountain, expresses the shadow (primitive, negative, socially unacceptable impulses and emotions, comprised of both personal and collective elements), then it is up to all of us to help transmute the darkness that is created. Spiritually-awake individuals, particularly initiates, are acutely aware that their *own* shadows must be acknowledged and transmuted to enable them to act as clear conduits for higher vibrational energies that serve others—and to heal, as Anna has shown, the world around us.

## Ann McCoy: Alchemical Transmutation

*At its essence, art is an alchemical process.*
*Alchemy is a process of transformation.*
~ **Julia Cameron**

Ann McCoy, painter and sculptor, has long created artworks that reflect mythology, symbology, archeology, and alchemy. Alchemy, a medieval precursor to modern chemistry, was more than rudimentary experimentation with various metals and chemical compounds. It was also about experiencing *ourselves* as the alchemical laboratory, where the transmutation of the lower bodies into higher states of being could be achieved. These are the same psychospiritual changes that occur in us as initiates, and accordingly, the themes and symbols of alchemy can be seen in the dreams of people even today. "Alchemy is very important to my work on a daily basis," Ann explains, "I study the relationship of my dreams to alchemical symbolism in a concentrated way. The actual making of the artworks is the end product of this process."[20]

Ann's large-scale, colored pencil drawings and bronze sculptures depict the profound transformational processes she herself has undergone, much of which occurred while she was in Jungian analysis. Over a span of time, she has dreamed of and then translated to her art:

- **Crossing the Red Sea in flames.** The crossing of the waters symbolized the beginning of her psychospiritual journey. The heating up of these waters denoted emotional turbulence.

- **Walking across a land of the dead.** Here corpses were being consumed by fire, representing the death of her old ego-state and way of life.

- **Having her heart exposed as a wolf tears away her sternum.** To Ann, this represented the recovery of the wisdom of the heart and a renewal after a long period of suffering.

- **Traveling to Alexandria, Egypt.** This dream led her to create drawings of resurrection, renewal, and healing (Alexandria was once an important center of alchemical knowledge and practice).

Ann's murals are created from her *lived* psychological processes. The images in her work carry the energy of the dreams borne out of her personal unconscious as well as from the broader collective unconscious, which is shared by all humans everywhere. In this way, her artworks fascinate, challenge, and sometimes frighten viewers. Ann has unearthed and rendered into art ancient archetypal images and patterns of the initiatory process which are both terrible and beautiful. They remain relevant to the modern individual, who is disturbed and awakened by Ann's work. Even if not completely understood, the spiritual numinosity (energy) of such symbolism acts as a catalyst for profound psychological change and spiritual renewal. Ann's innermost world is embodied in her artworks, which offer to others her authentic awareness of the alchemical changes wrought by the processes of spiritual unfoldment.

Ann's mural drawings and bronze sculptures represent the alchemical themes and symbols that many persons can witness in the imagery of their own dreams. The process of transmutation that we undergo is of the deep unconscious, which can be symbolized in our dreams, for example, by the imagery of:

- being embalmed, dismembered, or flayed
- transforming into a wild animal
- seeing oneself as a skeleton
- roasting in a blazing fire, such as on a funeral pyre
- climbing up and perching in a tree
- flying through the air
- visiting various realms of existence

These often bizarre images symbolize various states of purification, refinement, and enlightenment in ourselves. They are also aspects of alchemical operations that were once performed on substances in the medieval laboratory. Alchemy is alive and well within our psyches, and as persons on the initiatory path, we can observe these processes in our dreams as we undergo profound changes in every cell of our being.

## Deena Metzger:
## The Dark Night of the Soul

*Many, many artists have floundered in the depths,*
*but the sheer number of pieces of music, poems, and paintings...*
*bear evidence that they surface again, see the light again,*
*and make art again.*

~ **Sorina Higgins**

Novelist, poet, educator, and healer, Deena Metzger is also a survivor. In 1977, she was diagnosed with breast cancer. She had recently finalized a divorce and won a freedom of speech case in the California Supreme Court. While in the hospital recovering from breast surgery, and later during the post-operative weeks at home, Deena began writing the diary/novel *Tree*[21] in which she asked the questions: "*What was lethal in my psyche? What was killing me in the world? What were the inner and outer politics acting against the body and the psyche?*" Deena concluded that, "Cancer is the repression of the feminine, the repression of feminine values. Cancer is silence. For women, it is the rub between the need to speak and this society's refusal to listen." In *Tree*, Deena testifies that one can be healed through the compassion, the loyalty, and the loving intervention of others. "Tree," understood as both the tree of life and family tree, is what Deena calls the "frequency of love." On what is now a famous poster, Deena is pictured with her arms stretched out in celebration of her return to health, her upper torso bare except for the green vines tattooed where her right breast once was. A poem is written in the upper corner of the poster, part of which is below:

> "I am no longer afraid of mirrors where I see the sign of the Amazon, the one who shoots arrows... What grows in me now is vital and does not cause me harm... I have the body of a warrior

*who does not kill or wound. On the book of my body, I have permanently inscribed a tree."*[22]

Drawing on her experience with life-threatening illness, Deena founded "Healing Stories Workshops," during which she taught persons with serious illnesses to locate, explore, and modify their personal mythologies. Deena's book, *Writing for Your Life*,[23] characterizes the writing process as a spiritual discipline, a means to the discovery of story and self. In 2004, her work as a healer gave rise to ReVisioning Medicine, a program involving medical personnel along with alternative practitioners to evolve a medicine that does no harm to humans or the earth. The work is based on the *19 Ways to the 5th World* or "19 ways to create a viable future for all beings," a manifesto of how to nurture the land and each other through a training program of workshops, classes, books, council meetings, storytelling, and dream sharing.

Deena describes her work, including her many novels and poems, as always rooted in the underworld, in the dream life. For Women *Dreaming-Into-Art,* Deena shared three dreams that represented for her a *descent,* a psychological journey into the depths of the unconscious, or a Dark Night of the Soul. The dream trilogy below encapsulates her personal journey of death and rebirth experienced over several years:

- **Undergoing torture in a Latin American country.** This symbolized for Deena the beginning of her downward spiral into deep psychological despair.

- **Being forced by soldiers into a jail cell, deep underground.** To Deena, this dream was a metaphorical "dropping into" the underworld or Hades, epitomizing the nadir or bottommost of her Dark Night.

- **Experiencing rebirth and renewal.** In Deena's third dream, a voice ordered her to "make a child." (In actuality, she was beyond her child-bearing years.) She was to create "new life" to populate the devastated and barren land around her (a new stage of growth after a long, barren period of psychospiritual desolation).

The entire body of Deena's work emphasizes the unconscious as the source of creativity and psychological transformation. She is interested in individual transformation, and especially in how this corresponds to enhancing our relationships to one another and to the world in which we live. She sounds the alarm at the advent of oppression in any form. Her message urges us to integrate the psycholgical and political, the sexual and spiritual, the mythical imagination with contemporary world events. Her courage reminds us to engage in a serious struggle with the issue of darkness in the psyche and the world. She proposes that we do this by taking responsibility for lifting our own vibration through spiritual love, light, and sound.

Nearly everyone needs to embark on a Dark Night of the Soul as part of their initiatory path. Societal and global events in recent years have drawn attention to this process as a way for many to awaken to Spirit. The Dark Night varies in length, depth, how often it occurs in a single lifetime, and in what ways it specifically affects each person who struggles through it— but it is *always* life changing. Old, unresolved issues come up for review and resolution; unimaginable psychospiritual processes are experienced; and new awakenings and realizations occur. For myself, a prolonged Dark Night of the Soul experience in my early thirties was a pivotal turning point; everything I've worked with since as a psychotherapist, college professor, and author has referred back to this profoundly transformational period in my life. Initiates often find that they are forced to negotiate a Dark Night (in fact, often more than one) as they progress on the Serpentine Path. ***The old maxim that "we can only go as high as we have gone deep" refers to the need for us to grow as beings by honoring our plunges into the darkest depths as profoundly as our leaps into the light.*** The Dark Night of the Soul deepens and carves us out so that we are able to live with greater love, beauty, and understanding.

## Carolee Schneemann: Union

*One's art is just one's efforts
to wed oneself to the universe,
to unify oneself through union.*

~ **Robert Motherwell**

Painter, filmmaker, performance artist, and provocateur, Carolee Schneemann, who died in 2019, was one of the pioneers of *happenings* and body art, calling her work in this medium, "kinetic theater." In the New York art world of the 1960s and '70s, Carolee was concerned with artworks that addressed both sexual and personal freedom. Her well-known performance piece, *Meat Joy*,[24] a kinetic theater piece, was originally performed in Paris in 1964. The performance featured semi-nude performers who interacted with chickens, sausages, raw fish, wet paint, plastic, and paper while accompanied by the sound recordings of Paris street vendors, popular songs, and traffic noises. During the performance, the participants undressed and painted each other. Carolee had developed both the title and much of the content of *Meat Joy* from bits and pieces of dreams that she had collected for several years.

Carolee described her artistic process this way: "All of my work derives from the transition between dreaming and waking. Without opening my eyes, I write or scrawl dream messages or drawings on notepads, or even on the walls."[25] She often portrayed the intersection of various realities and experiences in her artworks by constructing simultaneous overlays and interconnected patterns. As a child, she once experimented with painting underwater: submerged in a pond, and floating her tablet and a little wooden tray on top of the water, she practiced painting watery tableaus. This desire to unify her inner and outer worlds translated into her films, as well as to her paintings and performance art pieces. In her 1967 film, *Fuses*, (the first of an *Autobiographical Trilogy* of films),[26] she juxtaposed scenes of sexual and domestic activity with environmental imagery, manipulating the recorded footage to resemble the abstract expressionism of her paintings. This film and the next two of her *Trilogy* are produced with a similar layering of complex sounds and visuals, resulting in a kaleidoscopic, dreamlike sensory experience for the viewer.

Carolee's desire to unify and connect everything in her life and work could be traced, perhaps, to her Scottish nanny, who told her when she was a child that in each lifetime, humans search the world over for their other halves, experiencing much unhappiness until they have found those particular beings to complete them. This significant memory may be reflected in Carolee's emphasis, particularly in film, of the nature and intensity of male-female relationships. She shared, "I have always connected to the natural world and to my sense of my own physicality, my sexuality. I can remember orgasm as a child, and a feeling that my genital was my soul, as a sacred place…this is where God dwelled."[27] Carolee's artworks, often by challenging and defying collective norms, point the way to a greater acceptance of the body, sexuality, the unconscious, and the transformative feminine.

Along the *Labyrinthine Way*, union is experienced in multiple ways: as the psychological integration of the splintered parts of ourselves; the inner unification of our lower and higher selves; the marriage of the masculine and feminine principles within ourselves; and the merger of Soul and Spirit in Self-Realization. The yearning for the "other" in physical life is more truly the desire for spiritual completion, which is accomplished by the eventual reunion with our inner partner on an advanced spiritual plane. The intimacy experienced via physical union is an approximation—and a promise—of what we most profoundly long for, a wholeness that is only found in reunification with the Divine.

# INITIATION THEMES IN FILM

*No form of art goes beyond ordinary consciousness as film does,*
*straight to our emotions,*
*deep into the twilight room of the soul.*

~ **Ingmar Bergman**

Films are all-encompassing, immersive experiences. The medium of film offers a sensory surround that we viscerally feel and portrays human journeys that, for two hours or so, we vicariously *live*. Certain films introduce universal themes that uplift and transform us; they are usually based on the Path of Initiation, also known in mythology as the Hero's Journey. The following films include a few of the elements presented in previous chapters that characterize the human unfoldment process.

## *Chasing Mavericks:* Finding A Mentor

*Every great soul had a great mentor.*

~ **Lailah Gifty Akita**

The initiation theme of the Spiritual Guide as teacher and mentor is exemplified in the biographical film, *Chasing Mavericks* (2012), directed by Curtis Hanson and Michael Apted, with Johnny Weston portraying real-life surfer Jay Moriarity and Gerard Butler as his mentor, surfer Frosty Hesson. Saved from drowning by Frosty when he was only eight years old,[28] teenager Jay asked veteran surfer Frosty to train him to surf Mavericks, a formidable reef break with surf in the 50-foot range,[29] located at Half Moon Bay, about 25 miles south of San Francisco. Frosty only agreed to train Jay if he was willing to embark on a sometimes grueling program of physical, mental, and spiritual training,[30] which included the "foundation pillars" of surfing. The pillars included successfully paddleboarding 36 miles across Monterey Bay, treading water for 40 minutes. and holding his breath for four minutes. In addition, Jay was expected to learn the arts of positive visualization and thoughtful reflection. During the nearly four years[31] Frosty prepared Jay to ride Mavericks, he required Jay to write on various topics regarding life and surfing, writings which eventually totaled 55 essays or 330 pages. Each essay, a minimum of two pages or more, was followed by a lengthy discussion held in Frosty's van or at the beach.

Frosty was 45 when he became mentor, guide, and teacher to 13-year-old Jay. Jay's father was absent during much of his early life, and when his mother and father separated, he turned to surfing as a way to cope with his difficult family life. In many ways, Frosty filled a father's place in Jay's life, not only teaching him how to become a premier surfer, but how to live life as an exceptionally kindhearted and strong-minded young man. Jay loved surfing because he experienced it as "…an art, by the way you can express yourself on a wave. It's a sport because you can compete with it, and it's spiritual because it's just you and Mother Nature. For me, it's very spiritual."[32] Frosty's mentorship fostered in Jay this love for surfing and for life.

Jay Moriarity died in June, 2001, one day before turning 23, while free diving in the Indian Ocean off the coast of the Maldives. Just days after his death, hundreds of Jay's friends and fellow surfers paddled out into the waters of Pleasure Point near Santa Cruz, California, to scatter his ashes and hold a memorial service. Even today, there are signs and bumper stickers seen around Santa Cruz that urge people to "Live like Jay."

Being taught by a Master Teacher who has "been there and back" is important in any profession where skill, attitude, and approach are important, and even more so when someone walks the unknown Path of Initiation. Just like surfing Mavericks, there are dangers, challenges, and thrills for which only an expert in the field, someone who has "walked the walk," can prepare us. When we are ready, many of us are contacted by the Master or Guide we have known in a previous lifetime, who is part of our (known or unknown) spiritual lineage (many modern initiates have partially walked The Path in earlier lives). Or, we may come upon a certain Master and know that in our hearts that *this* is the Teacher who has been meant for us. A few initiates find someone who is fitting at the beginning stages of the path and another who is better suited at later stages. (Casual, persistent, and frequent "shopping around," though, can be harmful to the unfoldment process.) Some of us decide to climb the ladder by ourselves, but without help, we can progress only to a point. To realize our own limitations is to learn humility, a quality needed by all Initiates, the Lovers of God.

## *Seven Years in Tibet:* Learning Humility

> *It's not the mountain we conquer, but ourselves.*
> **~ Sir Edmund Hillary**

You can be sure that, once you are on The Path, you will gradually undergo such a complete transformation that at some point, you will look back and not even recognize the person you once were. The changes you experience include dropping negative patterns of your lower nature, such as self-importance or vanity. *Seven Years in Tibet* (1997), directed by Jean-Jacques Annaud, and starring Brad Pitt and David Thewlis, is the true story of the Austrian mountain climber Heinrich Harrer, whose pride and arrogance were transformed by the development of a profound friendship with the 14th Dalai Lama. A desire for fame leads Harrer (Pitt) and his partner Peter Aufschnaiter (Thewlis) to join a 1939 expedition to climb Nanga Parbat, one of the highest peaks in the Himalayas. However, their plans were at first frustrated by bad weather and an avalanche, and later interrupted by the start of World War II. Harrer and his climbing partner, Aufschnaiter, escaped a British internment camp in India to find sanctuary in the holy city of Lhasa, Tibet, the "Land of Snows."

While adjusting to the ways of the Tibetan people, Harrer and Aufschnaiter eventually adopted the dress as well as some of the language and customs of the local Tibetans who showed both men patience, generosity, and kindness. The Dalai Lama (also known as Gyalwa Rinpoche) invited Harrer to the Portola Palace to make a film on ice skating, which Harrer had introduced to the Tibetans. When the yellow-haired Austrian met the 14-year-old Dalai Lama (played by the actor Jamyang Jamtsho Wangchuk), both began a program of cultural exchange and an interchange of mutual respect. Harrer became the Dalai Lama's tutor in English, geography, and the sciences, and even built a cinema for him, with the projector powered by a Jeep engine. In return, the Dalai Lama taught Harrer the ways of Buddhism, including the virtues of humility, gratitude, and compassion. A bond was forged between the two men that brought fulfillment and meaning to Harrer's life. Slowly, the egocentric and boastful Harrer transformed into a person of quality and substance.

This story appears to bear witness to the maxim that "Spirituality is not so much taught as it is caught." Even while Harrer was performing the role as "the knowledgeable Westerner" by imparting his academic learning to His Holiness, the Dalai Lama's spiritual influence on Harrer was subtle yet unequivocal. The lessons on Buddhism imparted to Harrer were persuasive, but the daily loving presence of the Dalai Lama was inexorably transformational. At the end of the seven years that Harrer remained in Tibet, he was no longer the egocentric braggart who was once summoned to the Portola Palace. When Chinese troops invaded Tibet in 1951, both men were forced to flee; the Dalai Lama settled at Dharamsala in Northern India and Harrer returned to Austria. The Dalai Lama and Harrer continued to meet periodically over the years, their friendship enduring until Harrer's death at 93 in January, 2006.[33]

To be humble as a spiritual student is to acknowledge our *truest* role in life, which is always as *learner*. There is always one more step on the spiritual path, no matter how spiritually advanced we are (I read once that there are 352 levels, though I am not sure exactly what these "levels" refer to, along the gradient back to the Source!) We are all travelers on the Road to God, and the individual ego-self only helps us to navigate our way on this Road while we are still functioning in the human body. One of the main tasks of initiation is learning how to establish the lower self in "correct" relationship to the Self (or Soul)—and that relationship always requires reverence, devotion, and humility.

## *The Whale Rider:*
## Going Your Own Way

*To walk the spiritual path is
to continually step out into the unknown.*

**~ Wallace Huey**

Wending one's way along the Path of Initiation sometimes requires that you give up certain detrimental habits, separate from friends who no longer resonate with your spiritual goals, or possibly, painfully break with the traditions of your family or culture. You are forced to go your own way. The movie, *The Whale Rider* (2002), directed by Niki Caro, stars Keisha Castle-Hughes as Paikea Apriana ("Pai"), a 12-year-old Maori girl who dreamed of becoming her tribe's first female chief. This notion was vehemently rejected by her grandfather, Koro, the current village leader. Only males were allowed to ascend to chiefdom and had to be in direct patrilineal descent from the mythic Whale Rider, Paikea, who rode to coastal New Zealand on the back of a whale (the *Taniwha*). Pai's twin brother, the natural heir to this leadership role, died at birth, and now Noro deeply feared that the tribe would decline unless a suitable male was found.

Against her grandfather's commands, Pai surreptitiously learned tribal lore and skills that her grandfather was teaching to a group of boys, hoping to find the future village leader among them. Pai soon passed several tests of courage customarily reserved for Maori males: She successfully wielded the fighting stick or *taiaha* in a contest with a boy and recovered the *rei puta* (whale tooth) after it is thrown into the ocean, a task traditionally distinguishing someone as a worthy leader. But Pai's real test came when a number of Southern right whales were beached; she climbed onto the back of the largest whale (associated with the legendary Paikea) and coaxed the whale out to sea, which is then followed by the entire pod. Koro finally recognized that his granddaughter was truly the rightful chief of the tribe. The entire village was restored and reinvigorated by the celebrations and rituals held in recognition of Pai's installment as leader.

Early in the film, Pai was alone in her conviction that she was destined for her singular path as tribal leader. She experiences rejection by those she dearly loves as well as general disapproval from members of her tribe for her "inappropriate" and disrespectful behavior. Pai continued unaided, and was never distracted or disheartened to the point of straying from achieving her calling. Her ultimate ascension as tribal leader is not only a spiritual step up for her but a renascence for her entire village.

There may be times when the initiate needs the strength to strike out on his or her own in order to follow the road less traveled. There is a "call" from the "still, small voice within," sometimes so insistent that there seems to be no other choice! In my late twenties, I felt so estranged from my life—and from myself—that I knew I might not even make it through life without answering the inner pressure to know who I was. Those around me were puzzled by this, as I had so much: job, husband, house, and friends. To want something more probably seemed ungrateful and privileged. Yet day after day, I would drive home after work and sit in my car inside the garage and cry inconsolable tears, wondering how to feel at one with myself. I began to look for a life that more closely "resembled me," even if this eventually required that I go my own way.

## *Dune:*
## Facing Your Fears

*Love is what we are born with.*
*Fear is what we have learned here.*
*The spiritual journey is the unlearning of fear*
*and the acceptance of love*
*back into our hearts.*

~ **Marianne Williamson**

*I will not fear. Fear is the mind killer. I will face my fear.*
*I will let it pass through me.*
*When the fear has gone, there shall be nothing.*
*Only I will remain.*

~ **Frank Herbert**

The movie, *Dune: Part I* (2021), the first of two parts, is the latest adaptation of the 1965 book by Frank Herbert, (the first version came out in 1984) and is directed by Denis Villeneuve.[34] In the year, 10191, the House of Atreides from the planet Caladan was tasked by the Galactic Padishah Empire (the Imperium) with relocating to the desert planet of Arrakis, or Dune, for the purpose of supervising the production of mélange, or "spice." Created beneath the planet's surface by a process for which monstrous-sized sandworms were vital, spice was a highly addictive substance that extended life, expanded consciousness, and was the key to interstellar space travel. The enormously profitable spice harvesting industry had been previously overseen on Arrakis by House Harkonnen, whose members, in collusion with the Emperor, now set out to destroy the Atreides.

Members of the House of Atreides were Duke Leto and Lady Jessica, the parents of Paul Atreides, the main protagonist in the Dune saga. When Paul had prescient dreams and visions, there was speculation by the mystical order of women, the *Bene Gesserit* (to which Lady Jessica belongs) that he might be the Chosen One, or *Kwisatz Haderach*, a male who can bridge both space and time. When the Harkonnens assassinated Duke Leto, Paul and his mother fled into the desert and, after winning a combat challenge between Paul and a Fremen warrior, were taken in by the Fremen, nomadic peoples of Dune, who had long held the prophesy of a savior figure who would free them from the rule of the Emperor.

At this point in the film, *Dune: Part 1*, ends. *Dune: Part 2* (relying on the book) will undoubtably include that while living with the Fremen, Paul rises as a leader, chooses the name Muad'Dib, forms an army, falls in love with Chani (daughter of the esteemed Fremen, Liet), and vows to avenge his father's murder. To gain greater powers of precognition, Paul drinks the *Water of Life,* a blue liquid variously described as an illuminating poison, or an "awareness spectrum narcotic," which is used by the Bene Gesserits to become Reverend Mothers; drinking the liquid is generally fatal to men. After weeks in a coma-like state, Paul regains consciousness with the power to control the sandworms and a deeper understanding of the spice. He has also experienced a vision of the Emperor's plan to regain control of Dune with an invasion fleet. He has awakened as the *Kwisatz Haderach*.

With the Fremen riding the sandworms, Paul launches a final attack against the Harkonnens and the emperor's elite military force, the *Sardaukar*, at Dune's capital city of Arrakeen. Paul and the Fremen triumph, and with Paul's marriage to the emperor's daughter, Irulan Corrino, (even though he continues to love his consort and mother to his children, Chani), he has cleared the way for his own ascendancy to the position of emperor. There is more to the epic, *Dune*, but I will leave off here.

**Paul had to face and overcome many fears:**

- He confronts pain via the Gom Jabbar Test for Humanity, given to all women who enter the Bene Gesserit order. With the poisoned needle (gom jabbar) at his neck, he is directed to put his right hand into a nerve-induction box to test whether he is able to withstand extreme pain by controlling his instincts to escape it.

- After his father is betrayed and murdered, Paul must face the unknown to protect himself and his mother as they escape deeply into the desert.

- Paul drinks the Water of Life. It is an especially dangerous act for men, who usually die after drinking the liquid.

- Paul envisions a possible future that, as the "One," he is fated to lead the Fremen in a jihad, or holy war, that will spread across the known universe, killing millions in its path. He is fearful that the jihad will be the fulfillment of what he senses is his "terrible purpose," a destiny he hopes to circumvent.

Facing one's greatest fears is an important part of the initiatory journey. The Labyrinthine Path teaches us that fears are only illusions and that overcoming them strengthens us to meet any and every eventuality in life. ***It is said that to travel into outer space is the physical parallel to the great adventure of entering inner space, where we undergo deeply spiritual transformations that will lead us all back to the Far Country of God.***

## CHAPTER SIX EXERCISES

**Your Life is a Story, Too**

*You have to have the guts to engage with your own spiritual journey,
which is what life is for. It can be reflected in art,
but art won't take you there on its own. It's not good enough.
You actually have to use your inquiring mind and question yourself...
You have to avoid getting tied up in intellectual and ironic gameplay,
which will not liberate you... You're going to get it through authentic engagement.*
~ **Billy Childish**

You do not need to only rely on books, art, and films to supply you with human narratives, life dramas, and transformational encounters. Your life is a story, too. One of the most therapeutic exercises that you can do is to *write an autobiography*. When I did this, I gained an invaluable perspective, as writing allowed me to set things down in an objective manner. You can more easily see repetitive patterns and unexpected connections to gain fresh insights. This can be fun to do, as you are the protagonist (hero) in your own plot line! Try to find incidents in your life that parallel some of the facets of the initiation process, and journal about them. For example:

1. Think of the particular **fears** that you've had to face this lifetime—fear of public speaking; fear that others will reject you (so you reject them first); fear of failure or success, etc. What have you done (or could you do) to resolve these fears?

2. Name as many of your **inner selves** as possible, especially those that you have hidden from public view (for example, the Rebel, the Scaredy-Cat, the Bully, the Great Artist, etc.) How can you work with these inner selves to recognize and integrate them into your personality?

3. Discuss times when you were really **disillusioned**; you had thought something or someone was one way and found out that they were altogether something else. What were the circumstances, and what did you learn to see more clearly?

4. Think of an anecdote that clearly illustrates your **shadow** characteristics, such as when you took something that belonged to a sibling and later denied it, or you took credit for someone else's idea at school or work, etc. What did you learn about yourself, and what are the lessons?

5. What did someone do or say in your early life to guide or **mentor** you? This could be a parent, a teacher, a family member, an older friend. How did they make a difference in the trajectory of your life?

6. When did you experience a lesson in **humility**? (Sometimes this is related to learning gratitude). What was your most important takeaway from this situation?

7. Have you ever felt that you were in a **Dark Night of the Soul**? What did you experience physically and psychologically? What help/support did your find? At the end of this ordeal, what changed in your life? How did *you* change?

8. In what ways have you become more **detached**? These might include the areas of:

   - political conflicts
   - friendships you no longer resonate with
   - old scores that you were formerly determined to settle
   - mistakes you've regretted
   - love relationships that you've needed to release
   - your outer appearance as a priority

9. How are you being of **service**? Have you begun thinking more in the context of "we" than in "me"? What have you done (or plan to do) to put service into action? Examples might be:

- helping the senior living near you with her grocery shopping needs
- volunteering at the local food distribution center which feeds the impoverished or the homeless
- joining Habitat for Humanity in your local area
- working with a wounded warrior
- tending the lawns of people who no longer can keep them up

# CHAPTER SIX ENDNOTES

1. *The Call of the Wild* has been adapted to film at least five times, while *The Secret Garden* has been made into four distinct movies since its publication in 1911.

2. Cheryl Strayed. *Wild: From Lost to Found on the Pacific Crest Trail.* New York: Vintage Books, 2012.

3. Abu Hamid al-Ghazzali, trans. R. J. McCarthy. *Al-Ghazali's Path to Sufism: The Deliverance from Error.* Louisville, KY: Fons Vitae, 1999.

4. Ibid., p. 53.

5. Ibid., p. 54.

6. Doris Lessing. *The Golden Notebook.* New York: Simon & Schuster, 1962.

7. Ibid., p. x.

8. Ibid., p.61.

9. Karan Bajaj. *The Yoga of Max's Discontent.* New York: Random House, 2016.

10. Ibid., p. 23

11. Ibid., p. 187

12. Ibid., p. 211

13. Ibid., p. 254

14. After Anna Halprin's 1981 "In and On the Mountain" dream-based community dance ritual was perfomed, the murderer of seven women killed on Mount Tamalais' trails was caught. Following the advice of a Huichol Indian shaman, the ritual was repeatedly performed on Mount Tamalpais by local community members to collectively reclaim and purify the mountain.

Anna Halprin was an American choreographer and dancer who created innovative directions for dance from the 1930's until her death at 100 years in 2021. She helped to pioneer postmodern dance, founding the San Francisco's Dancers Workshop in the 1950s. She pushed the boundaries of dance to address social issues ("Ceremony of Us"); build community in the world ("Circle the Earth" community dance rituals); nurture physical and emotional healing ("Intensive Care: Reflections on Death and Dying"), and connect people to nature ("Experiments in the Environment"). In 1978, with her daughter, Daria, she founded the Tamalpa Institute in Marin County, California, which offers workshops and training in the

Life/Art process. Over her decades-long career, Anna created over 150 dance theater works and wrote several books. She is also included in a number of films celebrating her life and many contributions. (See EndNote 19).

[15.] Ann McCoy, painter and sculptor, grew up as the adopted child of a chemist who worked with rare earths. One of her earliest dreams as a child was of a king who was knocked on the head and pulverized. It wasn't until Ann studied alchemy as an adult that she realized that this motif refers to an alchemical (deep-seated psychological change) stage during which the ego undergoes death and dissolution. This dream, and many more of this nature, foreshadowed her adult process of psychological transformation and informed the themes and symbols of her art.

Ann is a New York-based working artist, art critic, and educator who is a lecturer at the Yale School of Drama, where she teaches art history, mythology, and the use of projection technique in art. Her large-scale pencil drawings are based on her dreams, studies in alchemy, and depth psychology (which emphasizes the unconscious). Her work is in the collections of the Metropolitan Museum of Art, the Los Angeles County Museum of Art, San Francisco Museum of Modern Art, and many others. Ann has won numerous awards, including; the Prix de Rome, the National Endowment for the Arts, and the New Talent Award from the Los Angeles County Museum of Art.

Currently, Ann is offering working seminars for artists, playwrights, and film makers. During her 6-week course, "Accessing the Unconscious," she guides participants in "techniques for accessing the unconscious, using drawings, different art mediums, journals, meditations, and readings." Her classes are taught from a Jungian perspective, but include reading material from a variety of texts (from her introductory brochure).

[16.] Deena Metzger once dreamed that a woman lifted her hand, and Deena was shocked to see that the woman had absolutely no lines on her palm. The words, The Woman Who Slept with Men, then trailed across her vision like the tile of a movie. Shortly after, Deena rented a cabin in Mendocino, CA, and spent a summer outlining a drama/novel by that name. (See Note 21).

Writer, healer, and teacher, Deena Metzger has made noteworthy contributions in various genres, including novels, poetry, non-fiction, and plays. In 2012, her novel *La Negra y Blanca* won the Oakland Pen Award for Literature. In 1999 Deena introduced the concept and practice of Daré: monthly gatherings for community and individual healing. Deena's continued interest in promoting healing for persons and the communities they live in led her to establish ReVisioning Medicine in 2004, a coalition of traditional, indigenous, and alternative medicine practitioners. In 2009, she began teaching the *19 Ways to the 5th World*, a manifesto of resolutions leading to practices that sustain our planet and each other.

17. Carolee Schneemann performed *Up to and Including Her Limits* nine times between 1971 and 1976, before establishing it as an installation. For this work, she "functioned as a pencil," (p.231 in *More Than Meat Joy*) scrawling on the floors and walls of her environment as she swung, suspended and nude, via a harness attached to the ceiling. She incorporated double-screen projections of one her black and white films, video relays, slides, and writings relevant to her project. In her book, *More Than Meat Joy*, Schneemann characterized her process as "private movement meditations," (p.277) which emerged from her liminal state induced while swinging. Schneemann was a New York-based visual experimental artist, known for her multi-media works, (primarily as a painter and performance artist) on the topics of body, narrative, sexuality, and gender. She died in 2019 (see EndNote 19).

18. Patricia Ariadne. *Women Dreaming-into Art: Seven Artists Who Create from Dreams.* Lakeville, Minnesota: Galde Press, 2013.

19. Anna Halprin died in May, 2021 at the age of 100 in Kentfield, CA. Pauline Oliveros, celebrated composer of experimental and electronic music, died at 84 years old in 2016 in Kingston, New York. Carolee Schneemann, died in March, 2019 in New Paltz, New York, at the age of 79. Mary Beth Edelson, a pioneer of the feminist art movement, died at 88 years in April, 2021. The artists who are living at the time of this book's publication are: Deena Metzger, 85, who lives in Topanga Canyon, CA; Ann McCoy, who is 75 and is New York-based; and the scholar and author Christine Downing, 89, who is currently living in Washington state.

20. These statements are excerpted from notes written by Ann McCoy for a 1987 exhibition catalog for the Edinburgh International, Scottish Arts Council.

21. Deena Metzger. The diary-novel, *Tree*, is paired with the drama-novel, *The Woman Who Slept with Men to Take the War Our of Them.* Berkeley, CA: Wingbow Press, 1981.

22. Ibid., p. 219.

23. Deena Metzger. *Writing for Your Life.* New York: HarperOne, 1992.

24. Carolee Schneemann. Read more about the "kinetic theater" piece, *Meat Joy*, in Schneemann's book, *More Than Meat Joy.* New York: McPherson & Co., 1979.

25. From my September, 1986 interview with Carolee Schneemann in her New York apartment, for the book, *Women Dreaming-into-Art*.

26. Carolee Schneemann's first major film was *Fuses*, which was Part I of an *Autobiographical Trilogy* (1964–67) and was screened at the Cannes Film Festival in 1969. For the film she recorded and then collaged together both filmed and painted frames of sexual intimacies between herself and her husband at the time (to the outrage of the audience at Cannes). The

second film of her *Autobiographical Trilogy* was *Plumb Line* (1968–71), about the dissolution of her marriage, and the third was titled, *Kitch's Last Meal* (1973–78), chronicling the day-to-day life of her cat, Kitch, until his death.

27. From my 1986 interview with Carolee Schneemann.

28. In the movie, Jay's water rescue as a boy by Frosty is creative license and did not actually happen in Jay's life.

29. It's been reported that when the Mavericks waves are at their biggest (they can be as tall as a five-story building), they crash down on the North American plate with enough force to register on the UC Berkeley seismograph.

30. Jay was not Frosty's only pupil; Frosty trained dozens of young men about life and surfing.

31. The film, *Chasing Mavericks*, relates that Frosty trained Jay for Mavericks for only 12 weeks. Sources also differ in their accounts of how long Frosty's training was: some say four years and others say two years. If Jay was only 13 when he began his training, then I lean toward the accounts that report four years, as he was 16 when he first surfed Mavericks.

32. Quoted from "The Compelling Surf Life Story of Jay Moriarity," *SurferToday*, April 18, 2017 https://www.surfertoday.com/surfing/the-compelling-surf-life-story-of-jay-moriarity

33. It has come to the forefront in recent years that Heinreich Harrer was a member of the Nazi Party, though he claimed he was not active and had only worn his SS uniform once, when he was married. Harrer was cleared of pre-war crimes and supported by Simon Wisenthal, who was a fellow Austrian, well-known Holocaust survivor, Nazi hunter, and writer. Harrer stated that his Nazi Party membership was a youthful mistake that he regretted.

34. Other adaptations of *Dune* include a three-part miniseries written and directed by John Harrison. The TV series debuted in 2000 and starred Alec Newman as Paul Atreides. This miniseries was followed by another in 2003, *Frank Herbert's Children of Dune* (starring James McAvoy), which was based on Frank Herbert's novels *Dune Messiah* (1969) and *Children of Dune* (1976).

# CHAPTER SEVEN

# The World Labyrinth: The New Human

*Whether it is to be Utopia or Oblivion will be a touch-and-go relay race
right up to the final moment...
Humanity is in a final exam as to whether or not
it qualifies for continuance in the Universe.*

~ R. Buckminster Fuller

*Trying to change social, national, or global realities
without working on human consciousness
means there is no serious intention.*

~ Sadhguru

## CH-CH-CH-CH-CHANGES (David Bowie)

*Crisis, catastrophe, and disaster
are part of evolution's rich repertoire.
Stress creates evolution; often life's setbacks set the stage
for a new evolutionary advance.*

~ Carter Phipps

> *The consciousness of each of us is evolution*
> *looking at itself and reflecting upon itself.*
> ~ **Teilhard de Chardin**

Over the year that I have been writing this book, it's been interesting to ask random people how their lives have changed during the first few years of the 20s decade. How have they been personally affected by the various crises—biological, social, economical, political, and global—that have disrupted, which for many in the U.S., were admittedly over-scheduled, excessively social, and aggressively materialistic lifestyles? I asked questions about their lives during 2020-2022, such as, "*What changes have you made in your home life, health, job, and relationships? What have you gained and what have you lost over the beginning years of the 2020s decade? Do you think differently in some ways now? If so, give examples. Have any changes occurred in your spiritual life? Are you more optimistic or more pessimistic about the future of the U.S?*"

I have been struck by the number of people who reported they realized that they wanted new jobs that gave them more time with their families, even if some of those jobs would pay less. They did not want to continue the rat race pace of life that does not allow for meaningful relationships or for individual time and reflection. Others planned to hold out for jobs which offered better pay and benefits, flexible work settings, and increased family-leave allowances. A number of the people I talked to had gone into psychotherapy; some began journaling; and others began a meditation practice; quite a few seemed determined to put more attention on their physical well-being with weight-loss programs and renewed exercise routines. A few of those I talked to seemed more pessimistic about the future of the U.S., primarily those who believed that the U.S. government was set on taking away their freedoms by mandating public health policies. Others expressed concerns about rising crime, inflated prices, diminished personal freedoms, and potential nuclear aggression. Those who were optimistic usually had a spiritual orientation of some kind. They believed that there were valuable lessons inherent in the difficulties they were facing, and that critical circumstances had impelled them to make important and timely changes for the better. More than half of the people I spoke with had renewed their commitment to their life partner and families. In contrast, some decided that it was high time to exit a marriage that had become merely habitual; a few of these same individuals reported that they had ended a zero-sum relationship (where one person's gain is always the other person's loss) to seek a relationship that was more equitable and mutually fulfilling.

Others, especially young people, were having difficulty coping. (I hear firsthand of this ongoing problem, as I teach college psychology courses to a student population that includes many Generation Z students). They seemed especially affected by the spread of unregulated (and sometimes targeted) social media content, unleashed viruses, unchecked school shootings, unprecendented threats to individual freedoms, unbridled cultural, political, and global conflicts, and unremitting social isolation.

While I was only able to talk to a few dozen people, the American Psychological Association reported in a 2021 survey[1] that, the majority of adults (81%) indicated that they were most stressed about the future of our nation (nine in ten adults said they hoped our country moved toward greater unity). In addition, the coronavirus pandemic (80%) and the country's general political unrest (74%) were causes of a sharp increase in stress. In their attempts to cope with the crises of the early 2020s, the survey showed that significant numbers of Americans were drinking more alcohol, had gained or lost weight, and were losing excessive amounts of sleep. These health impacts have been particularly true of young people, parents, essential workers, and people of color. Many people have suffered an increase in health and mental issues, such as chronic illnesses and difficulties in resolving grief.[2]

The shattering crises faced by millions in the U.S. (and in the world) during the last few years have involuntarily pulled some into the Dark Night of the Soul, which can begin a cycle of experience that leads people into the depths of their own beings. Some people will not be ready to confront the transformative forces that this process awakens and will abort it with medication or seek in other ways to alleviate or compromise the psychological demands such a process requires. This is to be expected, as it is a serious and sometimes dangerous process, and not all are prepared to participate in it. For those with sufficient psychospiritual maturity and commitment, the survival of the identity disintegration that a Dark Night often engenders may lead to a new level of integration and cohesiveness (what earlier has been called a "death and rebirth" process). The few who are able to go to the *nadir*, or descend to the "bottom of their own wells," can ultimately reemerge with greater clarity and well-being, having undergone a transmutation that is cell deep and culture wide. For just as individuals experience this cycle of death and renewal, so do cultures.

## THE FOURTH TURNING

> *Crisis, catastrophe, and disaster*
> *are part of evolution's rich repertoire.*
> *Stress creates evolution;*
> *often life's setbacks set the stage*
> *for a new evolutionary advance.*
>
> ~ **Carter Phipps**

A generational theory published in 1977 seems to have predicted a crisis in America occurring on or near 2020. In their book, *The Fourth Turning*,[3] Neil Howe and William Strauss wrote that sometime before 2025, America would pass through a great gate in history during which the very survival of the nation could be at stake. They predicted that the climax of this period would take place around 2020 and the resolution, which includes the restructuring of many of the country's institutions, would occur around 2026.

The Strauss-Howe generational theory holds that history moves in 80-year cycles (corresponding to the general length of a human lifetime), called a "saeculum" by the Romans. It posits that each 80-year saeculum is divided into four 20-year cycles, each identified as a "turning." At the beginning of each turning, there is a change in how people view themselves, society, and the future. The First Turning is called *Growth* (a "high"), an era during which institutions are strong, and society is based more on collectivism and conformity than on individualism. The Second Turning is *Maturation* (an "awakening"), a period that both exemplifies a peak period of public progress and the condemnation of institutions by those seeking greater personal and spiritual autonomy. The Third Turning is identified as *Entropy* (an "unraveling"), during which people mistrust institutions and lean toward individualism. The Fourth Turning, which we can identify with now, is the *Destruction* (or "crisis") era. This is a 20-year period which, according to the authors, began in 2008 and will extend to around the year 2030.

## THE CURRENT CRISIS ERA

*In several decades, humanity will be*
*at a fork in the road: utopia or oblivion.*
*Either a utopia of abundance or an oblivion of destruction.*
~ R. Buckminster Fuller (1969)

The Fourth Turning crisis response, claim Howe and Strauss, occurs in the face of a perceived threat to the nation's very survival. During this era, the old culture disintegrates and gives way to a transitional period of hardship, stress, and the clash of class, race, and national goals and policies. Howe and Strauss predict that during the current Fourth Turning, America will experience a passage similar in impact to that of the American Revolution, the Civil War, the Great Depression, and World War ll. They caution that the risk of catastrophe is high, with the possibility of revolutions and civil wars. Stresses during the current time of crisis include economic issues (wide disparities in wealth; increased poverty); social unrest (race and class inequalities, militias, nationalism); cultural deterioration (degeneration of media); ecological crises (global warming); political turmoil (extreme bipartisanship, threat of authoritarianism); bio-distress (the pandemic and its variants), and global upheaval (conflicts and wars).

On the more positive side, Strauss and Howe suggest that the contemporary crisis era is an opportunity for America's institutional life to be overhauled, to be rebuilt from the ground up (much like our external infrastructure). The authors submit that the successful resolution of the Fourth Turning can bring new founding movements that ultimately contribute to a new national identity, the reshaping of our politics, economy, social policies, educational and medical systems, and our relationship to the world. People once again find themselves a part of a larger whole as the culture begins a process of *regeneracy*. Within 15-25 years between the triggering events or catalysts leading to *destruction* (and a possible crisis *resolution)*, American society will have moved on to either tragedy or triumph, "apocalypse or glory."[4] Just as individuals experience death and rebirth during an existential crisis (The Dark Night of the Soul), America as a nation could be said to be doing the same. A radical "turning" that leads to the rebirth of America will require a new psychospiritual attitude, a cultural sea change in consciousness.

We have been focusing here on the United States, but in view of the 2022 war in Eastern Europe and the subsequent coalition of most of the world behind Ukraine, perhaps we should look at a possible transformative change on a worldwide level. Collective change, in addition to individualistic shifts, will be a notable characteristic of the 20s decade.

# THE SHIFT AGE

> *We are at that inflection point,*
> *the nexus of change, the historical moment*
> *which will set civilization on its path*
> *for the remainder of the 21st century.*
> *The 2020s will define the direction for humanity,*
> *including our survival as a species.*
>
> ~ **David Houle**

Futurist David Houle cautions us not to use the term "new normal" when speaking about life changes during the 2020s. He maintains that, "There will not be anything remotely normal in quite a while…Abnormality is the new normal."[5] Houle labels the 2020s as the *Shift Age*, a transition period which he believes began in 2005 and will continue until the 2030s. Houle defines this decade as "the most disruptive and transformative decade in history," one which will "set the direction of civilization for the rest of the century."[6] Houle posits that this historical moment, or nexus of change, will also determine our very survival as a species.[7]

During the 2020s decade, Houle claims that we will experience shifts in virtually every aspect of our lives: methods of communication; types of occupations; monetary systems and global economy; content and delivery of education; systems of healthcare (incorporating preventative medicine and new treatments for mental disorders); forms of transportation and energy; social values and concepts; new perspectives on geopolitics; and relationships of all kinds (racial, ethnicity, gender-fluid recognition/acceptance).

# ISSUES OF THE SHIFT AGE

**The primary issues that demand resolution in the 2020s decade:**

- **Climate change.** The U.S. Energy Information Administration predicts that the current world energy consumption will increase by 56% between 2010 and 2040.

- **Immigration.** It's estimated that by 2050, 200 million climate refugees may have fled their homes,[8] but this number will undoubtably be larger due to unforeseen global conflicts and wars.

- **Wealth inequality.** As of 2021, the top one percent held about half of total U.S. net worth, while the bottom 50% held about two percent of all U.S. wealth).[9] Houle suggests that the 240 years-old concept of capitalism needs to be reinvented to be relevant to the Shift Age and beyond.

- **Pollution, including ocean degradation.** According to online research, chemicals and trash, (80% of which comes from land sources) are the two main types of ocean pollutants.[10]

- **Social injustice.** This area of concern includes affordable healthcare, food insecurity and hunger, LGBTQ+ rights, racial inequality, income disparity, climate change issues, and more.[11]

- **Population control**, on both national and global levels. Global population is growing by more than 80 million a year; population today is nearing 8 billion, more than double what it was in 1970.[12]

- **World relationships.** International relationships will need to evolve to reflect greater interdependence in the areas of geopolitics and geoeconomics, including the strategic containment of nuclear aggression with the active promotion of peace among the world's nations.

Author and Buddhist teacher Jack Kornfield states that the root cause of such problems is essentially due to the world's *spiritual crisis*. Societal ills, Kornfield contends, are caused by "greed, fear, hatred, prejudice, and delusion" and are resolved with solutions that include "compassion, understanding, kindness, and reverence for life."[13] The psychiatrist Carl Jung saw that "the psychological problem of our time"[14] would involve the meaning of life itself. He posited that the human individuation process, what we are recognizing in this book as initiation, is a "road to freedom," and that the psychological health of humanity relies on mitigating individual and collective shadow elements and formulating a new relationship to Source.

## CYCLES OF EVOLUTION

*When there is a set process,*
*you cannot change things so easily.*
*But when there is a periodic destabilization of the system,*
*there is a great possibility for change.*

~ **Sadhguru**

The Shift Age is a transitional period leading us into the dawning of the Age of Aquarius, which is alternately called the Wisdom Age or the Age of the Sages. This period also sees the end of the Kali Yuga (Iron Age), which is crossing over to the Satya Yuga (Golden Age). The calendar date of December 12, 2012, marked the completion of a 5,126-year Great Cycle (the end of the Mayan Long Count Calendar), a date interpreted by some as heralding a world cycle of positive transformation and a collective unfoldment or initiation for humanity. In addition, the Great Conjunction of Jupiter and Saturn on December 21, 2020 (also the date of the Winter Solstice), was considered the true dawning of the Aquarian Age,[17] marking the end of the Piscean Age, a cycle of approximately 2,160 years. This smaller cycle converges with a Great Cycle of 26,000 years, during which there is a steady change in the orientation of the axis rotation of the Earth, known as the precession of the equinoxes. In my book, *Drinking the Dragon*, I wrote about the Aquarian Age and its influences:

> "In 2020, we experienced (the onset of) the Dark Night as a culture. If we successfully process the many trials and lessons of this period, we will mature as a nation. This translates to a decrease in materialism, an ability to embrace diversity, a heightened sense of responsibility to the Earth, a renewed spirituality, greater appreciation and sponsorship of the arts, and an awakened awareness of our own darkness and that of others (so that we can better protect and uphold the light). The Age of Aquarius is about embracing values based on love, unity, integrity, humanitarianism, freedom, and truth."[15]

The many adjacent and intersecting cycles occurring during this era denotes it as a time of significance. Of this time, medical anthropologist Alberto Villoldo remarks, "Many prophecies in the indigenous world speak of this time in human history as a period of great transformation; a new human is emerging on earth."[16] This momentous, wide-sweeping change in human consciousness has been anticipated by sages and philosophers such as Teilhard de Chardin, Sri Aurobindo, and Jean Gebser, and is embedded in the myths and lore of the Maya, Hopi, Hindu, Inca, Cherokee, Algonquin, Egyptian, Aborigine, and more.

The Nobel-winning chemist Ilya Prigogine, noted for his work on complex systems, confirmed that periods of chaos are likely to reorder themselves into more complex and creative patterns. As far back as the twentieth century, Prigogine remarked that the current age could be a turning point for humanity. The philosopher Jean Gebser suggested that a new consciousness, transitioning from mental/rational to "integral" would soon allow humans to assimilate human experience as an integrated whole rather than as a fragmented reality. All told, the themes of chaos and disaster are often linked to the convergence of cycles during stages of transition, but they also presage processes of transformation and renewal. ***Humans face an existential choice: actively seek out ways to facilitate and collaborate with evolutionary changes in consciousness or refuse to make positive accommodations to a new society that will move forward, with or without them.***

## CONSCIOUSNESS RISING

>*…we are living in history*
>*and history is living in us.*
>**~ Carter Phipps**

Houle theorizes that in the 2020s, we will need to manage two realities: physical reality and screen reality.[17] I would add that as we increasingly encounter spiritual experiences, we will also need to acknowledge and integrate a newly recognized *spiritual reality* as well. Houle points out that while technology defined the previous Information Age, consciousness will define the Shift Age. He predicts that humanity will experience both a common and an individual altering of consciousness or what he terms a "collective global brain." Houle attributes this development primarily to an accelerating interconnectedness affected by increasingly high-speed global communication and travel.[19]

The uptick in global consciousness is partially due to technological advancement, as changes in consciousness are often a part of a reciprocal process of inner and outer factors. **I would also like to submit that this increase in global consciousness is due to several other causes, among them:**

- ***Growing perception of oneself as a global actor,*** *interested in the common welfare and the belief that the individual is capable of making a positive contribution to the world. This is an artifact of increasing globalization.*

- ***A move toward greater inclusivity,*** *superseding differences of race, gender, class, generation, or geography. This is a trend in which humans become "world citizens," less nation-centric and more world-centric. Currently, we seem caught in unending dissension and conflict, but as Jung taught, whenever there is a radical change, whether occurring individually or in large groups, conditions tend to get worse before they get better. He used the term,* **enantiodromia,** *to refer to the phenomena of things going to their utmost extremes, only to suddenly turn into their opposites (think about how it's said that love and hate are two sides of the same coin). A healing crisis (or creative illness) often occurs, and for a time, it may seem as if we are going backward rather than forward. However, this abrupt changeover can eventually work for the better, surmounting our differences.*

- ***The birth of highly-advanced and unusually-intuitive children,*** *especially those born after 1982: Millennials (those born 1982-2000 who make up around 31 million people in the U.S.); Generation Z (born 1997-2012); and continuing into the "Alphas" (born 2010-2033). These children, especially Generation Z and the younger generation of Alphas, have been variously identified as indigo, crystal, starseed, rainbow, psychic, and cosmic.*[20]

- ***The increase in unusual paranormal and/or spiritual experiences,*** *which often serve as triggers to an "awakening." Such events include out-of-body experiences (OBEs); near-death experiences (NDEs); extraterrestrial encounters; meetings with deceased loved ones in the dream state; kundalini awakenings; the opening of senses beyond the usual five (such as clairvoyance); a Dark Night of the Soul experience; and more.*

- ***The influence of those who have awakened,*** *called "thresholders" by author Mary Rodwell,*[21] *to the necessity of focusing on and developing the spiritual quadrant*[22] *in their lives. Some researchers argue that* it requires four to five percent of any group, condition, or situation to change the entire unit of which it is a part; others posit that we only need one percent of the global population, or 78 million people, to affect a change in consciousness worldwide.

- **The perspective and sensibility of the feminine principle** (*yin*) becoming more prevalent in today's world (emphasizing cooperation, collaboration, mediation, and the welfare of the collective). The greater balance between the yin and yang principles in the world is interrelated to the progressive fusing of Eastern and Western cultures on this planet.

- **The increasing number of stressors of the 20s decade.** Stress creates consciousness. Crisis, catastrophe, and cataclysms can often set the stage for evolutionary advancement. The extreme stressors of the first few years of the 20s decade, while at times devastating, can also contribute to what author Carter Phipps terms the "progress of meaning."

- **The very real possibility of engaging with higher intelligences in this decade or the next.** In fact, many humans claim to have already been contacted by extraterrestrial beings.[23] Benevolent ETs (and most, though not all, have our best interests at heart) have observed us (and at times, have interacted with us) for eons. We are preparing to take our place as galactic members of a much larger panoply of beings, thus the uptick in events that are acclimating us to this eventuality. In the end, the fact that we are part of a wide array of beings existing in the multiverse, though momentous, should not be a distraction from a more significant truth: **All forms of life and consciousness, residing in every dusty corner of the cosmos, eventually long for and begin to travel the Return Journey to God.**

Inventor and futurist Ray Kurzweil, who famously predicted a moment (*the singularity*) when machines will become smarter than humans, proposes that progress in the next 100 years of the 21$^{st}$ century will equal, at today's rate, around 20,000 years of human advancement in the past. Kurzweil focuses primarily on the field of technology, but there is no doubt that human beings themselves will need to quickly advance to meet the challenges of the coming decades. The *new human* will need to develop in deeply spiritual ways that merely merging humans with tech (one of Kurzweil's areas of study) doesn't necessarily address. The new human will also be known as the *Initiate*.

## THE NEW HUMAN

*I think the sages are the growing tip of the secret impulse to evolution.*
*I think they are the leading edge of the self-transcending drive*
*that always goes beyond what went before.*
*I think they embody the very drive of the cosmos*
*toward greater depth and expanding consciousness.*
*I think they disclose the face of tomorrow.*

~ **Ken Wilbur**

During this epoch and the next, we may begin to see the rise of a new human, one who has transcended the conventional ego, retaining it while recognizing the preeminence of the Self. The new human will have achieved self-realized individuality while concurrently recognizing a universality with all beings. The evolved human will seek the greater good and transformation for all of humankind. The new humans, like Wilbur's sages, are the "growing tip" of humanity. They have been variously named *Homo noeticus* (consciousness researcher John White); *Homo deus* (historian Yuval Harari); *Homo universalis* (futurist Barbara Marx Hubbard); *Galactic Human* (popularized by many); *Homo evolutis* (author Juan Enriquez); *Gnostic being* (philosopher and maharishi Aurobindo Ghose); and *The Initiate* (purported by Theosophist Helena Blavatsky to be the true name of humanity).

The evolutionary impulse itself is not only personal: It is an objective process of "creativity, dynamism, and forward movement that comes alive in the personality,"[24] but this innate urge toward growth also profoundly affects and includes the shared moral, social, and practical aspects of society itself. There is a reciprocity between all beings and the world around them. The actualizing drive is innate within the individual, but it is only fully realized and expressed in *connectivity*. Cosmologist Brian Swimme aptly expresses this seeming paradox: "The universe isn't a place, it's *a movement*…we are individuals who are part of cultures, but at the same time, *we are a dimension of the entire universe.*"[25]

# CONNECTIVITY

> *To awaken spiritual unity,*
> *and to spread to others the love*
> *that is our inherent nature,*
> *is the true goal of human life.*
> ~ Amma

> *Progress has not followed a straight line,*
> *but a spiral with rhythms of progress and retrogression,*
> *of evolution and dissolution.*
> ~ Goethe

Dancing the Labyrinth of Initiation leads into the very depths of our being, awakens our reverence for world and cosmos, reveals the mysteries of death and birth (and rebirth), and ultimately, brings order out of chaos. The enfolding turns of the labyrinth, mimicking the complexities of the brain, shift our consciousness into new perspectives. We begin to realize our connectedness to nature, to animal life, to one another, to the cosmos.

One of the visionary founders of the Human Potential Movement (including the establishment of a modern Mystery School program), Jean Houston remarked that when she was a young girl she met a kindly gentleman in Central Park. She only him as "Mr. Tayer," but later discovered he was the philosopher-theologian Pierre Teilhard de Chardin. Jean would meet with him over a series of visits during which he taught her that all life was "a spiral of becoming." They spoke of:

> *"...spirals and nature and art, snail shells and galaxies, the labyrinth in the floor of Chartres Cathedral... and the Rose Window and the convolutions of the brain, the whirl of flowers and the circulation of the heart's blood. It was all taken up in a great hymn to the spiraling evolution of spirit and matter."* [26]

The more we grow in consciousness, the greater we realize our connectivity to all life. Our perspective broadens to accommodate the world and all the living beings within it (and eventually, the universe and its denizens). **If you go back just 29 generations, we are all related.** What we do as individuals matters; we are part of a larger evolutionary blueprint. Once humans have truly realized their bonded humanity, their connectivity, we will begin to rely more on nonverbal communication (and know that our hidden thoughts and attitudes will stand revealed); develop greater empathy for the plight of others; have increased reverence for life, including the Earth itself; and become more collaborative and less willing to go to war. The new human will realize a greater accountability for their emotions, words, and actions.

The Sufi Irina Tweedie characterized this connectivity as a profound responsibility:

> *"The realization that every act, every word, every thought of ours not only influences our environment but for some mysterious reason forms an integral and important part of the Universe, fits into it as if by necessity, so to say, in the very moment we*

*do, or say, or think it—is an overwhelming and even shattering experience…The tremendous responsibility of it is terrifying… If we know it deeply and absolutely, if this realization becomes engraved permanently on our hearts, on our minds, how careful we would act and speak and think…How precious life would become in its integral oneness."* [27]

To become a Self-Realized being is the immediate goal of the initiation process, but this aim is not for ourselves only. "Humanity itself is in transition on such a large scale that our survival depends on the consciousness of each and every individual." [28] The Labyrinthine Path of Initiation connects us to our divinity so that it lives within us, influencing individuals we have never met but to whom we are, as human beings, intrinsically related. ***If you are committed to a program of continual transformation; if you recognize that all of life's experiences are lessons to be learned; if you acknowledge the God divinity within yourself; if you are actively developing the qualities of compassion, generosity, patience, and love—then <u>you</u> are becoming the new human.***

# THE NEW RELIGION

> *If we live in our oneness-heart,*
> *We will feel the essence of all religions*
> *which is the love of God.*
> *Forgiveness, compassion, tolerance, brotherhood*
> *and the feeling of oneness*
> *Are the signs of a true religion.*
>
> ~ Sri Chinmoy

It is possible that, in the future, churches will be patterned after the ancient mystery schools, offering a universalized religion that incorporates the initiation process. These spiritual schools of the past include the Egyptian Rites of Osiris and Isis, and the Eleusinian, Orphic, and Dionysian Mysteries of Greece. The New Religion will not simply be a wholesale transplant of the past, however, as humans have increased in consciousness over the millennia since these schools existed. The steady increase of higher awareness in the world will make it possible to bring spiritual knowledge and higher influences down to earth in practical ways; past efforts were made only by the few and were largely limited to attempts at raising the initiate's consciousness to reach the high spiritual realms.

Mystery schools once imparted teachings on different levels or tiers, identified in the past as the Lessor and Greater Mysteries. In the future, the Lessor Mysteries will likely involve the entire community and include the dissemination of basic spiritual practices and knowledge regarding "right living." This level of instruction might incorporate commitment rituals such as baptisms and confirmations. The Greater Mysteries will encompass advanced esoteric knowledge and practices relating to the higher spiritual realms, including the Earth's purpose in a universal or cosmic context. At all levels of learning, it is possible that ceremonial rites and rituals will be interjected, but these sacred sacraments will mark profound psychospiritual changes transpiring *within* the spiritual student (initiations) and will not merely be ritualized allegories. Such transformational changes during the initiation process will occur, as they do now, via individual efforts as well as through certain galvanizing effects administered by the Initiator or Master Teacher (in the past, known as the Hierophant).

**How would this new, universal religion be integrated into everyday life? Some of the practical applications involved in the curricula of future Mystery Schools might be:**

- *Ecological and environmental relationships and stewardship.*

- *Early assessment of vocational leanings and propensities* based on temperament, innate abilities, and interests. Individuals are voluntarily funneled into appropriate avenues of study and apprenticeship.

- *Meditation, movement, and other esoteric practices* are taught, with the understanding of their impact on body-mind-spirit.

- *Understandings of basic human psychology.* Lessons in self-control, anger management, mediation skills, and emotional balance in the lower self. How to work with the separate selves of the ego-personality, including its shadow aspects.

- *Human psychology as it relates to the Self.* The fostering of positive emotions and thoughts and their influence toward spiritual progress. Advanced levels of education that emphasize the integration of heart and mind, the union of the Lower Self with the Higher Self.

- *Cultivation of a greater understanding of human expression and connectivity through art*—music, visual art, dance, theater and more. Regardless of our race, language, or religion, art assists us to focus on that inner part of ourselves where the urge to both create art and to explore ourselves has its origins.

- **Understanding of the importance and interpretation of dreams,** including how to bridge dream messages to the physical life.

- **Responsible development and application of special extrasensory abilities and skills:** telepathy, precognition, psychometry, and soul travel, to name a few.

- **Death seen as a passage,** to be experienced as a sacrament and without fear.

- **Greater understanding and progressive treatments of emotional and mental malfunctioning,** including the differentiation of spiritual crises from psychological impairment.

- **Light and sound used as healing treatments** for greater health and well-being.

The religion of tomorrow, according to philosopher Ken Wilbur, will incorporate many religions while guiding participants toward greater oneness within ourselves and with Source. The new, or *integral religion,* must include the science learned in the modern age regarding the mind, brain, emotions, and the development of consciousness. It should also encompass recent discoveries in psychology and religion. Moreover, Wilbur identifies four processes necessary to an integral religion: *Waking Up, Growing Up, Cleaning Up*, and *Showing Up*. The first category has to do with the "states of consciousness," traditionally emphasized in Eastern religions and are often involved, for example, in waking up to higher states of awareness, such as enlightenment and union with the Divine. The second category refers to "developmental stages," which are associated with Western models of human growth from infancy to maturity. In the new religion, these states and stages, once regarded separately, are recognized and *integrated*. The third category, *Cleaning Up*, is concerned with dysfunctions and shadow elements that are experienced at various levels of spiritual growth (discussed in an earlier chapter). For the last category,

*Showing Up,* Wilbur instructs that the new religion must be an intrinsic part of everyday aspects (or quadrants) of human life experience, which is the very definition of an integral spirituality—the experience of a *living* religion.[29]

## PRACTICAL SPIRITUALITY

> *The test of maturity, for nations as well as individuals,*
> *is not the increase in power, but the increase in self-understanding,*
> *self-control, self-direction, and self-transcendence.*
> *For in a mature society, man himself,*
> *and not his machines or his organizations,*
> *is the chief work of art.*
>
> **~ Lewis Mumford**

I woke up from a dream one morning remembering that I had been darting here and there, urgently telling various people to "wake up, wake up." A couple of weeks later, I watched the Netflix movie *Don't Look Up*, a 2021 satirical comedy directed by Adam McKay. In the movie, a planet-killing comet is careening toward Earth, and all efforts to alert society by astronomers played by Leonardo DiCaprio and Jennifer Lawrence are ignored, derided, trivialized, or exploited. The news media plays off the urgent reality of an extinction level event to create entertainment value; social media distractions trivialize and sideline any concerns about a looming disaster; the super-wealthy elites assess the rogue comet for its commercial potential; and warnings of the ominous oncoming comet are dismissed ("don't look up") or manipulated by politicians to win votes.

As I watched the movie, I thought of my "wake-up" dream. The events suffered during the last few years (all but excluding a comet crashing into the planet) have indeed been a wake-up call. It is vital that people prioritize what is truly important in life (a point made by showcasing family relationships during a dinner scene at the end of the movie), and to wake up to the realities of the climate crisis and other existential threats. Most importantly, humans need to spiritually mature.

The time for transformation is now upon us, and the life we once led is gone forever. **We will not be returning to business as usual. In order to grow and flourish as a world civilization, there are important transitions to make:**

- *Our social values must expand to include everyone on this planet.*

- *We need to go beyond living as limited five-sensory humans to develop intuition, insight, and purpose. (Rudolf Steiner claimed we actually have 12 senses).*[30]

- *Our materialistic values need to evolve into more creative, inspirational, and spiritual values, rather than the superficial values mirrored in some of the reality shows currently on TV. While a system of capitalism thrives on a healthy market economy of supply and demand, there is so much more than shopping and buying to a meaningful existence.*

- *We need to see more (and vote for) persons in public life who model (or who demonstrate an effort toward) an upright character,* nobility (now there's an old-fashioned word), dignity, grace, decency, altruism, and integrity. And we need to model these behaviors ourselves! All humans are flawed, but there are exceptional people in recent history whom we can admire and emulate such as the individuals in the list below (I did not include world spiritual leaders, such as the Dalai Lama and Pope Francis):

    - **Nelson Mandela**—*anti-apartheid revolutionary and head of state, who persisted despite spending 27 years in prison for his political activism.*

- *Maya Angelou*—writer, performer, and social activist, Angelou was known for her inspiring poems and autobiographical novels.
- *Malala Yousafzai*—defied the Taliban as an outspoken defender of female rights to education; shot on a school bus, she recovered and continues her activism.
- *Aung San Suu Kyi*—under house arrest for nearly two decades, she gave up her freedom to protest military rule in Myanmar (formerly Burma).
- *David Attenborough*—broadcaster, explorer, historian, and naturalist, Attenborough raised significant awareness about the plight of our environment in numerous films and documentaries
- *Volodymyr Zelensky*—former actor and comedian; as president of Ukraine, he exemplified a profile in courage and leadership during an unprovoked assault on his country.

What people of quality would you add to this brief list? What can we do to collaborate with the realization of a new, positive progression of life on this planet? How can we wake up?

**Practically speaking, we can contribute to the advancement of the planet by:**

- ***Realizing that we are responsible for our own circumstances.*** Our most relished and repetitive thoughts have established our current experiences. (Blaming others is no longer tenable when this understanding truly sets in). Learning from our circumstances is the key to psychospiritual growth.

- ***Comprehending that there are many planes of existence;*** and that there are, in fact, many levels of life correlating with varying degrees of consciousness.

- ***Fathoming that the multiverse is teeming with beings and lifeforms;*** we are not alone. (This statement will be confronting us as fact in the not-too-distant future).

- ***Understanding that all life is connected by the forcefield of love;*** science is seeking to produce a theorem (*the unified theory of everything*) to explain the physical connectivity of all life, but *this bond is essentially a spiritual one.*

- ***Knowing that, at some point, we will confront our own words, thoughts, and deeds*** as mirroring experiences in the world. Even though it may seem so to others, no one gets away with anything; we cannot ditch personal responsibility. (Yes, this can be thought of as *karma*; karma as cause and effect also includes the positive influences we demonstrate and experience in our lives).

- ***Working at identifying and cleaning up our "hungry ghosts,"*** those negative habits and desires that drain our energy and keep us mentally dulled and easily manipulated by outer influences.

- ***Doing our best to be of service to others,*** in big ways and small, which is the hallmark of an advanced human being.

- ***Making concerted efforts to be kinder, more compassionate, more forgiving, and more courteous.*** (It's true that the little things, such as simply saying "thank you," are sometimes the most important).

- ***Spending time and effort in meditation, contemplation, prayer or other spiritual practices;*** reading spiritually-oriented books, watching spiritually-focused videos, or working with your dreams. Look for a group of like-minded people with whom to share and compare dreams, remarkable outer-life occurrences, and spiritual experiences of all kinds.

- ***Grasping that our ego consciousness is not all that we are;*** there are "higher," more inclusive levels of human awareness. Awakening to the innate spiritual quality that lies hidden within each and every one of us can lead us to grow into these advanced levels of consciousness. What Ken Wilbur calls the "evolutionary imperative" is the stadial, integrative process of human spiritual development that transcends but includes earlier stages. In this book, that process is known as the Path of Initiation.

It is not an effortless or passive process to wake up from the collective sleep state: It requires struggle, commitment, and effort to throw off the inertia of conditioned reality (think how Neo in *Matrix Resurrections*, the fourth film in the Matrix franchise, initially resists the idea that he's once again living in a fabricated world). Once we "wake up," (the first of Wilbur's four categories), the work of authentic spiritual unfoldment has only begun.

Jean Houston was asked in an interview what she looks for as evidence of genuine evolution in human beings. She responded, "To me the proof of the pudding is: *are they kinder?* (author's emphasis). Like the Dalai Lama says, 'My religion is kindness.' Also, *what is the service to the world that people are giving? Are they trying to make a difference and make this a better world?* I feel that it really comes down to that."[31] Authentic spirituality has to show up in our daily lives, which means we must *embody* it; the initiation process transforms our very being, so that acting in principled ways is intrinsic to who we are. We no longer have to make an effort to be "good."

It takes great courage and honesty to know that the work of a better world first begins with purifying ourselves (Wilbur's "cleaning up") as this parable illustrates:

*Nasrudin was sitting with friends, drinking tea, and elaborating on his life and times. He related that when he was young, he was something of a firebrand, wishing to awaken everyone he happened upon. "I asked Allah to help me change the world," he shared. But when he reached midlife, Nasrudin realized that he had not changed anyone, not even those he loved most. He confessed that today he is older and much wiser: "I now simply ask Allah to help me with the difficult task of changing myself!"*

*Dancing the Labyrinth,* as a metaphor for treading the Path of Initiation, is our next evolutionary step—it's the only dance there is. Initiation is a world-embracing, forward-moving, creative program designed to assist us in growing into wholeness and moving toward God. It entails finding the essential Self, which then becomes the executor of the many levels of the personality. It's the path of human spiritual development that has existed throughout eons, and it is available today to the many rather than the few. **Once we commit to such a path, we can anticipate stepping into the future as the "new human" --always with guidance and never without hope.**

# CHAPTER SEVEN EXERCISES

### Reflecting On Your Spiritual Journey

**As you think about what you have read in** *Dancing the Labyrinth,* **explore the following questions in your journal.**

1. What stood out for you as you read the book? Were there parts of the book that you feel applied to your own life? Which tasks of the initiation process seemed the most meaningful to you?

2. In what ways do you feel you have grown and changed spiritually? Describe in what ways you feel connected to Source.

3. How have you grown and matured in spirituality over time? For example, what qualities, such as love and compassion, have you developed?

4. What aspects of your shadow have you identified, faced, and changed?

5. In what ways do you "show up" for your friends, family, and community?

6. How would your life be different if you lived an integrated spirituality—one in which awareness, generosity, empathy, and kindness were embedded in every aspect of your life?

7. How will you be remembered by those who love you?

# CHAPTER SEVEN ENDNOTES

1. American Psychological Association, "Stress in America," report based on the Feb., 2021 Harris Poll.

2. These statistics from : "APA: U.S. Adults Report Highest Stress Level Since Early Days of COVID-19 Pandemic," *Stress in America,* Stress Snapshot, conducted by The Harris Poll for APA.

3. Neil Strauss and Neil Howe. *The Fourth Turning: What the Cycles of History Tell Us About America's Next Rendezvous with Destiny.* New York: Broadway Books, 1997. Some have taken exception to the Straus-Howe theory, but there is no doubt that cyclic changes do occur, and when they do, there are upheavals and tumult.

4. Ibid., p. 7.

5. David Houle. *The 2020s: A Decade of Cognitive Dissonance*, Book 2. David Houle and Associates, 2021, p. 28.

6. *The 2020s: The Most Disruptive Decade in History,* Book 1. Houle & Associates, 2020, p. 3.

7. Ibid., p. 29.

8. Moira Lavelle. "By 2050, 200 Million Climate Refugees May Have Fled Their Homes, But International Laws Offer Them Little Protection," *Inside Climate News,* November 2, 2021. https://insideclimatenews.org/news/02112021/climate-refugees-international-law-cop26/

9. According to *Statista*: "As of Q1 of 2021, the top 10 percent held 69.8 percent of total U.S. net worth (which is the value of all assets a person holds minus all their liabilities). The top 1 percent held about half of that wealth, 32.1 percent, while the next 9 percent held approximately another half at 37.7 percent. The bottom 50 percent of U.S. residents only held 2 percent of all of U.S. wealth." https://www.statista.com/chart/19635/wealth-distribution-percentiles-in-the-us/

10. "What is the biggest source of pollution in the ocean?" National Ocean Service, national Oceanic and Atmospheric Administration, U. S. Department of Commerce. https://ocean-service.noaa.gov/facts/pollution.html

11. "Human Relations," *Sintellyapp*. August, 31, 2021. https://sintelly.com/categories/human-relations

12. *PopulationMatters:* https://populationmatters.org

13. Jack Kornfield. *A Path with Heart.* New York: Bantam Books, 1993, p. 295.

14. See Carl Jung's seminal book, *Modern Man In Search of a Soul*, New York: Harcourt, Brace & World, Inc., 1933 (as true today as it was in the 30's) and *Jung's Psychology and Its Social Meaning* by Ira Progoff, New York: Anchor Books, 1973.

15. Patricia Ariadne. *Drinking the Dragon*, Encinitas, CA: Sothis Press, 2021, pp. 254-255.

16. Alberto Villoldo. "Homo Luminous: The New Human," *The Four Winds*. November 1, 2016. https://thefourwinds.com/blog/shamanism/homo-luminous-new-human/

17. In my readings, I have alternately run across the year 2050 as the true beginning of the Aquarian Age.

18. op. cit., 2020, pp. 23-24 & 105; 2021, pp. 47-55 and pp. 91-95.

19. Houle, op. cit., 2021, Ch. 10, pp. 107-109.

20. P. M. H. Atwater. *Children of the Fifth World: A Guide to the Coming Changes in Human Consciousness*. Rochester Vermont: Bear & Co., 2012.

21. Mary Rodwell. *The New Human: Awakening to Our Cosmic Heritage*. New Mind Publishers, 2017. https://www.bookdepository.com/publishers/New-Mind-Publishers

22. The American philosopher Ken Wilbur put forward that humans develop via *Four Quadrants of Knowing*:

- *Interior* (**Individual-SELF**)-"I" language-with a focus on philosophy, art, psychology, spirituality.
- *Exterior* (**Individual-SCIENCE**)-"It" language-which focuses on physics, chemistry, biology, cosmology, etc.).
- *Interior* (**Collective-CULTURE**)-"We" language-focusing on literature, philosophy, religion, morals, etc.).
- *Exterior* (**Collective-SOCIAL SCIENCE**)-"They" language-the focus is on sociology, economics, anthropology, etc.

*Importantly, Wilbur holds that one quadrant cannot be affected without impacting the remaining quadrants.*

23. About two-thirds of Americans (65%) say they believe that intelligent life likely exists on other planets, according to a Pew Research Center survey. It can be added that an increasing number of people believe they have experienced Encounters of the Fifth Kind, which is defined as voluntary bilateral contact between humans and extraterrestrials. An interesting platform for learning more about this subject is Gaia.com, which advertises itself as the "largest online resource of consciousness-expanding videos—over 8,000 informative and enlightening films, original shows, yoga and meditation" videos and more.

(Reported June 30, 2021) https://www.pewresearch.org/fact-tank/2021/06/30/most-americans-believe-in-intelligent-life-beyond-earth-few-see-ufos-as-a-major-national-security-threat/

[24.] Carter Phipps. *Evolutionaries*. New York: Harper Perennial, 2012, p. 186.

[25.] See Brian Swimme's video, "Journey of the Universe." May 5, 2016. https://youtu.be/YOlkkMxAhj4

[26.] Amy Edelstein. "Orchestrating Our Many Selves: Interview with Jean Houston," originally published in *What is Enlightenment?* magazine (renamed *EnlightenNext Magazine*), Summer, Issue 15 pp.108-109 and later published in blog format, *Cultural Development, Featured Posts, Philosophers & Mystics: "Jean Houston on the Fallacy of Self Mastery,"* April 12, 2013. https://amyedelstein.com/orchestrating-our-many-selves-interview-with-jean-houston/ (An interesting note is that Jean Houston chose the labyrinth as the symbol for her various projects.)

[27.] Irina Tweedie. *Daughter of Fire*. Nevada City, CA: Blue Dolphin Publishing, 1986, p. 812.

[28.] Louise Carus Mahdi. *Betwixt and Between: Patterns of Masculine and Feminine Initiation*. LaSalle, Il: Open Court, Inc., 1987: p. xiv.

[29.] Ken Wilbur. *The Religion of Tomorrow: A Vision for the Future of the Great Traditions—More Inclusive, More Comprehensive, More Complete*. Boulder, CO: Shambhala Publications, 2017. Read a brief explanation of Wilbur's framework of quadrants in above Endnote 22.

[30.] Rudolf Steiner (1861-1925) was the founder of Anthroposophy. Steiner developed an entire framework of integrated spiritual living, including a therapeutic clinical center, research centers for science and math; and schools of drama, speech, painting, and sculpture. In addition, he created an expressive movement art called Eurythmy and an education system, the Waldorf School. Among Steiner's writings are *Knowledge of The Higher Worlds and Its Attainment (1947)* and *Occult Science: An Outline* (1913).

[31.] Amy Edelstein. op. cit.

# EPILOGUE

*We have not even to risk the adventure alone,
for the heroes of all time have come before us;
the labyrinth is thoroughly known;
we have only to follow the thread of the hero-path.
And where we had thought to find an abomination, we shall find a god;
where we had thought to slay another, we shall slay ourselves;
we had thought to travel towards, we shall come to the center of our own existence;
where we had thought to be alone, we shall be with all the world.*
~ **Joseph Campbell**

*As it gradually dawns on people, one by one,
that the transformation of God is not just an interesting idea
but is a living reality,
it may begin to function as a new myth.
Whoever recognizes this myth as his own personal reality
will put his life in the service of this process.
Such an individual offers himself as a vessel for the [continuing] incarnation of deity
and thereby promotes the ongoing transformation of God
by giving Him human manifestation.*
~ **Edward Edinger**

If you know mythology, you will have noticed that my last name, Ariadne, is the name of the Mistress of the Labyrinth in ancient Crete. She was the Cretan princess, daughter of King Minos, who naively fell in love with the Athenian hero Theseus and helped him to escape the labyrinth after he killed her half-brother, the half-man/half-bull Minotaur. She had given Theseus a ball of thread to unwind along his path as she held on to the thread's end outside the labyrinth, enabling him to make a quick exit. Theseus had promised her that he would take her with him to Athens, but when they stopped at the island of Naxos for the night, she discovered the following morning that he had set sail with his crew while she slept. Abandoned and alone on the island, Ariadne wept. She was soon rescued, however, by the God Dionysius, who married her and moved her to Mt. Olympus to live.

When I divorced at 31, I had the choice to keep my married name, revert to my maiden name, or choose a new name altogether. I was finishing my doctorate in psychology, studying mythology, reading the works of Carl Jung, and regularly seeing a Jungian analyst. I was deeply immersed in the world's ancient myths and legends. I was preparing to become a licensed psychotherapist, and Ariadne's name appealed to me because she represented (to me) the archetype of the healer, one who helped persons through the maze of their own beings so that they might discover their true Selves at the center. I also related the Ariadne reference to what I understood to be women's growing influence (the advancing feminine principle), which would, in time, help to change the culture by guiding people forward into new, more balanced ways of being. (To an extent, these were legitimate notions, but quite idealistic and romantic).

I am the first to say I was just as naïve as Ariadne to think that I could simply choose a name out of mythology and not have to *live* that myth. Abandonment was a theme in my childhood (as it is in so many others' lives). As a mature adult, I now see that the "saving God" (Dionysius) is not another rescuing hero at all, but a metaphor for the Immortal Self. I understand the labyrinth as the Path of Initiation, the spiraling patterns symbolizing not only the inner psyche but life itself! Dionysius, (known as *the twice-born,* which is a name for initiates*)*, is far more than the god of the concrete or material ideas of fertility, ecstasy, and wine. He represents the tumultuous transmutation undergone during the initiation process. To be married to him is to experience union with the Self. On the other hand, the beast who inhabits the labyrinth symbolizes the negativity within ourselves, which we must meet and redeem as part of the initiatory process. I

## Epilogue

did not know at 31 that I would shortly be going through a two-year ordeal of devastating loss and failure (feeling abandoned again, but this time by God) during which I would be "meeting self," including everything that needed to be squarely confronted and cleansed. I had no clue that in later life, I would be writing books about the Dark Night of the Soul and the initiation process. In a mysterious and unforeseeable way, the Cretan myth with a labyrinth at its center has held sway in my life.

I have felt a great urgency to complete this book. I know that to successfully transition into a positive and expansive future, we must change *ourselves*. You might be surprised to know what Charles Darwin *really* said about those who survive: "It isn't the strongest of the species that survive, nor the most intelligent, but the ones *most responsive to change*" (author's italics). The world belongs to those who can quickly adapt. We must take this opportune time, the critical moment (what the ancient Greeks called *Kairos*) to *choose* to make a change; otherwise, the change will occur without our conscious consent (and not all change is forward moving or growth producing).

We are here to become conduits for spiritual energies that bless the world and all of its inhabitants. Initiation is both a science and an art; in the coming years, the process of Self-Realization via initiation will be better understood and more integrated into the everyday fabric of the modern world. Initiation is the process that will prepare us to not only meet the future but to create it. ***It's time to remember that Earth is a school, to understand that the hard knocks of life are lessons to be learned, and to embrace our larger purpose: to become Self-Realized beings. Many more of us, hungry for a living religion that incorporates authentic spiritual experiences and transformations, will be walking the winding path into the mysterious labyrinth of our own beings.***

*A call to reflect upon a new era, a new task,
and accordingly, upon a totally different initiation-mystery,
is now resounding over the entire world to all those who are spiritually sensitive...
In this lies the key to the universal mystery that is 'the same yesterday and today'
and to the frequently used aphorism, 'when the pupil is ready, the master is there'.
If you truly wish to walk the path of this universal mystery,
and you know that this path means transfiguration, then these words will also
become true for you:
'seek and you shall find; knock and it shall be opened unto you'.*
~ Jan van Rijckenborgh & Catharose de Petri


*Generations do not cease to be born,
and we are responsible to them
because we are the only witnesses they have.
The sea rises, the light fails, lovers cling to each other,
and children cling to us.
The moment we cease to hold each other,
the sea engulfs us and the light goes out.*
~ James Baldwin

# ABOUT THE AUTHOR
## Patricia Ariadne, Ph.D., LMFT

Dr. Patricia Ariadne is a licensed psychotherapist in private practice in North County San Diego, California. Known as *The Transition Therapist*, Patricia focuses on helping people deal with the many challenges in everyday life. The difficulties she works with often include crises of the Dark Night of the Soul, which many persons are currently facing as catalysts to higher consciousness.

Patricia is also an associate professor of psychology and the author of several books designed to help people navigate the inevitable upheavals of life. She is a long-time initiate and member of the clergy for *ECKANKAR, The Path of Spiritual Freedom*.

Her books include: *Drinking the Dragon: Stories of the Dark Night of the Soul* (and accompanying *Workbook*); *Women Dreaming-into-Art: Seven Artists Who Create from Dreams*; and *Marjorie Klemp: Her Spiritual Journey through Service (ebook)*. She has also written guidebooks that are reader friendly and interactive, including: *The Transition Series: Bridging Night and Day: Decoding the Hidden Messages of Your Dreams*; and *Navigating Change: How to Go from Trauma to Transformation*.

One of Patricia's many therapeutic tools is dream work. Her unique approach to dreams and psychotherapy have been featured on television, radio, and in print media as well as at professional conferences and seminars across the country.

**Patricia is available for phone or online sessions.**
Patrica@Dr.Ariadne.com
TransitionTherapist.com

www.ingramcontent.com/pod-product-compliance
Lightning Source LLC
Chambersburg PA
CBHW070735170426
43200CB00007B/535